Lecture Notes in Computer Science 13852

Founding Editors

Gerhard Goos
Juris Hartmanis

Editorial Board Members

Elisa Bertino, *Purdue University, West Lafayette, IN, USA*
Wen Gao, *Peking University, Beijing, China*
Bernhard Steffen ⓘ, *TU Dortmund University, Dortmund, Germany*
Moti Yung ⓘ, *Columbia University, New York, NY, USA*

The series Lecture Notes in Computer Science (LNCS), including its subseries Lecture Notes in Artificial Intelligence (LNAI) and Lecture Notes in Bioinformatics (LNBI), has established itself as a medium for the publication of new developments in computer science and information technology research, teaching, and education.

LNCS enjoys close cooperation with the computer science R & D community, the series counts many renowned academics among its volume editors and paper authors, and collaborates with prestigious societies. Its mission is to serve this international community by providing an invaluable service, mainly focused on the publication of conference and workshop proceedings and postproceedings. LNCS commenced publication in 1973.

Ana Gainaru · Ce Zhang · Chunjie Luo

Editors

Benchmarking, Measuring, and Optimizing

14th BenchCouncil International Symposium, Bench 2022
Virtual Event, November 7–9, 2022
Revised Selected Papers

Editors
Ana Gainaru
Oak Ridge National Laboratory
Oak Ridge, TN, USA

Ce Zhang
ETH Zurich
Zürich, Switzerland

Chunjie Luo
Chinese Academy of Sciences
Beijing, China

ISSN 0302-9743   ISSN 1611-3349 (electronic)
Lecture Notes in Computer Science
ISBN 978-3-031-31179-6   ISBN 978-3-031-31180-2 (eBook)
https://doi.org/10.1007/978-3-031-31180-2

This Springer imprint is published by the registered company Springer Nature Switzerland AG
The registered company address is: Gewerbestrasse 11, 6330 Cham, Switzerland

Preface

This volume contains the papers presented at Bench 2022. The Steering Committee decided to describe Bench 2022 as the 14th symposium in the series. The first nine events constituted the BPOE workshops, which were held in conjunction with ASPLOS, VLDB, and ICS. The Bench symposia, which started in 2018, evolved from the BPOE workshops. The Bench symposium has three defining characteristics. First, it provides a high-quality, single-track forum for presenting results and discussing ideas that further the knowledge and understanding of the benchmark community. Second, it is a multi-disciplinary conference. This edition of the conference attracted researchers and practitioners from different communities, including architecture, systems, algorithms, and applications. Third, the program features both invited and contributed talks.

The Bench symposium solicits papers that address pressing problems in benchmarking, measuring, and optimizing systems. The call for papers for the Bench 2022 conference attracted a large number of high-quality submissions. During a rigorous review process, in which each paper was reviewed by at least four experts, the program committee selected 10 papers for the Bench 2022 conference. The papers in this volume include revisions requested by program committee members. Bench 2022 had two keynote lectures. John L. Henning, Secretary of the SPEC CPU Subcommittee, drew lessons from the history of CPU benchmarking to reveal difficulties that are commonly encountered when trying to develop meaningful benchmarks. Douwe Kiela, the Head of Research at Hugging Face, introduced the open source Evaluate library and the Evaluation on the Hub project, as well as Dynabench, a research platform that facilitates human and model in the loop data collection and evaluation. Moreover, our program included one invited talk by Kai Shu from the Illinois Institute of Technology, who presented the challenges to build fair models with incomplete, unknown, and unreliable information, and stressed the need for interdisciplinary research. There were two workshops in Bench 2022, the OpenBench Workshop and OpenCS Workshop.

During the conference, the International Open Benchmark Council (BenchCouncil) sponsored four different types of awards to recognize important contributions to the area of benchmarking, measuring, and optimizing. The BenchCouncil Achievement Award recognizes a senior member who has made long-standing contributions to the field. John L. Henning was named the 2022 recipient of the achievement award. The BenchCouncil Rising Star Award recognizes a young researcher who demonstrates outstanding research and practice related to the theme of the conference. Douwe Kiela was named the 2022 recipient of the rising star award. The BenchCouncil Best Paper Award is to recognize a paper presented at our conference with high potential impact. Tony Hey generously donated to the BenchCouncil Award committee to spin off the best student paper award. And this award is to a student as the first author who publishes a paper that has a potential impact. Majid Salimi Beni and Biagio Cosenza from the University of Salerno received the Bench 2022 Best Paper Award for their paper "An Analysis of Long-tailed Network Latency Distribution and Background Traffic on Dragonfly+". Sierra Wang, Fatih

Bakir, Tyler Ekaireb, Jack Pearson, Chandra Krintz, and Rich Wolski from University of California Santa Barbara received the Bench 2022 Tony Hey Best Student Paper Award for their paper "MSDBench: Understanding the Performance Impact of Isolation Domains on Microservice-based IoT Deployments". There was one candidate for the BenchCouncil Distinguished Doctoral Dissertation Award in Computer Architecture, Akshitha Sriraman from Carnegie Mellon University. There is also one candidate for the BenchCouncil Distinguished Doctoral Dissertation Award in Other Areas, Markus Schuß from Graz University of Technology, Austria.

We are very grateful to all authors for contributing such excellent papers to the Bench 2022 conference. We appreciate the indispensable support of the Bench 2022 Program Committee and thank its members for the time and effort they invested in maintaining the high standards of the Bench symposium.

December 2022

Ana Gainaru
Ce Zhang
Chunjie Luo

Organization

General Chairs

Peter Mattson   Google, USA
Emmanuel Jeannot   INRIA, France
Wanling Gao   University of Chinese Academy of Sciences,
         China

Program Chairs

Ana Gainaru   Oak Ridge National Laboratory, USA
Ce Zhang   ETH Zurich, Switzerland
Chunjie Luo   Institute of Computing Technology, Chinese
         Academy of Sciences, China

Program Committee

Woongki Baek   UNIST, Republic of Korea
Greg Diamos   Landing.AI, USA
Murali Krishna Emani   Argonne National Laboratory, USA
Steve Farrell   NERSC, USA
Vladimir Getov   University of Westminster, UK
Sascha Hunold   TU Wien, Austria
Yunyou Huang   Guangxi Normal University, China
Miaoqing Huang   University of Arkansas, USA
Bin Hu   ICT, CAS, China
Khaled Ibrahim   Lawrence Berkeley National Laboratory, USA
Zhen Jia   Amazon, USA
Gwangsun Kim   POSTECH, Republic of Korea
Piotr Luszczek   University of Tennessee, USA
Shin-ying Lee   AMD, USA
Gang Lu   Tencent, China
Xiaoyi Lu   University of California, Merced, USA
Mario Marino   Leeds Beckett University, UK
Krishnakumar Nair   Meta, USA
Bin Ren   William & Mary, USA

Rui Ren	Beijing Open Source IC Academy, China
Nicolas Rougier	INRIA, France
Fei Sun	Alibaba, USA
Narayanan Sundaram	Facebook, USA
Nana Wang	Henan University, China
Lei Wang	ICT, CAS, China
Biwei Xie	ICT, CAS, China
Shengen Yan	SenseTime, China
Chen Zheng	Institute of Software, Chinese Academy of Sciences, China

Invited Talks

BenchCouncil Achievement Award Lecture: Benchmarking: An Incomparable Science?

John L. Henning

Secretary, SPEC CPU Subcommittee and Performance Engineer, Oracle

Abstract: Why are some of us so attracted to computer benchmarks? In part, it is the self-sustaining cycle of empirical methods: hypothesis, experiment, numerical result, which leads to the next hypothesis. But that's not good enough: instead of simply "numerical results", we need "meaningful numerical results". This talk draws lessons from the history of CPU benchmarking to reveal difficulties that are commonly encountered when trying to develop meaningful benchmarks.

Biography: John L. Henning is currently a performance engineer at Oracle, Nashua, NH, USA, and has been the Secretary for the SPEC CPU Subcommittee since 1998. In his first performance optimization experience, he trimmed a DOS/360 job from 8 hours to 45 minutes.

BenchCouncil Rising Star Award Lecture: Rethinking Benchmarking in AI: Evaluation-as-a-Service and Dynamic Adversarial Data Collection

Douwe Kiela

Head of Research at Hugging Face
and Adjunct Professor at Stanford University

Abstract: The current benchmarking paradigm in AI has many issues: benchmarks saturate quickly, are susceptible to overfitting, contain exploitable annotator artifacts, have unclear or imperfect evaluation metrics, and do not measure what we really care about. I will talk about my work on trying to rethink the way we do benchmarking in AI. First, I'll go into our work at Hugging Face on establishing better best practices for the comprehensive evaluation of data and models, through the open source Evaluate library and the Evaluation on the Hub project. Second, I'll talk about Dynabench, a research platform that facilitates human and model in the loop data collection and evaluation, as well as the progress the team has been making in exploring the dynamic adversarial data collection paradigm.

Biography: Douwe Kiela is the Head of Research at Hugging Face. He is also an Adjunct Professor at Stanford University. Before, he was a Research Scientist at Facebook AI Research. His current research interests lie in developing better models for (grounded, multi-agent) language understanding and better tools for evaluation and benchmarking. He received his PhD and MPhil from the University of Cambridge. Before that, he did a BSc in Liberal Arts & Sciences at Utrecht University with a double major in Cognitive Artificial Intelligence and Philosophy; and an MSc in Logic at the University of Amsterdam's ILLC.

Towards Fair Machine Learning with Imperfect Information

Kai Shu

Assistant Professor at Illinois Institute of Technology

Abstract: Modern machine learning (ML) models are becoming increasingly popular and are widely used in decision-making systems. Though ML models are achieving great success, critical issues of ML discrimination and unfairness are revealed, which hinder their adoption on high-stake applications. Recent research on fair machine learning has drawn significant attention to develop effective algorithms to achieve fairness and good prediction performance. However, sensitive attributes are often incomplete or unavailable due to privacy, legal or regulation restrictions. In addition, practitioners trying to audit group-based criteria can easily face the problem of noisy or manipulated sensitive attributes. In this talk, we look into some of the challenges to build fair models with incomplete, unknown, and unreliable information, and urge the need for interdisciplinary research.

Biography: Dr. Kai Shu is a Gladwin Development Chair Assistant Professor in the Department of Computer Science at Illinois Institute of Technology since Fall 2020. He obtained his Ph.D. in Computer Science at Arizona State University. He was the recipient of the 2020 ASU Engineering Dean's Dissertation Award, 2021 Google Cloud Research Credits Award, 2021 Finalist of Meta Research Faculty Award, 2021 Finalist of BenchCouncil Distinguished Doctoral Dissertation Award, 2022 Cisco Research Faculty Award, 2022 AMiner AI 2000 Most Influential Scholar Honorable Mention, and 2022 Baidu AI Global High-Potential Young Scholar Award. His research addresses challenges and applications such as big data, social media, trustworthy AI, fake news detection, social network analysis, cybersecurity, and health informatics. He has published innovative works in highly ranked journals and top conference proceedings such as ACM KDD, SIGIR, WSDM, WWW, EMNLP, NAACL, CIKM, IEEE ICDM, IJCAI, and AAAI.

Contents

Architecture and System

Algorithm and Dataset

Network and Memory

Architecture and System

A Quantitative Analysis of OpenMP Task Runtime Systems

Sascha Hunold(✉)🆔 and Klaus Kraßnitzer🆔

Research Group for Parallel Computing, Faculty of Informatics,
TU Wien, Vienna, Austria
{hunold,krassnitzer}@par.tuwien.ac.at

Abstract. Although OpenMP is heavily used to parallelize for-loops, it also supports task-parallel programming, which is important for parallelizing irregular applications. In this work, we focus on the performance of OpenMP runtime systems for task-based applications. In particular, we investigate the performance of different OpenMP runtime systems when scheduling a large set independent tasks of different granularity. To that end, we propose a new OpenMP benchmark, which features profiling and tracing options that help developers to reason about the observed performance differences. We compare the execution times measured for a variety of compilers, such as gcc, icc, clang, aocc, and pgcc, for both homogeneous and heterogeneous workloads. Our study shows that there are significant performance differences between the different OpenMP implementations. We also show that the performance attainable with a compiler strongly depends on the machine architecture, the number of threads, the thread-pinning strategy, and the task granularity.

Keywords: OpenMP tasks · Benchmarking · Scheduling

1 Introduction

In high-performance computing (HPC), OpenMP is the de-facto standard for parallelizing applications at the level of a compute node. In this work, we focus on parallel OpenMP applications that run on shared-memory parallel, multi-core machines. The most common type of today's multi-core machines are cache-coherent NUMA systems (ccNUMA), i.e., the multi-core processors typically have several DRAM memory controllers and partitioned last-level caches (e.g., Level 3 data caches). As a consequence of this ccNUMA architecture, the latency for reading from and writing to memory depends on the actual location of a core and the memory address. The traditional way of parallelizing applications with OpenMP is marking the compute-heavy for-loops with specific OpenMP pragmas. Compilers are then able to transform the programs into data-parallel

K. Kraßnitzer—This work was partially supported by the Austrian Science Fund (FWF): project P 33884-N.

fork-join applications, where each thread is responsible for specific chunks of the overall, global iteration space. The other, later introduced parallelization strategy in OpenMP is task-parallel programming. This strategy is particularly helpful for parallelizing recursive computational patterns or irregular applications in general, where tasks of different type and granularity can be dispatched by individual threads. The concept of OpenMP tasks increases the potential degree of parallelism that can be exploited by programmers, yet they also increase the scheduling complexity for the OpenMP runtime systems.

In this paper, we want to answer the question of how efficiently current C/C++ compilers (with OpenMP support) handle a large number of parallel tasks. To that end, we propose the OMPTB benchmark suite, which contains three basic OpenMP task processing strategies (inspired by the EPCC microbenchmarks [1]):

1. `MasterTask`: the master thread creates all tasks, but tasks are executed by all worker threads,
2. `ParallelTask`: all threads both emit and execute tasks, and
3. `ParallelFor`: the actual task code is executed using a single parallel for-loop. No OpenMP tasks are created, but the same number of instructions is executed. This strategy serves as a performance baseline.

We perform a large set of experiments with these three task processing strategies and address the following questions:

- How efficiently do current compilers process a large number of tasks? The compilers examined in this study are: gcc, icc, aocc, clang, and pgcc.
- How much does the task granularity (i.e., the runtime of each task) impact the performance difference between the different compilers?
- How do the different compilers deal with heterogeneous tasks, i.e., if the runtime of the tasks varies significantly?
- What is the impact of the thread mapping strategy on the performance of the task benchmark?
- How is the task workload balanced across the threads? Our hypothesis is that the more balanced the tasks are across the different threads the shorter the runtime should be (cf. Terboven et al. [13]).
- Is the runtime of the task benchmark correlated with the number of cache misses? This is a reasonable assumption considering the fact that we run on highly partitioned ccNUMA systems where compute nodes have up to 16 NUMA nodes.

In this paper, we make the following contributions:

- We present a benchmark for assessing the performance of OpenMP runtime systems. The benchmark features profiling and tracing capabilities, which help to investigate performance differences between compilers. The design of the benchmark is compiler-fair, i.e., the code executed by each OpenMP task is compiled with one fixed compiler to avoid assembly differences, while the OpenMP part is compiled with every investigated OpenMP compiler.

– We present an in-depth experimental study of the performance difference of various compilers for scheduling OpenMP tasks on shared-memory systems. We assess the performance of the OpenMP runtime systems when scheduling OpenMP tasks in the presence of heterogeneous tasks.

The remainder of the paper is structured as follows. In Sect. 2, we discuss the related work and indicate how previous work has influenced our benchmarking setup. In Sect. 3, we give a brief overview of our benchmark suite OMPTB, before we explain our experimental setup in Sect. 4. As we put an emphasis on empirical results, we show a large set of experiments in Sect. 5 and draw conclusions in Sect. 6.

2   Related Work

Several other works have already evaluated OpenMP task runtime systems in different contexts. A pioneering work in this field was published by Bull et al. [1], who proposed a set of OpenMP benchmarks to evaluate the cost of applying OpenMP pragmas in various settings. In particular, they proposed the `taskbench` benchmark, which can be used to assess the overhead associated with creating and processing OpenMP tasks. Bull et al. [1] use the sequential time for executing a loop with a fixed work W as the reference time. They measure the time to execute the same loop with various task creation strategies, e.g., only the master threads or all threads create a set of tasks. For evaluating the overhead of using OpenMP tasks, `taskbench` performs weak-scaling experiments, i.e., the number of tasks per thread that is created initially stays constant. The time difference between the parallel execution of work pW on p cores and the sequential execution of work W is called the overhead. In contrast, in our present work, we focus on a strong scaling analysis and keep the overall work exactly the same in each experiment. The benchmark `taskbench` fixes the "work time" of a loop iteration, i.e., how long each iteration should take. In order to estimate the waiting time, Bull et al. [1] use a nested busy loop that executes k iterations, where these k iterations should match this waiting/work time. In `taskbench`, this value of k is estimated every time the benchmark starts, leading to variances of the so-created homogeneous workload between different experimental runs.

Terboven et al. [13] compared how well different OpenMP implementations execute task-parallel OpenMP codes on NUMA machines. They compared performance results obtained with compilers from Intel, GNU, Oracle, and PGI. Similar to our approach, they investigated how load imbalance impacts the performance. To this end, they created a specific heterogeneous workload, where the time for executing a task increases linearly with the number of tasks. Each task internally reads data from memory to examine both load imbalance and data locality effects on NUMA machines. They showed that spawning OpenMP tasks concurrently by all threads often leads to a better performance than if only one thread is creating the tasks.

Olivier et al. [10] analyzed the scalability behavior of different task scheduling systems. In particular, they compared the performance results obtained with

Intel's icc and GNU's gcc to the ones obtained with the Qthreads library. The Qthreads library allows them to use different scheduling strategies at different levels of the NUMA architecture, i.e., they have an implementation with a single LIFO queue or with multiple queues and different work stealing strategies. They showed strong scaling results for a variety of benchmarks from the Barcelona OpenMP Tasks Suite (BOTS) [4].

Clet-Ortega et al. [3] presented an orthogonal work to Olivier et al. [10], where the authors analyze different scheduling strategies of OpenMP tasks on NUMA systems in their own customizable OpenMP runtime system called MPC. The idea is that the number of task queues could be a parameter, e.g., there could be one queue per system, one queue per socket, or one queue per core. The authors studied the performance of the different granularity options for the tasks queues and different work stealing strategies for BOTS applications.

Schuchart et al. [12] extended the EPCC OpenMP MicroBenchmark Suite to analyze the performance of OpenMP task runtimes in the presence of task dependencies. To that end, they defined several task dependency patterns, which were evaluated independently.

Gautier et al. [6] investigated the internal overheads of managing tasks in OpenMP. They instrumented the LLVM OpenMP runtime libOMP to measure the delay of different steps in the task creation process. The authors examined the impact of internal implementation choices on the performance, such as the maximum length of task queues or the hashtable size. Gautier et al. [6] also reported that a substantial fraction of the overhead can be attributed to checking task dependencies (in case dependent tasks are used).

Several commonly used multicore benchmarks are collected in the PARSEC benchmark suite [15]. Since task-based programming has gained importance, task-centric modifications of the PARSEC benchmarks were devised to examine the scaling behavior when expressing the parallel work in the form of tasks [2,8].

Lastly, Yang and He [14] present an extensive survey on work stealing approaches in the context of task-parallel programming on multicore machines.

3 OMPTB: The OpenMP Task Benchmark

Now, we introduce the OpenMP Task Benchmark (OMPTB) and the supported task creation strategies.[1] The overall design and structure of the microbenchmarks have been inspired by the works of Bull et al. [1], Terboven et al. [13], and Olivier et al. [10].

Micro-benchmark Structure. Our main objective is to create a stress test for the OpenMP scheduling system. Therefore, we focus on scheduling a large number of independent tasks onto a set of homogeneous cores. In Graham's scheduling notation, we are interested in the problems $P \,||\, C_{\max}$ and $P \,|\, \bar{p}_i = \bar{p} \,|\, C_{\max}$ [7], where $\bar{p}_i = \bar{p}$ is a special case, in which all tasks (jobs) have the same running

---

[1] https://github.com/parlab-tuwien/omp-task-bench.

Listing 3.1. Version `MasterTask`

```
#pragma omp parallel firstprivate(m)
{
#pragma omp master
  for (i = 0; i < n; i++) {
    if( hetero_workload )
      m = get_work(i);
#pragma omp task firstprivate(m)
    res[ridx] = add_bench(m);
  }
#pragma omp taskwait
}
```

Listing 3.2. Version `ParallelTask`

```
#pragma omp parallel firstprivate(m)
{
#pragma omp for
  for (i = 0; i < n; i++) {
    if( hetero_workload )
      m = get_work(i);
#pragma omp task firstprivate(m)
    res[ridx] = add_bench(m);
  }
#pragma omp taskwait
}
```

Listing 3.3. Version `ParallelFor`

```
#pragma omp parallel firstprivate(m)
{
#pragma omp for
  for (i = 0; i < n; i++) {
    if( hetero_workload )
      m = get_work(i);
    res[ridx] = add_bench(m);
  }
}
```

time $\bar{p}$. From an implementation standpoint, we would like to create the simplest way of testing the scheduling system with the smallest amount of noise introduced by experimental factors. In our context, a scheduling instance for homogeneous tasks is defined by three variables: n denotes the number of tasks to be created, m denotes the work done in each task, and p denotes the number of threads to be created. Since each thread is mapped to one core exclusively, p also defines the number of cores used to schedule this instance. We also consider the more general case, where each task can have a different amount of work. In this heterogeneous case, the work of each task is drawn randomly from a given distribution, which will be discussed later (cf. Sect. 4).

In order to test the scheduling system, our benchmark executes n jobs of work m on p cores. Our benchmark suite supports two commonly used task creation strategies:

- `MasterTask`: The master thread creates all n tasks, as shown in Listing 3.1.
- `ParallelTask`: All p threads create all n tasks, which is outlined in Listing 3.2.

As a performance baseline, we execute the same n function calls, instead of using OpenMP tasks, in a parallel For-loop (cf. `ParallelFor` in Listing 3.3). Since all loop iterations are independent, the parallel For-loop will provide a lower bound on the performance of the task scheduling system in the case of homogeneous tasks.

Workload Options. The actual work of each task is done by the `add_bench` function, which takes m as an input and computes $\sum_i^m i$ in a for loop, and the result is returned as a double value. When we test the heterogeneous problem

Table 1. Multi-core machines and compilers used in our study.

machine	*Hydra*	*Nebula*	*VSC-5*
processor	Intel Xeon 6130F	AMD EPYC 7551	AMD Epyc 7713
core frequency	2.10 GHz	2.00 GHz	2.00 GHz
nb of sockets	2	2	2
nb of cores per node	32	64	128
compilers	gcc 12.1.0	gcc 12.1.0	gcc 11.2.0
	clang 14.0.4	clang 14.0.4	clang 12.0.1
	pgcc 22.5	pgcc 22.5	pgcc 22.5
	icc 2021.7.0	aocc 3.2.0	aocc 3.2.0

instances, the value of m is selected independently for each task. The add_bench function should mimic a real function call, and thus, it returns an actual result. In our benchmark, we always store the result of the add_bench function in a variable, which the compiler cannot optimize away. However, if we just stored the latest result of each add_bench function from all threads in one global variable, we would create a false sharing issue among the threads. Therefore, each thread stores the latest result of add_bench in its own part of the global res array. The index ridx ensures that each thread accesses a different cache line.

Due to its simplicity, our benchmark setup has two advantages compared to the previous benchmarks. First, the work m is always the same for different executions of the benchmark, which reduces noise and improves reproducibility. Second, the add_bench function only needs to read one integer value (m) from memory, and thus, the benchmark is insensitive to the different bandwidths that typically occur between the various NUMA nodes on current multi-core processors.

Considerations for Compiler Fairness. Our study should reveal differences in the OpenMP runtime systems when scheduling a large number of independent tasks. Therefore, the actual code that each task executes should be exactly the same. For this reason, we compile the task's code into a separate, dynamic library with exactly one compiler (gcc in all cases), to ensure that the assembly code of the individual tasks is identical. The rest of the benchmark, in particular the OpenMP pragmas, is compiled with each tested compiler.

4   Experimental Setup

Now, we explain our experimental, hardware, and software setup for comparing various OpenMP runtime systems.

Hardware and Software Setup. We conduct experiments on three different multi-core, shared-memory systems that comprise 32, 64, and 128 physical cores, which are called *Hydra*, *Nebula*, and *VSC-5*, respectively. We provide an overview of

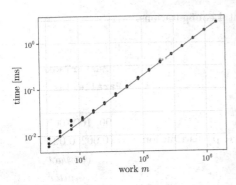
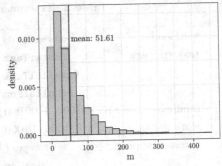

(a) Running time of computational kernel for growing work m; *Hydra*   (b) Exponentially distributed heterogeneous workload per task m_i; $\lambda = 0.02$

Fig. 1. Example workloads for parameter m.

the hardware and software details in Table 1. On the Intel system, *Hydra*, we compare the Intel icc compiler to the compilers gcc, pgcc, and clang, while on the AMD systems, *Nebula* and *VSC-5*, we use the aocc compiler instead of the Intel icc. Since aocc is built on top of the clang infrastructure and also uses `libomp`, we expect similar performance results from clang and aocc. The most important difference between the Intel processor and both AMD processors, which are used in our experiments, is the number of NUMA nodes. The Intel processor only has one NUMA node per socket, while the AMD processors have either four (*Nebula*) or two (*VSC-5*) NUMA nodes per socket.

Workload Options. A central parameter of our benchmark is the work done per task. If the work is small, the fraction of the overall time spent in the OpenMP runtime system grows, and differences in the scheduling methods become more pronounced. Figure 1a shows how the runtime of our `add_bench` function depends on the work parameter m. In this experiment, we increase the work m and measure the running time of `add_bench` for each m. We can observe that the runtime grows linearly with m, exactly as it should.

As already mentioned, we also investigate how well the OpenMP runtime systems perform for heterogeneous workloads. In particular, we would like to answer whether the scheduling results change if the workload is heterogeneous. Feitelson [5] points out that typical workloads, e.g., runtimes of jobs in batch systems, do not follow a uniform distribution, as the distributions are often heavy-tailed. Jain [9] states that exponential service times are commonly used. Outsterhout et al. [11] examine the performance of Spark schedulers, where the duration of spark jobs are exponentially distributed.

We also use workloads that follow an exponential distribution. An example workload is shown in Fig. 1b, where the rate parameter λ is set to 0.02, which leads to a mean work per task of 50 iterations.

From an implementation point of view, we have to be careful that the random number generator does not influence the performance results when creating

Table 2. Experimental configurations.

workload	homogeneous	heterogeneous
task strategy	MasterTask	MasterTask
	ParallelTask	ParallelTask
	ParallelFor	
number of tasks n	100 000, 1 000 000	100 000, 1 000 000
work per task m	1, 1000, 10 000	exp. distribution $\lambda = \{0.002, 0.02\}$
thread mapping	*compact*	*compact*
	scatter	*scatter*

OpenMP tasks. For this reason, a list of k heterogeneous task sizes are precomputed before each heterogeneous experiment and stored in a global array (we currently use $k = 10\,000$). When a task is spawned, we know its global task number $0 \leq i < n$, and we use the i to pick the next task size from the global list (with a wrap-around if i becomes larger than k).

Experimental Configurations. We provide an overview of the experimental parameters in Table 2. For space constraints, we can only show plots for a subset of the experiments conducted. The task size parameter m is the most crucial one for comparing the OpenMP runtime systems. With $m = 1$, the time spent in each task is extremely short, and structural differences in the runtime systems get emphasized. When increasing m to 1000 or 10 000, we would like to examine whether performance differences of the runtime system can still be seen for coarser-grained tasks.

Another important parameter for efficient, multi-threaded OpenMP applications on NUMA systems is the thread-to-core mapping strategy [13]. In order to exactly implement our desired mapping strategies, we rely on the OMP_PLACES environment variable and define our own *compact* and *scatter* mapping strategies. We consider the exposed NUMA nodes of the system to be the basic building blocks for thread-mapping. In the *compact* strategy, we start by filling up the first NUMA node, before we map threads to the second, third NUMA node, and so forth. In the *scatter* strategy, we allocate the threads in a round-robin fashion across the NUMA nodes.

5   Experimental Results

5.1   General Experimental Factors

While experimenting with the different OpenMP runtime systems, we made two important observations. The first concerns the thread mapping strategy. In virtually all cases, the variance of the running time of our task benchmark decreases significantly if threads are pinned to specific cores. Therefore, we used thread pinning in all our experiments to reduce the number of required repetitions to obtain consistent, reproducible performance numbers.

We also noticed that the gcc compiler, especially with the MasterTask strategy, performed significantly inferior to its competitors. Since it uses a central task queue, we experimented with adapting environment variables provided by OpenMP and libGOMP. We found that the wait policy had a huge positive impact on the performance of gcc, while the other compilers were unaffected. Therefore, we executed the experiments with all OpenMP runtime systems after setting the environment variable OMP_WAIT_POLICY to PASSIVE.

5.2 Homogeneous Workloads

In our first experimental analysis, we compare the performance of the different compilers on the Intel-based machine *Hydra*. Figure 2 presents strong scaling results for the case of executing $n = 100\,000$ independent tasks, each having work $m = 1$. We can observe that the MasterTask strategy, where the master thread creates all tasks, does not scale at all. When the number of threads increases the running time also grows, independently from the actual thread mapping strategy. Here, we can see that the larger overhead of gcc is already clearly visible starting with $p = 4$ threads.

A similar trend can be observed in the middle graphs of Fig. 2, where the ParallelTask version is analyzed. We can see that gcc's runtime is very unstable, as shown by the 95% confidence intervals, but gcc is very fast for 1 or 2 threads compared to clang and icc.

In the last row of this figure, we show the ParallelFor results as a baseline. We can observe that the task-based versions (shown in the middle row) add a significant overhead to the running time. In contrast, when applying the ParallelFor strategy, the parallel execution of the add_bench functions does show a good scaling behavior for all compilers.

In order to compare the measured runtimes in a more comprehensible way, we show the runtimes for the different compilers relative to the runtime of gcc. Thus, if a compiler has a ratio larger than 1, then this compiler was slower than gcc. On the contrary, if this ratio is below 1, the runtime of the OpenMP benchmark compiled with the respective compiler was shorter than the one compiled with gcc.

Figure 3 presents the runtime results for clang, icc, and pgcc, always relative to the runtime of gcc. In this experiment, we fixed the number of tasks to $n = 100\,000$ and used the *compact* mapping strategy. We can notice that the performance difference is relatively small if the task size m is 1000 or larger. For the task-based versions, we can observe that the other compilers outperform gcc for more than 2 threads. Yet, for two threads or less, gcc is overall the best. Interestingly, in the ParallelFor case, clang is clearly outperformed by both icc and gcc for virtually all thread counts.

We now turn to the AMD processors. Figure 4 presents the performance results for the 64-core machine *Nebula*. The architecture of this machine differs significantly from the Intel-based machine from before, as it has 8 NUMA nodes

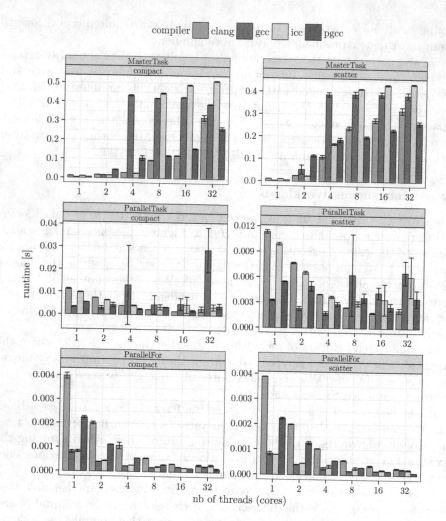

Fig. 2. Performance comparison of different compilers for $n = 100\,000$, $m = 1$; machine: *Hydra*. Error bars represent the 95% confidence interval of the mean.

in total, 4 per socket. The Intel-based machine *Hydra* from the previous experiment only has two NUMA nodes, one per socket. From this figure, we can observe that the gcc compiler outperforms the competitors for small threads counts (1 and 2). However, in the ParallelTask case, gcc is significantly slower than the competitors when the number of cores is between 32 and 64. In the benchmarks on the AMD machine, the pgcc compiler provided the best overall performance, while the benchmark times obtained with clang and aocc were often slower than the ones produced by pgcc and gcc.

Last, we show the performance results for the largest shared-memory node in our experiments, which has 128 cores. In Fig. 5, we only present the results

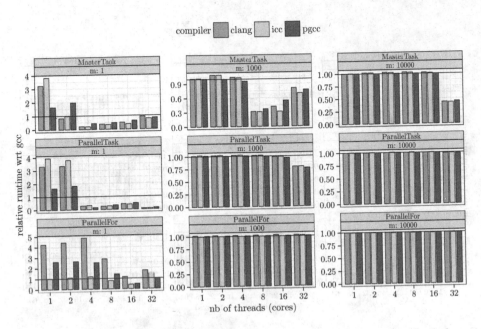

Fig. 3. Performance of compilers with respect to the runtime obtained with gcc, $n =$ 100 000, mapping: *compact*; *Hydra*.

with more than 32 cores, as these cases showed the largest differences. We can observe that gcc scales very well for the `MasterTask` strategy. More interestingly, pgcc was suddenly outperformed for 96 and 128 cores for the `ParallelTask` case (middle). This was surprising as pgcc was found to be the best compiler for the other machines in this case. For the `ParallelFor` case, the situation is very different, as pgcc outperforms the other compilers again significantly. We used the profiling option of our benchmark to assess how equally the tasks are balanced among the threads, in order to find the cause of the performance differences (especially for the `ParallelTask`). We could not find a correlation between the task imbalance and the running time.

5.3   Homogeneous Case: Correlation Analysis

We also wanted to assess whether the shortest running time translates to best load balanced schedule. In classic scheduling theory, a perfectly balanced schedule is a lower bound for an instance of $P \parallel C_{\max}$. However, our case is slightly different as we only have homogeneous cores, but the interconnect between the cores is heterogeneous.

In order to show the results of our study, we present one specific case that highlights our findings, which comprises $n = 100\,000$ tasks of size $m = 1$ and the `MasterTask` task creation strategy with $p = 64$ threads.

By leveraging the profiling and tracing capabilities of OMPTB, we analyzed the resulting load distribution across the different participating threads. In fact,

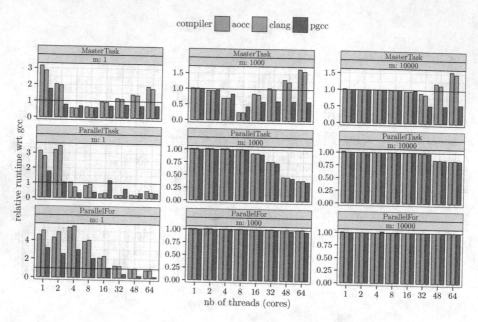

Fig. 4. Performance of compilers with respect to the runtime obtained with gcc, $n = 100\,000$, mapping: *compact*; *Nebula*.

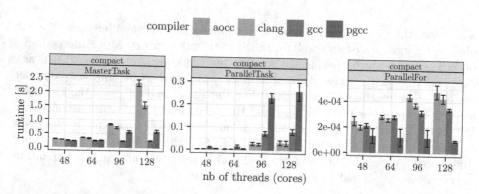

Fig. 5. Performance comparison of different compilers for $n = 100\,000$, $m = 1$ and $p > 32$; *VSC-5*. Error bars represent the 95% confidence interval of the mean.

we only used the profiling capability in this case, where the number of tasks that is executed per thread is counted. In contrast, when recording a trace, the start and finish timestamp of each task will be recorded, which introduced too much overhead to the overall running time if tasks only have size $m = 1$.

Figure 6a compares the running times measured for the different compilers. In Fig. 6b, we present the number of executed tasks per thread (top) and the total number of cache misses per core. The cores on the x-axis are ordered NUMA node

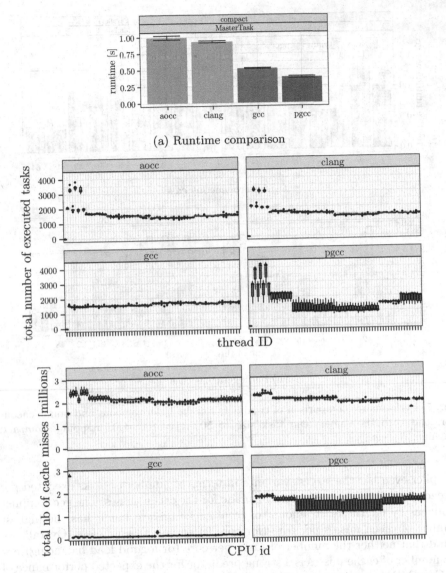

(a) Runtime comparison

(b) Executed tasks and cache misses per thread/core

Fig. 6. Compiler comparison for the specific case $n = 100\,000$, $m = 1$, $p = 64$, `MasterTask` (boxplots show results of 10 different runs), mapping: *compact*; machine: *Nebula*.

by NUMA node, where each NUMA node comprises 8 cores. We also ordered the thread IDs on the x-axis in the top graph to match the core ID in the graph at the bottom. In this case, the pgcc compiler is the fastest, but we can also observe that gcc produces the most balanced load distribution across all threads. The pgcc

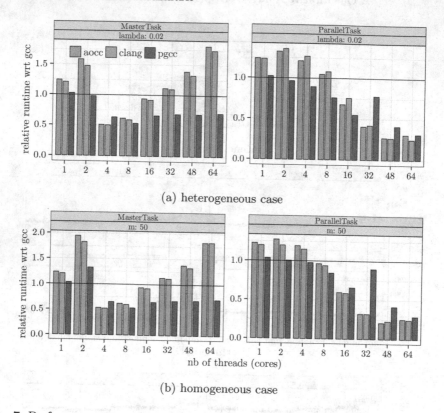

(a) heterogeneous case

(b) homogeneous case

Fig. 7. Performance comparison of compilers for the heterogeneous and homogeneous workload with the same mean task size of 50, $n = 1\,000\,000$, mapping: *compact*; machine: *Nebula*.

compiler even has the largest variance in terms of number of tasks executed per thread. A similar observation can be made for the cache misses. The gcc compiler produces by far the least amount of total cache misses, but it has the highest number of cache misses per core (for core 0) among all compilers. Overall, we found that neither the number of tasks per core (or a good load balancing) nor the number of cache misses is a strong predictor for the expected performance of an OpenMP runtime system. The individual implementations of data structures and locks used for the task queues also have to be taken into account.

5.4   Heterogeneous Workloads

We also investigated the scheduling performance of the different OpenMP runtime systems in the presence of heterogeneous workloads. Our initial question was whether the heterogeneity of the work done by each task fundamentally changes the performance numbers of the OpenMP runtime systems. To answer this question, we conducted experiments with two similar sets of workloads. The first workload contains heterogeneous task sizes, which are drawn from an exponential distribution with $\lambda = 0.02$ (cf. Sect. 4). This specific exponential distribution has a mean of 50. For comparison, we also conducted experiments with a homogeneous workload, where each task size has exactly the same work, i.e., $m = 50$.

The experimental results for running these two workloads are shown in Fig. 7. Although the graphs do not precisely match each other, the results for the heterogeneous case (top) are very similar to the ones obtained for the homogeneous case (bottom). We can observe that gcc is inferior for more than 16 cores for the `ParallelTask` case. However, for the `MasterTask` case, gcc outperforms both clang and aocc for many core counts. Similarly to the results shown before, the pgcc compiler offers the best overall performance for the cases considered. More importantly, the performance was mainly influenced by the number of cores (threads) and by the mean task size. The fact that the individual task sizes are distributed either homogeneously or heterogeneously only has a small impact. This finding was consistent with the other experiments that we have conducted.

6   Conclusions

We evaluated the task scheduling performance of OpenMP runtime systems found in modern compiler suites, such as gcc, icc, pgcc, or clang. We developed a benchmark called OMPTB to assess the performance of OpenMP runtime systems when processing a large number of independent tasks. In particular, we examined the scalability behavior of the runtime systems when increasing the number of cores. We also investigated the influence of the thread mapping strategy on the performance of the schedulers.

When the generated tasks have a small work, gcc is outperformed by the competitors. However, for 2 and 4 cores (threads), gcc often provides a very competitive performance. When comparing the other compilers, we observed that clang (and aocc) was often slower than icc or pgcc.

We also investigated whether the tread mapping strategy has a strong impact on the resulting performance. Here, we can give several answers. Using a thread mapping strategy improves reproducibility, as the runtime variance is significantly reduced. In our work, we examined the *compact* and the *scatter* mapping strategies. When comparing both, we cannot clearly state which one should be used, because there was no clear winner, as the better mapping strategy depends on the actual scheduling problem (e.g., number of tasks, number of cores).

We also examined the performance impact of executing heterogeneous workloads, i.e., the work of the generated OpenMP tasks differs (they have a different runtime). Surprisingly, the actual mean of the work distributions was far more important than heterogeneity, i.e., the performance numbers produced by the compilers were very similar for homogeneous and heterogeneous workloads if the mean work per task matched.

Acknowledgments. We thank Lukas Briem for helping to implement the heterogeneous workloads.

References

1. Bull, J.M., Reid, F., McDonnell, N.: A microbenchmark suite for OpenMP tasks. In: Chapman, B.M., Massaioli, F., Müller, M.S., Rorro, M. (eds.) IWOMP 2012. LNCS, vol. 7312, pp. 271–274. Springer, Heidelberg (2012). https://doi.org/10.1007/978-3-642-30961-8_24

2. Chasapis, D., et al.: PARSECSs: evaluating the impact of task parallelism in the PARSEC benchmark suite. ACM Trans. Archit. Code Optim. **12**(4), 1–22 (2016). https://doi.org/10.1145/2829952

3. Clet-Ortega, J., Carribault, P., Pérache, M.: Evaluation of OpenMP task scheduling algorithms for large NUMA architectures. In: Silva, F., Dutra, I., Santos Costa, V. (eds.) Euro-Par 2014. LNCS, vol. 8632, pp. 596–607. Springer, Cham (2014). https://doi.org/10.1007/978-3-319-09873-9_50

4. Duran, A., Teruel, X., Ferrer, R., Martorell, X., Ayguadé, E.: Barcelona OpenMP tasks suite: a set of benchmarks targeting the exploitation of task parallelism in OpenMP. In: Proceedings of the ICPP, pp. 124–131. IEEE Computer Society (2009). https://doi.org/10.1109/ICPP.2009.64

5. Feitelson, D.G.: Workload Modeling for Computer Systems Performance Evaluation. Cambridge University Press, Cambridge (2015)

6. Gautier, T., Perez, C., Richard, J.: On the impact of OpenMP task granularity. In: de Supinski, B.R., Valero-Lara, P., Martorell, X., Mateo Bellido, S., Labarta, J. (eds.) IWOMP 2018. LNCS, vol. 11128, pp. 205–221. Springer, Cham (2018). https://doi.org/10.1007/978-3-319-98521-3_14

7. Graham, R.L., Lawler, E.L., Lenstra, J.K., Kan, A.R.: Optimization and approximation in deterministic sequencing and scheduling: a survey. Ann. Discrete Math. **5**, 287–326 (1979)

8. Huynh, A., Helm, C., Iwasaki, S., Endo, W., Namsraijav, B., Taura, K.: TP-PARSEC: a task parallel PARSEC benchmark suite. J. Inf. Process. **27**, 211–220 (2019). https://doi.org/10.2197/ipsjjip.27.211

9. Jain, R.: The art of computer systems performance analysis - techniques for experimental design, measurement, simulation, and modeling. Wiley (1991)

10. Olivier, S., Porterfield, A., Wheeler, K.B., Spiegel, M., Prins, J.F.: OpenMP task scheduling strategies for multicore NUMA systems. Int. J. High Perform. Comput. Appl. **26**(2), 110–124 (2012). https://doi.org/10.1177/1094342011434065

11. Ousterhout, K., Wendell, P., Zaharia, M., Stoica, I.: Sparrow: distributed, low latency scheduling. In: Proceedings of the 24th SOSP, pp. 69–84. ACM (2013). https://doi.org/10.1145/2517349.2522716

12. Schuchart, J., Nachtmann, M., Gracia, J.: Patterns for OpenMP task data dependency overhead measurements. In: de Supinski, B.R., Olivier, S.L., Terboven, C., Chapman, B.M., Müller, M.S. (eds.) IWOMP 2017. LNCS, vol. 10468, pp. 156–168. Springer, Cham (2017). https://doi.org/10.1007/978-3-319-65578-9_11

13. Terboven, C., Schmidl, D., Cramer, T., an Mey, D.: Assessing OpenMP tasking implementations on NUMA architectures. In: Chapman, B.M., Massaioli, F., Müller, M.S., Rorro, M. (eds.) IWOMP 2012. LNCS, vol. 7312, pp. 182–195. Springer, Heidelberg (2012). https://doi.org/10.1007/978-3-642-30961-8_14

14. Yang, J., He, Q.: Scheduling parallel computations by work stealing: a survey. Int. J. Parallel Program. **46**(2), 173–197 (2018). https://doi.org/10.1007/s10766-016-0484-8

15. Zhan, X., Bao, Y., Bienia, C., Li, K.: PARSEC3.0: a multicore benchmark suite with network stacks and SPLASH-2X. SIGARCH Comput. Archit. News **44**(5), 1–16 (2016). https://doi.org/10.1145/3053277.3053279

EAIBench: An Energy Efficiency Benchmark for AI Training

Fan Zhang[1], Chuanxin Lan[1], Lei Wang[1,2,3], Fei Tang[1,3], Shaopeng Dai[1,2], Jiangtao Wang[4], Jiantao Ma[4], and Jianfeng Zhan[1,2,3]([⊠])

[1] Institute of Computing Technology, Chinese Academy of Sciences, Beijing 100190, China
{zhangfan,lanchuanxin,wanglei_2011,tangfei,daishaopeng, zhanjianfeng}@ict.ac.cn
[2] International Open Benchmark Council (BenchCouncil), Beijing, China
[3] School of Computer Science and Technology, University of Chinese Academy of Sciences, Beijing 100049, China
[4] Huawei, Shenzhen, China
{wangjiangtao,majiantao}@huawei.com

Abstract. The increase in computing power has prompted more considerable artificial intelligence (AI) model scales. From 341K multiply-accumulate operations (MACs) of LeNet-5 to 4.11G MACs of ResNet-50, the computational cost of image classification has increased by 10,000 times over two decades. On the other hand, it has inevitably brought about an increase in energy consumption, and benchmarking the energy efficiency of the modern AI workloads is also essential. Existing benchmarks, such as MLPerf and AIBench, focus on performance evaluation of AI computing, the time to the target accuracy (TTA) is the primary metric. Corresponding to the TTA metric, using the energy consumption, where the AI workload achieves the specific accuracy, is a straightforward energy measurement method. However, it is too time-consuming and power-hungry, which is unacceptable for energy efficiency benchmarking. This work introduces a new metric to quickly and accurately benchmark AI training workloads' energy efficiency, called the Energy-Delay Product of one Epoch (EEDP). The EEDP is calculated based on the product of the energy and time consumption within one training epoch, where one epoch refers to one training cycle through the entire training dataset. It can reflect not only the energy consumption but also the time efficiency and suit the energy efficiency of the AI training workloads. Then, we introduce an AI training energy efficiency benchmark named EAIBench, which covers different energy efficiency dimensions, including dominant layers, computation intensities, and memory accesses. Our evaluation results demonstrate that EAIBench can provide reproducible and meaningful results in only dozens of minutes, which is hundreds of times faster than the existing AI training benchmark method.

Keywords: Energy efficiency · AI training · Benchmark

© The Author(s), under exclusive license to Springer Nature Switzerland AG 2023
A. Gainaru et al. (Eds.): Bench 2022, LNCS 13852, pp. 19–34, 2023.
https://doi.org/10.1007/978-3-031-31180-2_2

1   Introduction

From the Data Center Frontier's report, from 2010 to 2018, the global energy consumption of data centers grew from 194TWh to 205TWh [23]. According, by 2030 the data centers will emit up to 720 million tons of CO_2 [21], where a considerable proportion is from AI training computing. Therefore, improving the energy efficiency of AI is essential, and building a benchmark is the first step.

AI computing is generally divided into training and inference. Some works focus on the energy efficiency of AI inference. MLPerf [22] released inference v1.0 results with power measurements, but they only reported the average power and energy consumption (Joule) without further analysis. Yao et al. [33] did in-depth research, including energy consumption ratio, layer-level analysis, operational intensity, and memory access intensity. Still, the research is limited to the image classification task. However, the training procedure differs from inference: (i) Training contains both forward (inference) and backward designs, so it is more computationally intensive and requires more storage space to store intermediate variables. (ii) Training consists of many epochs to iteratively update the model, leading to much larger computation and other data reuse than inference. In a word, the energy efficiency benchmark for AI training is necessary.

However, existing AI training benchmarks are focused on the time to train the model to the target accuracy (TTA). Mainstream benchmarks such as DAWN-Bench [8], MLPerf [22] and AIBench [29] all use TTA as the metric. For the energy efficiency measurement, mainstream benchmarks only use the energy that the AI training workload achieves the target accuracy as the metric [22]. TTA/Energy is a good metric that can directly compare different optimizations that may modify the training procedure and impact the final accuracy. However, the training time is days to get the target accuracy. For example, from our experiment, it takes 230 h and 20 kWh ($7.2*10^7$ Joules) to train ResNet50 [16] to 77% top1 accuracy on one V100. So, TTA/Energy is unsuitable for energy efficiency evaluation for AI training.

This paper introduces a new metric for AI training workloads' energy efficiency, called the Energy-Delay Product of one Epoch (EEDP). Then, we build an AI training energy efficiency benchmark named EAIBench, which covers different energy efficiency dimensions. Our contributions are as follows:

- We present a new methodology to benchmark the energy efficiency of AI training. Inspired by the energy-delay product (EDP), our new methodology is based on the EDP of one training epoch named EEDP. The EEDP is the product of the energy and time consumption within one training epoch, where one epoch refers to one training cycle through the entire training dataset. (i) First, we verify that EEDP represents the whole training process (Sect. 4.1). In detail, We reveal that from the first to the end epoch of the training, the EEDPs for different epochs are similar. (ii) Second, Only two essential parameters are open, batch size and worker, and others are fixed. We reveal that, compared with throughput, EEDP is robust to different configurations and a recommended way is given to set parameters. (iii) Finally, EEDP benchmarks different hardware platforms, not algorithmic optimizations. EEDP can measure any optimizations, where improvement ratios are used to compare different hardware platforms as we do in Sect. 4.4. However, the implementation should be identical for different hardware platforms under test.

– We propose an energy efficiency benchmark for AI training named EAIBench. Compared with MLPerf and AIBench, EAIBench is a benchmark specific to energy efficiency, which is built from different aspects of energy efficiency characteristics, including different dominant layers, computation intensities, and memory accesses. Seven workloads are finally selected for EAIBench. Compared with MLPerf and AIBench, EAIBench is aimed at energy efficiency and includes more representative tasks while keeping the benchmark subsets to a minimum.

– We explore configuration space and propose a uniform method to set critical parameters on different systems to improve the usability of EAIBench. Furthermore, we reveal that the Energy efficiency is less sensitive than throughput under different model parameters (Sect. 4.3), which implies that energy efficiency is robust to different configurations.

– Using EAIBench, we take the ResNet50 as an example to analyze the energy efficiency of AI training. We found that the highest average energy consumption in ResNet50 is the convolutional layer because it is compute-bound, and floating-point operations per second (FLOPS) is much larger than others (Sect. 4.5). The second highest is the whole connection layer because it is memory-bound, and the memory access strength is much larger than others (Sect. 4.5).

The rest of this paper is organized as follows. Section 2 summarizes the related work. Section 3 presents the methodology and implementation. Section 4 is the evaluations. Section 5 draws a conclusion.

2   Related Work

The existing AI benchmarks are listed in Table 1.

2.1   Benchmark

Existing AI benchmarks mainly focus on performance. MLPerf [22] and AIBench [29] are two systematic AI benchmarks. MLPerf performs the most large-scale testing by accepting and analyzing the results submitted by companies. AIBench is by far the most comprehensive AI benchmark, including 19 benchmarks. DAWNBench [8] is the first benchmark that proposes to use TTA as an end-to-end metric for AI training. Fathom [2] is the first benchmark that contains a collection of tasks instead of only a specific task. TBD [34] is a training benchmark for deep neural networks (DNNs). DeepBench [5] is an atomic benchmark that consists of basic operations such as matrix multiplies and convolutions. However, these works ignore the study of energy efficiency. Until 2021,

Table 1. AI benchmark comparison.

Benchmark	Metric		Energy Efficiency		Task						
	TRNG	INFR	TRNG	INFR	IC	IS	NLP	TR	SR	RA	RE
MLPerf [22]	TTA	Latency, Energy	✗	✓	✓	✓	✓	✗	✓	✓	✓
AIBench [29]	TTA	Latency	✗	✗	✓	✓	✓	✓	✓	✓	✓
DAWNBench [8]	TTA, Cost	Latency, Cost	✗	✗	✓	✗	✗	✗	✗	✗	✗
Fathom [2]	Throughput	Latency	✗	✗	✓	✗	✗	✓	✓	✗	✗
TBD [34]	Throughput	–	✗	✗	✓	✓	✗	✓	✓	✗	✓
DeepBench [5]	Throughput	Latency	✗	✗	✗	✗	✗	✗	✗	✗	✗
Yao [33]	–	Latency, Energy	✗	✓	✓	✗	✗	✗	✗	✗	✗
Wang [32]	Throughput, Energy	–	✓	✗	✓	✗	✗	✓	✓	✗	✗
EAIBench	EEDP	–	✓	✗	✓	✓	✓	✓	✓	✓	✓
Notes:	TRNG: Training										
	INFR: Inference										
	IC: Image Classification										
	IS: Image Segmentation										
	SR: Speech Recognization										
	TR: Translation										
	RA: Ranking										
	RE: Recommendation										

MLPerf joint SPEC [19] released the energy consumption analysis report, but it only contains the inference, not training.

There is some work focusing on AI energy efficiency. However, these works mainly analyze the inference procedure and lack training analysis. Yao [33] analyzes the energy efficiency of CNN inference on high-performance graphics processing unit (GPU). Few works involve energy efficiency for AI training. Wang [32] benchmarks the performance and energy efficiency of AI training, but there is very little analysis of the energy efficiency, which only contains the energy consumption under different batch sizes.

2.2   Metrics

Throughput and TTA are two dominant metrics for AI training. Some benchmarks [2,5,28] use throughput as a metric, where only running a mini-batch of data is enough. However, since DAWNBench [8] announced that TTA is a good metric for machine learning (ML) training in 2017, most performance benchmarks use TTA as a training metric. However, energy efficiency differs from performance benchmark (i) How to evaluate energy efficiency with limited time and energy cost is essential. (ii) Accuracy does not affect the energy consumption process for each epoch. This paper proposes that power-per-epoch (PPE) is a good metric, a kind of throughput metric.

Energy-delay product (EDP) was proposed in 1996 to test the energy efficiency of general-purpose microprocessors [12]. Compared with W and J, EDP considers both energy and delay simultaneously. Some recent works also use EDP to measure the energy efficiency of systems, primarily in the evaluation of DVFS technology [14].

3 Methodology and Implementation

The framework of EAIBench is shown in Fig. 1. The methodology of EAIBench consists of metric and measurement, benchmarks, configuration space design, monitor tools, and analyzer. The input of EAIBench is the benchmark workload, and the output is the energy efficiency analysis results.

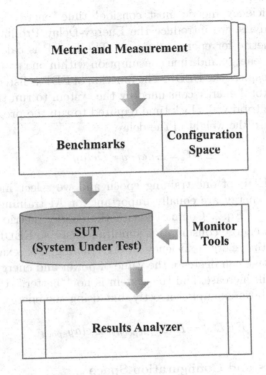

Fig. 1. The overview of the EAIBench framework.

3.1 Metric and Measurement

Most current AI models iteratively update model weights using algorithms such as stochastic gradient descent (SGD). A complete training process contains many epochs, where an epoch means one pass (forward and backward) of the whole training dataset. For example, it needs 90 epochs to train ResNet-50 [16] and 250 epochs to train DeepSpeech2 [4]. On the other hand, during the model training, each epoch passes the same process in calculation and memory access, which means that there is no difference in the energy consumption characteristics of each epoch. So, the behavior of one epoch can represent that of the entire execution process. Besides, compared with TTA, one epoch is more stable. Generally, Coefficient of Variation (CoV) can be used to measure stability, defined as the ratio of the standard deviation to the mean. More minor means more stable. Compared with 14% CoV of MLPerf's TTA metric, the CoV in time-per-epoch is less than 3% [7]. In the real test, we run two epochs and only record the last one because the first epoch may contain some model initialization work that others do not. Besides, the idle power (ready but not running program) is subtracted because different configurations have different idle powers and it has little to do with program running.

An energy efficiency metric must consider time, energy, and cost. Based on the above analysis, we introduce the Energy-Delay Product of one Epoch (EEDP) as the metric for energy efficiency. The EEDP is calculated based on the product of the energy and time consumption within one training epoch. The EDP metric also inspires the EEDP. The function of EDP is listed in Eq. 1, where the energy is the total energy consumed by the system to run the program, the delay refers to the total wall clock time required to run the program, and index x is used to increase the weight of the delay.

$$EDP = Energy * Delay^x \qquad (1)$$

EEDP is the EDP of one training epoch and we select index x with one because time and energy are equally important for AI training. The equation of EEDP is listed in Eq. 2. Compared with the energy metric (Joule), EEDP considers time and energy consumption simultaneously, so EEDP is more suited for evaluation of the energy efficiency of AI training. For example, reducing clock speed or voltage can decrease the value of power and energy. However, the procedure delay will increase, and the system is not "better." Using the EEDP can evaluate the above example correctly, but using the energy metric can not do it.

$$EEDP = Energy_{epoch} * Delay_{epoch} \qquad (2)$$

3.2 Benchmarks and Configuration Space

Benchmarks. We summarize the energy efficiency characteristic factors from the existing work [32,33] and choose the following key factors: task, model, layer, algorithm complexity, and memory access. Then we perform a detailed survey of those domains and select seven representative benchmarks shown in Table 2. In practical applications, those models are continuously updated. For example, Facebook incremental updates models daily or every couple of days [18]. So how to quickly and accurately bench-mark AI training workloads' energy efficiency is important. To further speed up the evaluation time, we use the reduced dataset as shown in Table 3.

Representative Tasks. We select seven representative tasks that encompass several vital areas, including image classification, image segmentation, natural language processing (NLP), text translation, speech recognition, learning to rank, and recommendation.

State-of-the-Art Models. For each task, we select the state-of-the-art models. For example, we select Mask R-CNN [15] instead of Fast R-CNN [11] because the accuracy is improved and the mask function is added. We select DLRM [24] instead of NCF [17] because the accuracy is improved, and DLRM is specifically proposed to predict click-through rate, which is a critical application of AI algorithms.

Dominant Layers. AI model consists of different layers that have different energy consumption characteristics. For example, compared with full connection, the convolutional layer is much more compute-bound, and more energy is spent on computations rather than memory fetches. EAIBench selects the different models with different dominant layers to cover different energy consumption modes. Convolutional layer (CONV), attention, recurrent neural network (RNN), and embedding are included. CONV is dominant in image processing tasks. Attention is widely used in NLP. RNN is famous for speech recognition. Embedding is mainly used in the recommendation.

Different Algorithm Complexity. The number of FLOPs and parameters are two critical metrics for algorithm complexity. EAIBench contains a vast space of FLOPs from 8E−4 to 1E−11 and parameters from 5 to 45 MB.

Different Memory Access. Memory access is different in two aspects: (i) The dataset size and the data type are different. (ii) Dominant layer is different. Different layers have different memory reuses and lead to different memory access characteristics.

Table 2. The benchmark workloads in EAIBench.

No.	Task	Model	Layer	FLOPs (G)	Params (M)
1	Image classification	ResNet-50 v1.5 [16]	CONV	4.11	25.56
2	Image segmentation	Mask R-CNN [15]	CONV	134.42	44.4
3	NLP	BERT [10]	Attention	−	−
4	Text translation	Transformer [31]	Attention	0.43	45.89
5	Speech recognition	DeepSpeech2 [4]	RNN	0.59	−
6	Learning to rank	Ranking distillation [30]	CONV	8.54E−05	5.58
7	Recommendation	DLRM [24]	Embedding	−	−

Configuration Space. From model to software and hardware, many parameters can be configured. For reproducibility, we only choose a few critical parameters for users for modification. The batch size is the most studied parameter, and it significantly affects the training time and final accuracy of the model [3,13]. Batch size is the number of training examples that GPU used to calculate loss

Table 3. The dataset of EAIBench.

No.	Task	Dataset	Traing Instances	Used Instances	Unit
1	Image classification	ImageNet [9]	1200000	50000	Image
2	Image segmentation	COCO [20]	82784	1333	Image
3	NLP	WMT EN-GE [1]	29000	29000	Sentence
4	Text translation	WMT EN-GE [1]	29000	29000	Sentence
5	Speech recognition	Librispeech [27]	281242	5567	Audio and text
6	Learning to rank	Gowalla [6]	433356	367611	User rating
7	Recommendation	Random	–	204812	Click record

Notes: EN-GE is English-German

and update weights. Learning rate is another parameter usually adjusted according to batch size, which affects the accuracy but does not affect each epoch's computation and memory access process. Another parameter that significantly affects throughput is the number of workers, and it is a positive integer that defines the number of CPU processes used to load data. In this paper, only batch size and the number of workers are open to being modified.

3.3 Monitor and Analyzer

While running the benchmark workloads, we collect three sets of information: (i) Program running information that contains model training records such as accuracy and throughput. Besides, the records are time-tagged to find GPU and power information at the corresponding time. (ii) GPU information. The information such as utilization, temperature, clock rate, etc., is recorded every second. (iii) Power information. We test and record power every second by a power meter, which is more accurate than using the NVIDIA system management interface (nvidia-smi). Finally, we calculate EEDP by recorded time and power to benchmark GPU energy efficiency and analyze the reasons behind the results based on the collected information.

3.4 System Under Test

Generally, the system under the test (SUT) platform is the CPU-based server with the GPU accelerator card. Now, the implementation of EAIBench is based on the GPU platform, but it is easy to extend to the other accelerator platform, such as the TPU or NPU. Whatever any accelerator platform, the AI workload is loaded by the OS of the CPU, so EAIBench can be ported to any accelerator platform in theory.

4 Experiment and Result

The model and dataset are listed in Sect. 3. We conduct experiments on two GPUs platforms: TITAN V and V100-PCIE. The detailed configurations of the servers and GPU cards are listed in Table 4. The fan mode of the server is set to max, and the idle power of the machine is about 250 W. The digital power analyzer is YOKOGAWA WT300EH, which is used to test the power of the whole server. The server outputs two files: "Program.txt", which contains benchmark running information with a timestamp for each epoch, and "GPU.CSV", which contains GPU profiling information per second. The power meter outputs the power value per second and saves the values to "Power.CSV".

Table 4. Hardware configuration details.

	Server1	Server2
OS Type	Ubuntu 16.04.7 LTS	Ubuntu 16.04.7 LTS
Physical CPU cores	12	12
CPU Type	Intel(R) Xeon(R) CPU E5-2620 v3 @ 2.40 GHz	Intel(R) Xeon(R) CPU E5-2620 v3 @ 2.40 GHz
	GPU1	GPU2
GPU Name	TITAN V	V100-PCIE
Processors	80	80
CUDA Cores	5120	5120
Base Clock (MHz)	1200	1230
Boost Clock (MHz)	1455	1380
FP32 (TFLOPS)	14	14
Memory Clock (MHz)	850	1752
Memory Bandwidth (GB/s)	652	897
L2 Cache Size (M)	4.6	6
Video Memory (GB)	12	30
TDP (W)	250	250

4.1 Experimental Methodology

We do four experiments: (i) To verify that one epoch is representative of the energy efficiency behavior of the whole training process, we take the ResNet50 as an example to illustrate the stability of epochs for the complete training process. Coefficient of Variation (CoV) is used to evaluate stability. More details are in Sect. 4.2. The whole training dataset of ImageNet is used to train the model to target accuracy. Still, in the remaining experiments, the reduced data set is used as listed in Sect. 3. (ii) AI training workload always has huge configuration space. In Sect. 4.3, to verify the energy efficiency is robust to different configurations, we select two important model parameters from the configuration space and explore an extensive range of them. (iii) In Sect. 4.4, we use EAIBench to evaluate two types of GPU platforms (TITAN V and V100). We illustrate that the EEDP metric and the EAIbench can quickly and efficiently benchmark the energy efficiency of AI training on different GPU platforms. (iv) In Sect. 4.5, to deeply analyze energy efficiency at the layer level, we take ResNet50 as an example to break down layers. We measure the power and energy consumed by individual layers and analyze the reasons according to GPU's computation and access features.

4.2 Stability of Epochs

We train ResNet50 to the target accuracy on two GPUs, where the final top1 accuracy is around 77% and the number of epochs is set to be 90 refer to NVIDIA's report [26]. CoV is used to measure stability, defined as the ratio of the standard deviation to the mean, and smaller means more stable. Our results show that the epoch's CoVs of time, power, and EEDP are all less than 6.5%.

Figure 2 shows that as the number of epochs increases, the accuracy improves, but the time and power remain stable. Besides, time and power are negatively correlated for each epoch. In detail, get out for the first epoch, which may contain the date or model initialization: (i) On TITAN V, the maximum power is 1.13 times the minimum power, and the CoV is 3.33%. The maximum epoch time is 1.12 times the minimum time, and the CoV is 3.59%. The CoV of EEDP is 3.79%. (ii) On V100, the maximum power is 1.26 times the minimum, and the CoV is 6.38%. The maximum epoch time is 1.18 times the minimum time, and the CoV is 4.18%. The CoV of EEDP is 6.21%.

Our results show that the power, time and EEDP is stability for each epoch, and the CoV is less than 6.5%. Therefore, one epoch is a good representation of the entire training.

4.3 Model Parameters Analysis

As described in Sect. 3.2, we select batch size and number of works to explore. We analyze the throughput (images/s), energy efficiency (images/J), GPU kernels, and memory utilization of ResNet50 v1.5 under different batch sizes and the number of workers. The batch size is from 1 to 256, where 256 is the max number that data already fills up GPU and larger values will cause "OutOfMemoryError". The workers are from 1 to 64, where the performance increases first and then decreases.

Figure 3 shows that: (i). For both throughput and energy efficiency, the larger the batch size the better the performance. Because with the increase of batch size, the utilization of kernels and memory of GPU becomes larger. So the batch size is set to be the largest that GPU can hold in our follow-up experiments. (ii). For number of workers, 4 is enough for one GPU and if the value is too large or too small, the performance will be degraded. Too small value causes low GPU utilization due to insufficient data supply. Too large value also causes insufficient data supply because of central processing unit (CPU) thread blocking. Our server has 12 physical CPU cores and 24 logical CPU cores. Exceeding the number of logical cores will result in thread blocking. Besides, the bottleneck of AI training process is usually in GPU computing not data loader. (iii). Energy efficiency is less sensitive than throughput under different model parameters. For throughput, there is 20x difference between best and worst performance as show in Fig. 3a. However, for energy efficiency, there is only 3x difference between best and worst performance as show in Fig. 3b. This is because the energy consumption mainly consists of the number of floating point operations (FLOPs) and

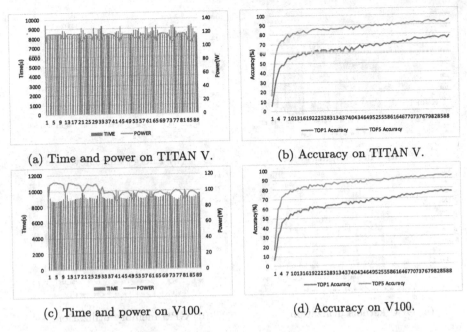

(a) Time and power on TITAN V.

(b) Accuracy on TITAN V.

(c) Time and power on V100.

(d) Accuracy on V100.

Fig. 2. Time, power and accuracy of ResNet50 training with 90 epochs.

memory accesses. However, batch size and workers dose not affect FLOPs and only affect memory access by different data reuse.

In summary, we not only provide a guidance method to set model parameters but also illustrate that the energy efficiency is robust to different configurations.

4.4 GPU Comparison

We benchmark two GPUs and use EEDP to do a comparative analysis. From Table 4, we can see that the computing power of two GPUs is equivalent, but V100 has a significant advantage in storage. The result of V100-PCIE is listed in Table 5, TITAN-V is in Table 6. We can see that EEDP scores for different models have large differences according to different model complexities and training data. Therefore, we use improvement ratios to compare two GPUs, which is listed in Table 7. Because the shorter the time and EEDP, the better, the values of time and EEDP in the Table 7 is the values of TITAN-V divided by V100-PCIE, and the rest is the opposite. We can see that: (i) EEDP of V100 is better than TITAN-V for all seven models. (ii) EEDP is a comprehensive metric that considers power and time at the same time. For the Transformer model, the throughput (Samples/s) of V100 is 99% of TITAN-V, while the energy efficiency (Samples/J) is 1.11 times, and the EEDP is a compromise value of 1.10. For

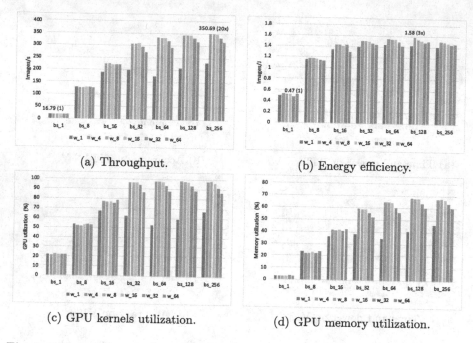

(a) Throughput.

(b) Energy efficiency.

(c) GPU kernels utilization.

(d) GPU memory utilization.

Fig. 3. Performance comparison of ResNet-50 under different batch size and workers on the V100 platform.

other models, both the throughput and energy efficiency of V100 are better than TITAN-V, so the improvement ratio of EEDP is much better.

So, using the EEDP metric, EAIbench can quickly and efficiently benchmark the energy efficiency of AI training on different GPU platforms. Besides, EEDP comprehensively considers time and energy, which is more suitable for AI training energy efficiency evaluation.

Table 5. The V100 platform results.

Model	Time	Power	Sample/s	Samples/J	EEDP
ResNet-50 v1.5	142.50	238.42	350.86	1.47	4842125.20
Mask R-CNN	6.87	188.59	11.64	0.06	139.24
BERT	9.65	74.00	3003.70	40.59	6928.32
Transformer	35.01	160.07	828.33	5.17	196133.38
DeepSpeech2	87.86	132.85	63.35	0.47	1025677.09
Ranking distillation	14.43	58.12	25629.86	440.62	12153.33
DLRM	68.77	53.25	2978.21	55.92	251877.27

Table 6. The TITAN-V platform results.

Model	Time	Power	Sample/s	Samples/J	EEDP
ResNet-50 v1.5	167.74	212.22	298.08	1.40	5971248.92
Mask R-CNN	9.00	171.95	8.88	0.05	218.07
BERT	10.58	137.99	2739.67	19.85	15446.10
Transformer	34.59	180.77	838.39	4.64	216285.54
DeepSpeech2	138.86	124.64	40.09	0.32	2403473.98
Ranking distillation	21.11	60.29	17417.13	288.92	26880.86
DLRM	86.97	61.07	2354.96	38.55	462134.06

Table 7. Speedup of V100 to TITAN-V.

Model	Time	Power	Sample/s	Samples/J	EEDP
ResNet-50 v1.5	1.18	1.12	1.18	1.05	1.23
Mask R-CNN	1.31	1.10	1.31	1.20	1.57
BERT	1.10	0.54	1.10	2.04	2.23
Transformer	0.99	0.89	0.99	1.11	1.10
DeepSpeech2	1.58	1.07	1.58	1.47	2.34
Ranking distillation	1.46	0.96	1.47	1.53	2.21
DLRM	1.26	0.87	1.26	1.45	1.83

4.5 Different Layers Analysis

To analyze energy efficiency at the layer level, we break down ResNet-50 into layers, including convolution, batch normalization, ReLU, full connection, pooling, and squeeze (Add the input to the current output). Time, power, energy consumption, FLOPS, and memory access are analyzed. In detail, NVIDIA's NVProf [25] tool is used to record FLOPS and memory access. In order to test the power of each layer, we: (i) Insert timestamps in the code, then find the output value of the power meter for the corresponding time. (ii) Repeat the execution of the target layer many times in each test, as one execution is too fast to be tested. For example, it is less than 0.01 s for one training pass of one batch for ResNet-50 on one V100.

Figure 4 shows that: (i) The dominant layer of ResNet50 is convolution, where the time accounts for 56%, and the energy consumption accounts for 67%. Batch normalization is the second dominant layer, where time accounts for 25%, and energy consumption accounts for 19%. (ii) The average power of the convolutional layer is the largest. Because it is compute-bound and the FLOPS is much larger than other layers, as shown in Fig. 4d. (iii) The average power of the full connection layer is the second largest. Because it is memory-bound and the memory access strength is much larger than other layers.

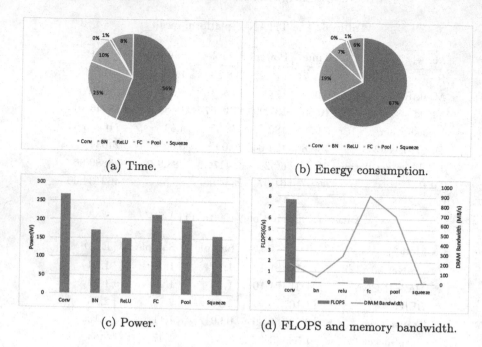

(a) Time.

(b) Energy consumption.

(c) Power.

(d) FLOPS and memory bandwidth.

Fig. 4. Layer analysis of ResNet50.

5   Conclusion

Existing AI training benchmarks, such as MLPerf and AIBench, mainly focus on the time to train the model to the target accuracy. However, it is not acceptable for the energy efficiency benchmark concerning time, energy, and costs. This paper presents a new benchmark named EAIBench and uses a new metric called EEDP to quickly and efficiently benchmark the energy efficiency of AI training. Besides, we use EAIBench to benchmark two GPU platforms and do a comparative analysis. Furthermore, we break down ResNet50 into layers for layer-level energy efficiency analysis.

References

1. https://nlp.stanford.edu/projects/nmt/
2. Adolf, R., Rama, S., Reagen, B., Wei, G.Y., Brooks, D.: Fathom: reference work-loads for modern deep learning methods. In: 2016 IEEE International Symposium on Workload Characterization (IISWC), pp. 1–10. IEEE (2016)
3. Akiba, T., Suzuki, S., Fukuda, K.: Extremely large minibatch SGD: training ResNet-50 on ImageNet in 15 minutes. arXiv preprint arXiv:1711.04325 (2017)
4. Amodei, D., et al.: Deep speech 2: end-to-end speech recognition in English and Mandarin. In: International Conference on Machine Learning, pp. 173–182. PMLR (2016)

5. Baidu: Deepbench: benchmarking deep learning operations on different hardware (2017). https://github.com/baidu-research/DeepBench
6. Cho, E., Myers, S.A., Leskovec, J.: Friendship and mobility: user movement in location-based social networks. In: Proceedings of the 17th ACM SIGKDD International Conference on Knowledge Discovery and Data Mining, pp. 1082–1090 (2011)
7. Coleman, C., et al.: Analysis of dawnbench, a time-to-accuracy machine learning performance benchmark. ACM SIGOPS Oper. Syst. Rev. **53**(1), 14–25 (2019)
8. Coleman, C., et al.: Dawnbench: an end-to-end deep learning benchmark and competition. Training **100**(101), 102 (2017)
9. Deng, J., Dong, W., Socher, R., Li, L.J., Li, K., Fei-Fei, L.: ImageNet: a large-scale hierarchical image database. In: 2009 IEEE Conference on Computer Vision and Pattern Recognition, pp. 248–255. IEEE (2009)
10. Devlin, J., Chang, M.W., Lee, K., Toutanova, K.: BERT: pre-training of deep bidirectional transformers for language understanding. arXiv preprint arXiv:1810.04805 (2018)
11. Girshick, R.: Fast R-CNN. In: Proceedings of the IEEE International Conference on Computer Vision, pp. 1440–1448 (2015)
12. Gonzalez, R., Horowitz, M.: Energy dissipation in general purpose microprocessors. IEEE J. Solid-State Circuits **31**(9), 1277–1284 (1996)
13. Goyal, P., et al.: Accurate, large minibatch SGD: training ImageNet in 1 hour. arXiv preprint arXiv:1706.02677 (2017)
14. Hajiamini, S., Shirazi, B.A.: A study of DVFS methodologies for multicore systems with islanding feature. In: Advances in Computers, vol. 119, pp. 35–71. Elsevier (2020)
15. He, K., Gkioxari, G., Dollár, P., Girshick, R.: Mask R-CNN. In: Proceedings of the IEEE International Conference on Computer Vision, pp. 2961–2969 (2017)
16. He, K., Zhang, X., Ren, S., Sun, J.: Deep residual learning for image recognition. In: Proceedings of the IEEE Conference on Computer Vision and Pattern Recognition, pp. 770–778 (2016)
17. He, X., Liao, L., Zhang, H., Nie, L., Hu, X., Chua, T.S.: Neural collaborative filtering. In: Proceedings of the 26th International Conference on World Wide Web, pp. 173–182 (2017)
18. He, X., et al.: Practical lessons from predicting clicks on ads at Facebook. In: Proceedings of the Eighth International Workshop on Data Mining for Online Advertising, pp. 1–9 (2014)
19. Henning, J.L.: SPEC CPU2006 benchmark descriptions. ACM SIGARCH Comput. Archit. News **34**(4), 1–17 (2006)
20. Lin, T.-Y., et al.: Microsoft COCO: common objects in context. In: Fleet, D., Pajdla, T., Schiele, B., Tuytelaars, T. (eds.) ECCV 2014. LNCS, vol. 8693, pp. 740–755. Springer, Cham (2014). https://doi.org/10.1007/978-3-319-10602-1_48
21. Liu, Y., Wei, X., Xiao, J., Liu, Z., Xu, Y., Tian, Y.: Energy consumption and emission mitigation prediction based on data center traffic and PUE for global data centers. Global Energy Interconnection **3**(3), 272–282 (2020)
22. Mattson, P., et al.: MLPerf training benchmark. Proc. Mach. Learn. Syst. **2**, 336–349 (2020)
23. Miller, R.: The sustainability imperative: green data centers and our cloudy future. Tech. Rep., Data Center Frontier (2020)
24. Naumov, M., et al.: Deep learning recommendation model for personalization and recommendation systems. arXiv preprint arXiv:1906.00091 (2019)

25. NVIDIA: https://docs.nvidia.com/cuda/profiler-users-guide/index.html
26. NVIDIA: Nvidia deeplearningexamples (2019). https://github.com/NVIDIA/DeepLearningExamples
27. Panayotov, V., Chen, G., Povey, D., Khudanpur, S.: LibriSpeech: an ASR corpus based on public domain audio books. In: 2015 IEEE International Conference on Acoustics, Speech and Signal Processing (ICASSP), pp. 5206–5210. IEEE (2015)
28. Shi, S., Wang, Q., Xu, P., Chu, X.: Benchmarking state-of-the-art deep learning software tools. In: 2016 7th International Conference on Cloud Computing and Big Data (CCBD), pp. 99–104. IEEE (2016)
29. Tang, F., et al.: AIBench training: balanced industry-standard AI training benchmarking. In: 2021 IEEE International Symposium on Performance Analysis of Systems and Software (ISPASS), pp. 24–35. IEEE (2021)
30. Tang, J., Wang, K.: Ranking distillation: learning compact ranking models with high performance for recommender system. In: Proceedings of the 24th ACM SIGKDD International Conference on Knowledge Discovery and Data Mining, pp. 2289–2298 (2018)
31. Vaswani, A., et al.: Attention is all you need. Adv. Neural Inf. Process. Syst. **30** (2017)
32. Wang, Y., et al.: Benchmarking the performance and energy efficiency of AI accelerators for AI training. In: 2020 20th IEEE/ACM International Symposium on Cluster, Cloud and Internet Computing (CCGRID), pp. 744–751. IEEE (2020)
33. Yao, C., et al.: Evaluating and analyzing the energy efficiency of CNN inference on high-performance GPU. Concurr. Comput. Pract. Exp. **33**(6), e6064 (2021)
34. Zhu, H., et al.: TBD: benchmarking and analyzing deep neural network training. arXiv preprint arXiv:1803.06905 (2018)

MSDBench: Understanding the Performance Impact of Isolation Domains on Microservice-Based IoT Deployments

Sierra Wang[✉], Fatih Bakir, Tyler Ekaireb, Jack Pearson, Chandra Krintz, and Rich Wolski

Computer Science Department, University of California, Santa Barbara, USA
sierrawang@ucsb.edu

Abstract. We present MSDBench – a set of benchmarks designed to illuminate the effects of deployment choices and operating system abstractions on microservices performance in IoT settings. The microservices architecture has emerged as a mainstay set of design principles for cloud-hosted, network-facing applications. Their utility as a design pattern for "The Internet of Things" (IoT) is less well understood.

We use MSDBench to show the performance impacts of different deployment choices and isolation domain assignments for Linux and Ambience, an experimental operating system specifically designed to support microservices for IoT. These results indicate that deployment choices can have a dramatic impact on microservices performance, and thus, MSDBench is a useful tool for developers and researchers in this space.

1 Introduction

As web service technologies have improved in performance and usability, the design of web/cloud service applications (often user-facing web venues) has evolved to make use of internal purpose-built web services as composable application components. This approach is often termed a *microservices* design or architecture, and the internal services themselves are called microservices.

Software architects find microservices attractive from a software engineering perspective because they promote software reuse [12,13,33], they naturally admit heterogeneous software languages and runtimes [12,16,35], and they improve the performance of software quality assurance mechanisms such as unit testing [12, 40]. They also enhance software robustness and facilitate distributed placement flexibility by incorporating modularity and service isolation into the internal design of the overall application [31,33,44].

The cost associated with these benefits, compared with monolithic application design in which the internal functionality is not a decomposition of microservices, is execution performance. Performance, in this context, refers (i) to the

A. Gainaru et al. (Eds.): Bench 2022, LNCS 13852, pp. 35–52, 2023.
https://doi.org/10.1007/978-3-031-31180-2_3

latency a user of the application observes when making individual requests to the application, (ii) to the computational and storage capacity that is necessary to support the application's functionality, and (iii) to the communication overhead of sending and processing network requests to/from other microservices and across isolation boundaries. As such, microservice designs tend to increase user-experienced request latency and application capacity requirements compared with their monolithic counterparts [16,41].

These costs are especially acute for applications designed to implement the "Internet of Things" (IoT). Microservices, as a fundamental design principle, is endemic in large-scale application hosting (e.g. cloud computing) contexts where web service technologies are well supported both from a performance and also a security perspective. Furthermore, many IoT applications use cloud-based services for scalable analysis, visualization, and user interactions. Thus, microservices have become a key architectural approach to building IoT applications due largely to the facility with which they can be deployed in the cloud.

However, the latency and capacity requirements for IoT applications differ considerably from other web service applications (e.g. e-commerce, social networking, web-content delivery, etc.). IoT applications almost always include data acquisition deadlines that arise from sensor duty cycles (e.g. a sensor produces a measurement with a periodicity measured in milliseconds to seconds) and sometimes include near real-time response deadlines (e.g. to operate an appliance as an automated response to analysis of sensor data). Thus, a careful understanding of application response latency is important to IoT application design, particularly when the design is microservice based.

For these reasons, IoT deployments are increasingly incorporating "edge" computing capabilities that augment cloud-based processing. By processing IoT data *in situ*, before traversing a long-haul network to a cloud, IoT applications can reduce response latency, decrease the needed long-haul bandwidth (e.g., by performing data aggregations at the edge), and improve scale. The edge resources, however, are typically not full-scale cloud resources but smaller, more resource restricted, single board computers or microcontrollers that can be inexpensively deployed near the "Things" in the Internet of Things. Therefore, the capacity requirements of microservices located at the edge must be considered.

The task of determining what each microservice does in an application (i.e., the service decomposition "boundaries") is typically a manual process that falls to the software architect. As such, the choices are design-time choices, and not deployment-time choices. In a cloud context, where computational, storage, network, and security topologies can be understood to be relatively static, design-time decomposition is effective. In an IoT context, *the same application may be deployed to many different infrastructures*, each with its own unique set of performance and security characteristics. Thus, it is critical for the designer to be able to anticipate the costs associated with service decomposition decisions for different IoT deployments.

To enable this, we present MSDBench – a set of microservice benchmarks specifically designed to capture the relevant performance characteristics for IoT applications. Our work is distinct from previous microservice benchmarking efforts [16,26,41] in that we focus specifically on the impact of using different isolation alternatives and placement decisions that consider devices, "the edge", and the cloud as possible execution sites. In particular, our benchmarks do not assume that the edge and device resources can run a common commodity operating system (e.g. Linux or Windows) since IoT deployments often incorporate devices requiring lightweight or real-time operating systems.

The benchmarks, described in Sect. 3, comprise a set of microbenchmarks that exercise cross-domain functionality and an end-to-end application benchmark based on the popular publish-subscribe IoT design pattern. To illustrate the diagnostic power of the benchmark suite, in Sect. 4, we compare the performance of the benchmarks using Linux as a host operating system to Ambience, an operating system specifically designed to support IoT microservices [3]. These results show the importance of different deployment decisions with respect to isolation domains and network connectivity. We also show (using Ambience) how the choice of isolation domain decomposition affects performance on devices that include only microcontrollers.

2   Related Work

Microservices is an application architecture that composes loosely coupled components that communicate using inter-/remote procedure calls or other REST APIs. Their loose coupling facilitates fault tolerance, scaling, and automatic orchestration [6,11,29] which enables independent development and enhanced software engineering benefits. As a result, microservices are widely used for development of web/cloud applications [8,14,29,32], and more recently for applications deployed across the cloud-edge continuum [24,28].

Given this widespread use, multiple benchmarking systems have emerged to help developers understand and reason about the performance implications of Linux-based microservices applications. DeathStarBench is a suite designed to explore how well the cloud system stack supports microservices, from the hardware to the application implementation [16]. The DeathStarBench applications were designed to be representative of large, language- and library-heterogeneous, end to end microservices applications that run primarily in the cloud. Their work compares microservices applications against monolithic applications and analyzes how well the cloud platform supports each application type.

Several benchmarking suites analyze the resource demands of specific application types, including scale out workloads, latency critical applications, and online data intensive microservices applications [15,20,25,26,34,41,43,45,48]. Ppbench examines how different languages, containerization, and a software defined networking affect microservices performance [26]. Other work explores techniques for benchmarking microservices and how to use this information to inform deployment decisions [1,17,18,21,23,47]. While several other benchmarking efforts describe IoT benchmarking suites for evaluating IoT architectures, IoT Gateway systems, IoT hardware devices, IoT database systems,

IoT sensor and analytics platforms, and distributed stream processing platforms [5,19,27,30,36,38], these latter suites are not designed for or tailored to the microservices architecture.

MSDBench differs from this prior work in both its focus and its content. It is unique in that it targets how runtime systems support microservices applications with regards to deployment options common to IoT settings (placement, isolation, cross-service optimization). To show its utility, we use the suite to evaluate and empirically compare the impact of different operating systems, RPC frameworks, hardware, and isolation domains across deployments that span the IoT cloud-edge continuum.

3   Benchmark Design

Microservices are useful for IoT because

- Microservices can be sized/decomposed to match the heterogeneous set of computing capacities in a target IoT deployment (e.g. one consisting of a resource constrained microcontroller, capacity limited edge device or edge cloud virtual machine (VM), or resource rich VM in a public or private cloud interconnected by low-power radio networks, WiFi, and wired networking).
- Microservices can be assigned to separate isolation domains (e.g. process- or service-level virtualization technologies) to implement site-specific security policies and to improve fault isolation.
- Microservices are decoupled from the operating system and other microservices, enabling independent development, distributed deployment, and use of a wide range of isolation options (e.g. IPC/RPC communication, process virtualization, or system virtualization); and
- Operating and build systems that are microservices-aware can exploit static information associated with deployments (e.g., co-location, service dependencies) to automatically optimize away various overheads associated with isolation and decoupling [3,22].

These features facilitate portability, rapid development, improved performance, and low maintenance. Moreover, this design enables horizontal scaling with little involvement from programmers, since a particular dependency of a service can be transparently replicated.

Developers must also face a number of new challenges when using microservices in distributed and heterogeneous IoT settings. In particular, service proximity can have a significant impact on overall application performance. For example, co-locating microservices on a single node (e.g. as a Kubernetes "pod" [29]) can enhance the inter-service communication, but also introduce security and/or fault isolation vulnerabilities. Further, in an IoT context where some of the services implement data acquisition, moving a microservice away from the data acquisition site to improve its inter-service messaging performance may degrade data acquisition latency. Moreover, these performance-impacting factors can be *deployment specific* meaning that the developer must code the microservices without knowing how they will ultimately be deployed.

To address these challenges, we have developed *MSDBench*, a pair of bench-mark suites for exploring the performance implications of different operating system, isolation, and placement alternatives for microservices applications deployed across the multi-tier IoT resources (microcontrollers, edge systems, and public/private clouds). MSDBench is unique in that it facilitates the study of different operating systems, devices, system-level virtualization, and isolation domains in combination. As described in the previous section, existing microservice benchmarking approaches [16,26,41,43] focus on resource-rich, relatively homogeneous cloud deployments and devices that run Linux. By addressing this gap, MSDBench enables developers to reason about the performance of emerging IoT deployments end-to-end and to interrogate the performance impact from using different isolation domains and operating systems.

MSDBench consists of a microbenchmark suite and end-to-end application suite. Both suites separate the client from the rest of the application (which we refer to as the server-side services) to allow for separate performance analysis (end-to-end versus server-side). We write microservices in C++ for device portability and implement them to be as efficient as possible.

C = client service
P = poll service

Fig. 1. MSDBench microbench-mark structure.

The microbenchmark suite consists of an application with two microservices depicted as triangles in Fig. 1. The client service makes requests to the poll service (dashed arrow in the figure). The poll service simply returns. The call benchmark includes a request payload, the size of which is parameterizable. This suite enables us to understand the overhead associated with calls and returns (local or remote) and any use of payload serialization.

The end-to-end application suite is a "Best Effort Pub/Sub (BEPS)" application consisting of six unique microservices. We provide a graphic of BEPS in Fig. 2; The microservices are triangles, and their dependencies are arrows. The dashed arrow is used by the client for requests to the BEPS entry point. The client service (C) makes requests to the server-side services which comprise the suite's benchmarks. The server-side services consist of a load balancer microservice (LB), 1+ workers (W), a user database service (DB), a payload database service (PDB), and a read endpoint (R). The client makes create_user, subscribe, publish, unsubscribe, and delete_user requests to the load balancer. Each request type benchmarks a different aggregate functionality from the microservice mesh. The load balancer distributes requests using round-robin among the workers. Each worker uses the payload database and the user database to service each request and publishes updates to the read endpoint as necessary. The number of workers is parameterizable; we use five in the evaluation herein.

We designed BEPS to represent several common microservices
design patterns [2, 9, 46]. The load
balancer is an "API Gateway (or
Proxy)" as it provides a uniform
interface to make requests to different services. Each worker is
an "Aggregator" since it combines
information from both databases to
update a user's feed in the read
endpoint. BEPS employs the "Data
Sharing" pattern since all of the

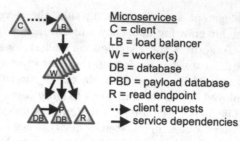

Fig. 2. MSDBench end-to-end application structure.

workers share the same two database instances. When the OS supports asyn-
chrony (e.g. Ambience does so via coroutines), all communication implements
the "Asynchronous messaging" pattern.

In this paper, we use MSDBench with Linux and Ambience [3]; the latter is an
experimental operating system specifically designed for IoT microservices. The
benchmark suites are coded as generically as possible to facilitate their porting
to other operating systems and software ecosystems. We choose these two examples to illustrate how the benchmarks allow a developer to assess the trade-off
between performance and technology risk. The MSDBench Linux benchmarks
use Thrift [39, 42] for RPC and argument serialization. They use Docker containers [10] for process-level isolation. MSDBench can use KVM VMs or physical
hosts for these deployments.

Ambience uses a "group" abstraction to isolate and co-locate microservices.
Microservices in the same group share an address space, are not isolated from
each other, and can be optimized together. Microservices in different groups
are isolated via protected address space regions. Ambience uses lidl, an interface
description language (IDL), to describe inter-service communication. lidl transparently specializes these interfaces as direct function calls, zero-copy shared
memory for calls across address spaces, or serialization for cross-machine calls.
Ambience is also more resource-scale independent than Linux. It is possible to
run Ambience on resource-restricted microcontrollers that do not have sufficient
functionality (e.g. an MMU) or resource capacity to run Linux. At the same
time, Ambience runs natively on the x86 and ARM architectures and on the
KVM hypervisor. Thus, it is possible to run Ambience as a single operating system on microcontrollers, single board computers at the edge, and cloud-based
VMs in a tiered IoT deployment. It is, however, highly experimental and supports a unique and potentially unfamiliar set of operating system abstractions
specifically for optimized microservices.

MSDBench is also unique in that it decouples the mapping of microservices
to isolation domain from the mapping of isolation domains to hosts. We dis-
tinguish the two because developers and operators typically have control over
the former (isolation domain assignment, i.e. containerization). The infrastructure provider (e.g. cloud vendor) may demand an additional level of isolation

Co-located   Tiered   Isolated

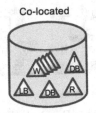  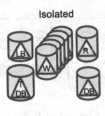

Fig. 3. BEPS Mapping of Microservices to Isolation Domains. An isolation domain provides process-level isolation (cylinders) for microservices (triangles). The letters in each triangle identify the BEPS microservice. For a Linux OS, the isolation domain is a Linux or Docker container. Ambience uses lightweight groups. MSDBench enables empirical evaluation and comparison for alternative isolation domain configurations, including those shown here: all co-located, tiered isolation (grouped), and full isolation.

to facilitate resource apportionment, decommissioning, and sharing of resources. Thus, MSDBench allows different combinations of these two mappings to be explored empirically. We refer to *isolation domains* when discussing operating-system implemented protection domains and *deployments* when discussing the assignment of microservices to isolation domains and the assignment of isolation domains to hosts. That is, a developer or application operator may decide on the assignment of microservices to isolation domains, and those isolation domains may either be implemented natively or placed in infrastructure-provided containers.

Mapping Microservices to Isolation Domains – We depict the three isolation domain configurations (*co-located*, *tiered*, and *isolated*) that we consider in our evaluation using the BEPS suite in Fig. 3 (the microbenchmark suite is similar). An isolation domain for the Linux OS is a Linux or Docker container; for Ambience, it is an Ambience group. In the co-located configuration, the load balancer, workers, databases, and read endpoint are all in the same isolation domain. In the tiered configuration, the load balancer and the workers are in an isolation domain, the databases are in an isolation domain, and the read endpoint is in an isolation domain. In the isolated configuration, every microservice is in its own isolation domain.

Deployments: Mapping Isolation Domains to Hosts – We depict the five deployments for the BEPS suite that we consider in our evaluation in Fig. 4 (we use the same deployments for the microbenchmark suite). For each deployment, we will evaluate the three isolation domain configurations above (co-located, tiered, and isolated). We represent these in the figures as a cloud icon marked "server-side." In deployment 1, we place the client within the load balancer's (LB's) isolation domain. All isolation domains in this deployment are co-located within a single VM on the same physical host. In deployment 2, we place the client in its own isolation domain, and co-locate that domain within the same VM and on the same physical host. In deployment 3, we modify deployment 2 so that the client and its isolation domain are in a separate VM but on the same physical host as the server-side VM. In deployment 4, we modify deployment 3 so that the client

Fig. 4. BEPS Mapping of Isolation Domains to Hosts (MSDBench deployment alternatives). MSDBench enables evaluation of different deployment options by mapping isolation domain configurations to infrastructure options (e.g. sensors, edge, cloud). We consider 5 common deployments (shown here) in our empirical evaluation. The server side configurations that we consider are shown in Fig. 3.

VM is on a separate physical host from that of the server-side microservices. Deployment 5 is the same as deployment 4 only the client service is executed directly on the physical host instead of in a VM.

MSDBench Configuration – MSDBench configuration uses a combination of scripting and deployment manifests to implement its benchmark deployments. Deployment configuration however, is currently manual (we are working on automation as part of future work). Linux VMs can be configured and deployed using any one of the many configuration management tools to automate server provisioning (e.g. puppet [37], ansible [4], chef [7], etc.). Moreover, Ambience has deployment support based on deployment manifests in which service interfaces and implementations are specified. It combines these with service manifests which specify service dependencies and hosts, to create an application deployment. We use qemu to instantiate virtual machines for both Linux and Ambience VM on KVM systems. For the microcontroller, we manually flash the devices with the Ambience images once they have been built. MSDBench leverages these tools for basic benchmark deployment scripting.

4 Empirical Evaluation

To generate informative results with minimal external noise, we run our experiments in a controlled environment. Our IoT setting consists of microcontrollers, edge devices, and a private cloud. In this study, we use the Nordic Semiconductor nRF52840 which has a 64 MHz Arm Cortex-M4 CPI with FPU. It has 1 MB of flash memory plus 256 KB of RAM. It communicates via Bluetooth 5.3 and zigbee (IEEE 802.15.4). The multi-host microcontroller deployments use zigbee for communication. Our edge and cloud servers are Intel NUC8i7HNK systems (NUCs) with 8 Core i7 CPUs (3.1 GHz), 32 GB of Memory, and 1 TB of disk. The multi-host edge/cloud experiments use a dedicated, isolated Ethernet network between hosts for communication. All devices run Ambience v1.0 [3] which runs on all devices that we consider herein. All devices except the microcontrollers are capable of supporting Linux. We use Fedora 35 and Fedora 36,

KVM for virtualization, and Thrift for RPC on the Linux systems. Ambience integrates virtualization internally (running directly on KVM or within a Linux process/container) and uses lidl for IPC/RPC.

We refer to the deployments that use the Intel NUCs as "edge/cloud" deployments, and the deployments that use the ARM devices as the "microcontroller" deployments in the evaluation that follows. Note that the nRF52840 microcontroller is not a Linux-capable single board computer (e.g. a device similar to a Raspberry Pi which also uses an ARM processor) but is a severely resource-restricted embedded device without an MMU.

For the microbenchmark edge/cloud deployments, the client makes 10,000 requests to the poll service per experiment. Our experiments evaluate different request payload sizes (0, 512, 1024, 2048, 4096, and 8192 bytes). Each request returns a 64-bit response payload. For the microcontroller deployments (due to resource constraints), the client makes 100 requests and we experiment with request payloads of 0 and 64 bytes.

For the edge/cloud deployments of the end-to-end benchmarks, we use MSDBench to measure the round trip request latency for BEPS by timing 10,000 create_user, 10,000 subscribe, 10,000 publish, 10,000 unsubscribe, and 10,000 delete_user requests from the client. The BEPS user names are 10 characters and the messages are 280 bytes. For the microcontroller deployments, we perform 10 requests each and use user names and messages of length 5 and 20 bytes, respectively. MSDBench can be used to measure both the internal (server-side) time and the end-to-end time experienced by the clients. We report the end-to-end times experienced by the client herein.

We use these benchmark suites to evaluate five deployments and three isolation domain configurations described in the previous section for our edge/cloud experiments (Sect. 3). We consider deployments 1, 2, and 4 and isolation domains co-located and tiered for the microcontroller deployments. All results, unless otherwise specified (e.g. for the throughput study), are in microseconds.

4.1   Microbenchmark Results

The MSDBench microbenchmark suite is useful for determining the performance impact associated with the microservice interface boundaries. Microservices typically communicate with each other through remote procedure call (RPC) or remote invocation mechanisms across their exported interfaces. The benchmark uses a single poll service that accepts a request via RPC and returns a timestamp to enable measurement of the RPC call and return performance. To evaluate the utility of this suite, we compare the overhead of RPC calls using different request payloads. Note that because RPC mechanisms are language level abstractions, they often convey typed data which must be serialized for transfer and then deserialized upon receipt. The benchmark includes serialization overhead.

For all experiments, the client and poll services are on the same machine and VM. Figure 5 and Fig. 6 show the average inter-service latency in microseconds for different payload sizes when deployed on the edge/cloud; Fig. 7 similarly shows the average inter-service latency when deployed on the microcontroller.

We use MSDBench to explore the performance differences of the no-isolation (co-located) and fully isolated isolation domains.

For the edge/cloud study, co-location reveals the impact of any optimization performed by the OS and/or microservices hosting framework. Note that Ambience uses compile and link time optimizations to automatically remove the messaging and serialization/deserialization code when microservices are co-located. In Linux, microservices use the same serialization and messaging code regardless of co-location. However, when co-located, Linux uses a "fast-path" for local network communication.

Ambience co-located thus achieves 73x better performance than fully isolated versus 1.3x for Linux. Ambience's group abstraction enables 6x better call performance (isolated configuration) compared to Linux because it is able to optimize across groups (using zero copy shared memory), a feature not available for Linux containers. Note that Ambience performs similarly regardless of the amount of data passed. This is because Ambience requires a deployment manifest that shows the location of microservices in a deployment so it can "compile-away" serialization and data copies when microservices share an address space. Each system runs an image that is compiled using the manifest and relocation of microservices requires new images to be created and deployed. For Linux, serialization (via Thrift) and messaging cause the microservices to slow as the payload size increases. However, Linux microservices do not need to be recompiled when they are moved between compatible architectures, and they may not need to be relinked (depending on the degree of software version compatibility between potential execution sites).

For the microcontroller, Ambience co-located outperforms isolated by 20x (versus 73x for edge/cloud). This is due to the slower clock rate (compared to the x86-based NUC) and the limited resources of the device. As noted previously, the microcontroller does not support Linux so we do not report results for Linux.

Microbenchmark Results

The following graphs show the average time for the client service to call the poll service (y-axis), with different payloads (x-axis), under different deployment configurations.

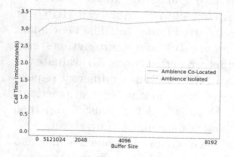

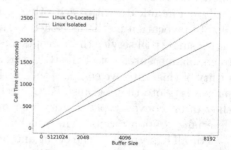

Fig. 5. Latency when isolating and co-locating Ambience services for edge/cloud.

Fig. 6. Latency when isolating and co-locating Linux services for edge/cloud.

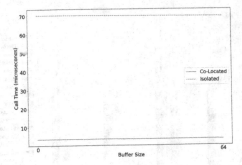

Fig. 7. Latency when isolating and co-locating the Ambience services for microcontrollers.

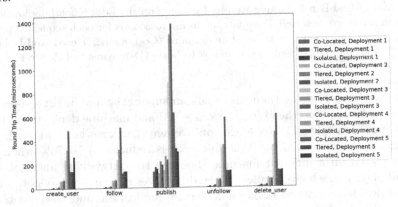

Fig. 8. End-to-End Benchmarking Results for Ambience on the Edge/Cloud deployments. The graph shows average round trip latency in microseconds for each request type, for each mapping of microservices to isolation domains (Co-Located, Tiered, and Isolated, see Fig. 3) and mapping of isolation domains to hosts (Deployments 1–5, see Fig. 4).

4.2   End to End Benchmark Results

We next use MSDBench to investigate a number of deployment related research questions using BEPS, the end-to-end benchmark suite. For these experiments, we consider the five deployments in Fig. 4 and the three isolation (ISO) domain configurations (co-located, tiered, and isolated) shown in Fig. 3. We benchmark both Ambience (Amb) and Linux (Lin) and report latency in microseconds observed by the client in terms of the average and standard deviation across 10,000 requests to each benchmark service function. The service functions are `create_user`, `subscribe`, `publish`, `unsubscribe`, and `delete_user`. Figure 8 shows the round trip times for each service function for all deployment configurations of Ambience. Figure 9 shows the corresponding results for Linux.

The data provides a number of different insights. First, the suite includes benchmarks with different resource requirements. For example, `publish` requires

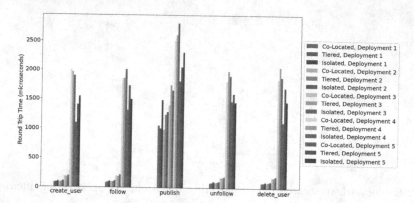

Fig. 9. End-to-End Benchmarking Results for Linux on the Edge/Cloud deployments. The graph shows average round trip latency in microseconds for each request type, for each mapping of microservices to isolation domains (Co-Located, Tiered, and Isolated, see Fig. 3) and mapping of isolation domains to hosts (Deployments 1–5, see Fig. 4).

more server-side processing than the others, `unsubscribe` and `delete_user` are impacted by network overhead (e.g. for cross-VM and machine deployments). As a result, `publish` takes 11–15x longer on average than `create_user` on Linux when within the same VM but this difference is reduced to 50–70% when the client is placed on a different machine (because the networking and isolation overhead plays a much larger role). These differences enable developers to make informed decisions about workload mix, service replication, and placement.

Next, the data shows the potential for performance optimization for co-located microservices. In every case, both Linux and Ambience show significantly better performance for co-located versus tiered (approximately 30–70% slower for Ambience, and 20% slower for Linux) or isolated (approximately 20–70% slower for Ambience, and 10–40% slower for Linux). Third, it enables us to understand the performance differences between the use of a general and special purpose operating system. On average, Ambience is at least an order of magnitude faster than Linux for all equivalent deployments, and the slowest Ambience experiment across deployments 4 and 5 (which traverse a network connection) is faster than the fastest Linux experiment in deployments 4 and 5 *across all experiments*, regardless of isolation domain assignment and service request type. We were surprised by these results, given the relatively highly optimized nature of the Linux networking stack and the maturity of its isolation implementations.

The differences per deployment are also interesting. Deployment 1 enables us to remove client interaction. Although this would not be used in an actual deployment (clients are typically separated and isolated from the server-side services for fault resiliency), it allows us (as developers) to focus on the server side performance of our deployments. This deployment with co-located isolation is the configuration with the best possible performance because maximal optimization is possible and minimal overhead is introduced to provide limited isolation. The

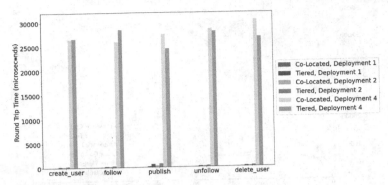

Fig. 10. End-to-End Benchmarking Results for Ambience on the microcontroller deployments. The graph shows round trip latency in microseconds for each mapping of microservices to isolation domains and a subset of the mappings of isolation domains to hosts (deployments 1, 2, and 4, see Fig. 4).

data across deployments shows that a large portion of the performance overhead end-to-end comes from separating the client from the server side.

Deployment 2 represents a more realistic edge case in which the microservices are co-located on the same device with the client isolated using only process-level virtualization (i.e. Linux containers or Ambience groups) and the server-side microservices isolated in various ways (all co-located, all isolated, or some combination (e.g. tiered)). Using deployment 2 as a baseline, Linux deployment 3 (isolating the client in its own VM) is 14–16x slower, and Linux deployment 4 (placing client and VM on a different host) is 65–68x slower. When we place the client on a different host without a VM (deployment 5), the end-to-end performance is only 45–56x slower. This latter result represents the overhead of system level virtualization (e.g. cloud use). For Ambience, deployment 3 and deployment 4 are 3–4x slower and 13–23x slower than deployment 2, respectively. The Ambience performance is also impacted by placing the client in a VM – deployment 5 is only 6–8x slower when the client is placed on bare metal vs 13–23x slower in an VM (deployment 4).

Figure 10 shows the end-to-end results for running Ambience on microcontrollers. In these experiments, we use deployments 1, 2, and 4 and the co-located and tiered isolation domains. The trends are similar, however, the differences are less stark due to the slower clock speed and severe resource constraints of the devices. Separating out the client (deployment 2 vs 1) introduces about 2x overhead across benchmarks. The performance for co-located and tiered is similar when the client is separated. Using deployment 2 as a baseline, the total average time across all benchmarks is approximately 134x slower for deployment 4 when co-located. Another interesting aspect revealed by this benchmark suite is the relative performance between microcontroller and edge/cloud deployments. For example, due to the limited capability of the microcontrollers, microcontroller deployment 1 exhibits performance that is similar to that of edge/cloud deployment 3 (which adds VM-level isolation to the client) for co-located isolation.

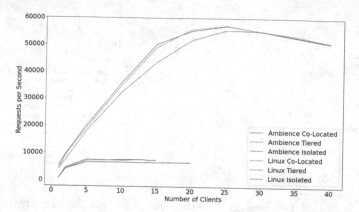

Fig. 11. MSDBench Throughput Experiments. This benchmark uses the edge/cloud deployment 5 to evaluate and compare three isolation domains co-located, tiered, and isolated for Ambience and Linux. The graphs show the average number of requests per second as the number of clients increases. The Linux system was unable to run workloads with more 15–20 clients for any configuration. Ambience achieves its peak throughput at 25 clients, Linux does so at 13. Such studies are a key component of capacity planning for IoT deployments.

4.3 Throughput Results

We next use MSDBench on the edge/cloud deployment 5 to test how the isolation domain configuration and platform supports different client workloads. In particular, we show how MSDBench can be used to support capacity planning for hosts in an IoT deployment. Capacity planning enables developers and deployment administrators to understand what the hosts in a deployment are capable of in terms of servicing microservice load.

To enable this, we use MSDBench to measure the performance of concurrent requests issued by multiple client processes simultaneously. For this study, we used an MSDBench client that is written in Python; Python simplifies the scripting of benchmark harnesses but adds considerable client-side latency (which is why we did not use it for the microbenchmark and end-to-end experiments). Our Python client is the same for Linux and Ambience except in its use of Thrift versus lidl for the respective RPC implementations. We invoke the clients concurrently. Each client "warms" the application by executing 50 `create_user` and `delete_user` requests each. It then times 105,000 requests of each type (210,000 total requests), then computes and outputs the throughput number. We repeat the experiment for an increasing number of clients until the number of requests per second stops increasing, indicating the host's saturation point for this benchmark. The resulting throughput "curve" indicates how microservices consume capacity as a function of offered request load for a given mix of service requests. A similar throughput curve can be generated for any individual or combination of the MSDBench microservices and target device.

Figure 11 shows the throughput in requests per second (rps) for each OS and isolation domain configuration as the number of clients increases. We use this benchmark to compare the co-located, tiered, and isolated configurations and the two OS's we consider (Ambience and Linux). The Linux system consistently crashed (we were unable to determine why) for client counts higher than 15 for co-located and tiered, and 20 for isolated. The throughput of the Linux system achieves a maximum throughput of 7587 rps with 13 clients for co-located, 7594 rps with 13 clients for tiered, and 6613 rps with 10 clients for isolated. At 5 clients, Ambience achieves 2.7x more throughput than Linux. Ambience saturates the capacity of the server-side host at 25 clients achieving a maximum throughput of 57083 rps for co-located, 57193 rps for tiered, and 55508 rps for isolated.

Note that all of the throughput experiments are for deployment 5, where the clients are executed on a separate host and communicate with the microservices over a 1 GB dedicated Ethernet network. Surprisingly, the throughput rate for Linux is not network dominated (it may be for Ambience, but we were unable to determine that it was conclusively). Indeed, the Linux networking stack is highly optimized compared to the nascent networking stack included in the Ambience runtime. Further, because requests are traversing the network, the Ambience requests include all serialization/deserialization and messaging overheads (the Ambience image compiler could not optimize these away). We expected that both Ambience and Linux would achieve the same saturation throughput (perhaps for different client counts) with the network as the performance bottleneck. This result illustrates both the impact of OS abstractions other than the networking abstractions on microservices as well as the relative capacity consumption of the two hosting operating systems.

5   Conclusion

We present MSDBench, a benchmarking suite for exploring the possibilities of deploying microservices in an IoT setting and understanding how deployment decisions impact microservices application performance. In our analysis, we study the effect of isolation domains, the assignment of isolation domains to hosts, operating systems abstractions, RPC Frameworks, and device types, revealing the strengths and weaknesses of each. We also investigate the performance associated with running microservices on resource-restricted devices (such as microcontrollers) that cannot host commodity service operating systems (e.g. Linux). The results indicate that the various deployment and operating system choices can have a dramatic effect of eventual application performance. This work enables us to understand how IoT technology supports microservices in terms of what is possible and what is optimal, informing future research and development on using microservices in an IoT setting.

References

1. Aderaldo, C.M., Mendonça, N.C., Pahl, C., Jamshidi, P.: Benchmark requirements for microservices architecture research. In: 2017 IEEE/ACM 1st International Workshop on Establishing the Community-Wide Infrastructure for Architecture-Based Software Engineering (ECASE), pp. 8–13. IEEE (2017)
2. Akbulut, A., Perros, H.G.: Performance analysis of microservice design patterns. IEEE Internet Comput. **23**(6), 19–27 (2019)
3. Ambience Microservices OS (2022). https://github.com/MAYHEM-Lab/ambience. Accessed 20 May 2022
4. Ansible configuration management. https://www.ansible.com. Accessed 20 July 2022
5. Arlitt, M., Marwah, M., Bellala, G., Shah, A., Healey, J., Vandiver, B.: IoTAbench: an internet of things analytics benchmark. In: Proceedings of the 6th ACM/SPEC International Conference on Performance Engineering, pp. 133–144 (2015)
6. AWS elastic container service. https://aws.amazon.com/ecs/. Accessed 20 July 2022
7. Chef configuration management. https://www.chef.io. Accessed 20 July 2022
8. Decomposing Twitter: Adventures in service-oriented architecture. https://www.slideshare.net/InfoQ/decomposing-twitter-adventures-in-serviceoriented-architecture. Accessed 19 July 2022
9. Everything you need to know about microservices design patterns. https://www.edureka.co/blog/microservices-design-patterns. Accessed 20 July 2022
10. Docker. https://www.docker.com. Accessed 12 Sept 2017
11. Docker Swarm. https://docs.docker.com/engine/swarm/. Accessed 20 July 2022
12. Dragoni, N., et al.: Microservices: yesterday, today, and tomorrow. In: Present and Ulterior Software Engineering, pp. 195–216. Springer, Cham (2017). https://doi.org/10.1007/978-3-319-67425-4_12
13. Dragoni, N., Lanese, I., Larsen, S.T., Mazzara, M., Mustafin, R., Safina, L.: Microservices: how to make your application scale. In: Petrenko, A.K., Voronkov, A. (eds.) PSI 2017. LNCS, vol. 10742, pp. 95–104. Springer, Cham (2018). https://doi.org/10.1007/978-3-319-74313-4_8
14. The evolution of microservices. https://www.slideshare.net/adriancockcroft/evolution-of-microservices-craft-conference. Accessed 19 July 2022
15. Ferdman, M., et al.: Clearing the clouds: a study of emerging scale-out workloads on modern hardware. ACM SIGPLAN Not. **47**(4), 37–48 (2012)
16. Gan, Y., et al.: An open-source benchmark suite for microservices and their hardware-software implications for cloud & edge systems. In: International Conference on Architectural Support for Programming Languages and Operating Systems (2019)
17. Grambow, M., Meusel, L., Wittern, E., Bermbach, D.: Benchmarking microservice performance: a pattern-based approach. In: Proceedings of the 35th Annual ACM Symposium on Applied Computing, pp. 232–241 (2020)
18. Grambow, M., Wittern, E., Bermbach, D.: Benchmarking the performance of microservice applications. ACM SIGAPP Appl. Comput. Rev. **20**(3), 20–34 (2020)
19. Gupta, P., Carey, M.J., Mehrotra, S., Yus, O.: SmartBench: a benchmark for data management in smart spaces. Proc. VLDB Endow. **13**(12), 1807–1820 (2020)
20. Hauswald, J., et al.: Sirius: an open end-to-end voice and vision personal assistant and its implications for future warehouse scale computers. In: International Conference on Architectural Support for Programming Languages and Operating Systems, pp. 223–238 (2015)

21. Henning, S., Hasselbring, W.: Theodolite: scalability benchmarking of distributed stream processing engines in microservice architectures. Big Data Res. **25**, 100209 (2021)
22. Jia, Z., Witchel, E.: Nightcore: efficient and scalable serverless computing for latency-sensitive, interactive microservices. In: International Conference on Architectural Support for Programming Languages and Operating Systems, pp. 152–166 (2021)
23. Jindal, A., Podolskiy, V., Gerndt, M.: Performance modeling for cloud microservice applications. In: Proceedings of the 2019 ACM/SPEC International Conference on Performance Engineering, pp. 25–32 (2019)
24. K3S. https://k3s.io. Accessed 19 July 2022
25. Kasture, H., Sanchez, D.: Tailbench: a benchmark suite and evaluation methodology for latency-critical applications. In: International Symposium on Workload Characterization (2016)
26. Kratzke, N., Quint, P.C.: Investigation of impacts on network performance in the advance of a microservice design. In: International Conference on Cloud Computing and Services Science, vol. 1 and 2, pp. 223–231 (2016)
27. Kruger, C.P., Hancke, G.P.: Benchmarking internet of things devices. In: 2014 12th IEEE International Conference on Industrial Informatics (INDIN), pp. 611–616. IEEE (2014)
28. KubeEdge. https://kubeedge.io. Accessed 19 July 2022
29. Kubernetes. https://kubernetes.io. Accessed 19 July 2022
30. Kumar, H.A., Rakshith, J., Shetty, R., Roy, S., Sitaram, D.: Comparison of IoT architectures using a smart city benchmark. Procedia Comput. Sci. **171**, 1507–1516 (2020)
31. Microservices. https://martinfowler.com/articles/microservices.html
32. Microservices workshop: why, what, and how to get there. http://www.slideshare.net/adriancockcroft/microservices-workshop-craft-conference. Accessed 19 July 2022
33. Newman, S.: Building Microservices. O'Reilly Media, Inc. (2021)
34. Papapanagiotou, I., Chella, V.: NDBench: benchmarking microservices at scale. arXiv preprint arXiv:1807.10792 (2018)
35. Paul, S.K., Jana, S., Bhaumik, P.: On solving heterogeneous tasks with microservices. J. Inst. Eng. (India) Ser. B **103**(2), 557–565 (2022)
36. Poess, M., Nambiar, R., Kulkarni, K., Narasimhadevara, C., Rabl, T., Jacobsen, H.A.: Analysis of TPCx-IoT: the first industry standard benchmark for IoT gateway systems. In: 2018 IEEE 34th International Conference on Data Engineering (ICDE), pp. 1519–1530. IEEE (2018)
37. Puppet configuration management. https://puppet.com. Accessed 20 July 2022
38. Shukla, A., Chaturvedi, S., Simmhan, Y.: Riotbench: a real-time IoT benchmark for distributed stream processing platforms. arXiv preprint arXiv:1701.08530 (2017)
39. Slee, M., Agarwal, A., Kwiatkowski, M.: Thrift: scalable cross-language services implementation (2007). Facebook White Paper
40. Soldani, J., Tamburri, D.A., Van Den Heuvel, W.J.: The pains and gains of microservices: a systematic grey literature review. J. Syst. Softw. **146**, 215–232 (2018)
41. Sriraman, A., Wenisch, T.F.: usuite: a benchmark suite for microservices. In: International Symposium on Workload Characterization, pp. 1–12 (2018)
42. Thrift software framework. http://wiki.apache.org/thrift/
43. Ueda, T., Nakaike, T., Ohara, M.: Workload characterization for microservices. In: International Symposium on Workload Characterization (2016)

44. Villamizar, M., et al.: Evaluating the monolithic and the microservice architecture pattern to deploy web applications in the cloud. In: 2015 10th Computing Colombian Conference (10CCC), pp. 583–590. IEEE (2015)
45. Wang, L., et al.: BigDataBench: a big data benchmark suite from internet services. In: Proceedings of the First International Symposium on High-Performance Computer Architecture, pp. 488–499 (2014)
46. Yeung, A.: The six most common microservice architecture design pattern (2020). https://medium.com/analytics-vidhya/the-six-most-common-microservice-architecture-design-pattern-1038299dc396. Accessed 20 July 2022
47. Zhou, X., et al.: Fault analysis and debugging of microservice systems: industrial survey, benchmark system, and empirical study. IEEE Trans. Softw. Eng. **47**(2), 243–260 (2018)
48. Zhou, X., et al.: Benchmarking microservice systems for software engineering research. In: International Conference on Software Engineering, pp. 323–324 (2018)

Algorithm and Dataset

ShoeMaster: A Benchmark for Sketch2Image Translation of Shoes

Shiyuan Xu, Yingjie Shi[✉], Tong Feng, and Huayi Yuan

Beijing Institute of Fashion Technology, Chaoyang, Beijing, China
shiyingjie1983@163.com

Abstract. The sketch2image translation of shoes innovatively generates natural shoe images that match the content and style of the input sketches, which is of important application value in the field of apparel e-commerce and auxiliary design. Training the translation model requires sketches and real images of shoes, however, the existing shoes datasets face the problems of small scale and unclear classification, which hinders the training of translation models. In this paper, we propose a benchmark for sketch2image translation of shoes called ShoeMaster, in the hope to facilitate the research of sketch2image translation of shoes, and provide a technical benchmark for fairly evaluate the progress of corresponding research works. ShoeMaster provides a large-scale daily shoe dataset covering all the categories of our proposed shoes classification knowledge hierarchy, which contains more than 50,000 real shoe images and corresponding sketches of different drawing styles. In order to comprehensively evaluate the quality of generated images, we propose the evaluation metrics from both qualitative and quantitative aspects. Based on ShoeMaster, we conduct comparison experiments on three state-of-the-art sketch2image models, the experiment results and analysis demonstrate the effectiveness of ShoeMaster. The ShowMaster benchmark including dataset, the metric questionnaire and calculating source code will be released at https://github.com/202oranger/ShoeMaster.

Keywords: sketch · image translation · shoes dataset

1 Introduction

Human hand-drawn sketches are highly concise and abstract, which can reflect the human brain's visual perception of the real world vividly and powerfully, so they are widely used by humans to describe objects and communicate with each other. The sketch2image (S2I) translation generates real natural images whose content and style are consistent with the input sketches, and completes the cross-domain conversion from abstract sparse lines to specific pixels. Shoes are one of the important apparel products. As shown in Fig. 1, the S2I translation of shoes generate real shoe images based on user's hand-drawn shoe sketches in practical application scenarios, which is of great practical application value. In the field of fashion design, the sketch2image translation of shoes can assist designers to quickly and intuitively visualize the design products, and can generate real shoe images with different effects based on different referenced style information such as textures, colors, material and so on. So it can provide designers with powerful reference information. In the field of e-commerce, the shoe sketch2image translation converts sketches drawn by consumers into real shoe images. On the one hand, it can help users to effectively search for similar online products of input sketches, thereby enhancing the consumption experience; on the other hand, it can provide important data support for merchants to analyze users' needs, so as to effectively promote the transaction volume of online shoes.

Fig. 1. Sketch2Image translation of shoes.

The S2I translation of shoes is a challenging problem. Firstly, the hand-drawn sketches consist of sparse strokes, which are highly abstract and always have noisy brushstrokes. While the real shoe image consists of dense pixels with precise boundaries. So the process has to realize the cross-domain translation which includes stroke correcting, coloring, and detail processing. Secondly, training the translation model requires sketches and real image of all categories of shoes, however, collecting shoe sketches are much harder than real images, the lack of shoe sketch-image dataset hinders the training of translation model. In this paper, we propose ShoeMaster - a benchmark for sketch2image translation of shoes, in the hope to benefit the researches in sketch2image translation of shoes. Our contributions are as follows: (1) Based on in-depth study with footwear designers of professional standards of footwear, online fashion communities and online sales platforms, we carefully define the daily shoes' category knowledge hierarchy, which is complete and mutually exclusive. (2) On the basis of the category knowledge hierarchy, we construct the shoes sketch-image dataset including 54,361 real shoe images and corresponding sketches of three representative drawing styles, which covers the whole shoe categories. (3) We propose the evaluate metrics of shoes' S2I translation from both qualitative and quantitative aspects. (4) Based on ShoeMaster, we conduct experiments on three state-of-the-art sketch2image translation models to demonstrate the effectiveness of ShoeMaster.

2   Related Work

2.1   Fashion Datasets

Several fashion datasets have been proposed to the advancement of fashion image understanding research, as summarized in Table 1. Most of the datasets focus on clothes images, such as FashionAI [2], Deepfashion [22] and DeepFashion2 [10], and they are different in scales and annotations. FashionAI and Deepfashion provide landmarks of clothes, while DeepFashion2 provides both landmarks and item masks. ModaNet [29] consists both clothes and shoes images, and the annotations include item masks. All the the aforementioned datasets enable tasks like clothes recognition, semantic segmentation, image-content-based retrieval. Some datasets for sketch2image translation are also proposed, the image categories include human faces, birds, and general types, few of them focus on fashion images. ShoeV2 [27] is the only sketch2image translation dataset for fashion, which provides 2000 real shoes images and 6648 sketches, each image has at least three sketches drawn by different individuals. ShoeV2 covers five types of shoes including boots, high-heels, ballerinas, formal and informal shoes. However, the shoe classification hierarchy is not complete or mutual exclusion, and the dataset scale is not large enough to train more sophisticated models. In this paper, we propose ShoeMaster, which contains large-scale shoe image-sketch pairs and covers the whole category of daily shoes.

2.2   Sketch2Image Translation

At early stages, the sketch2image translation was implemented through image retrieval, Sketch2Photo [7] and PhotoSketcher [9] search for corresponding image patches from large-scale image datasets according to the objects and backgrounds given by the sketches, and then fuse these image patches together. The disadvantage is that they cannot generate completely new images. In recent years, Generative Adversarial Networks (GAN) [13] has made transformative progress in the effect and performance of image generation, which is widely used in S2I translation. GAN-based S2I translation research work can be divided into three categories: the methods based on Pix2Pix [14], the methods based on CycleGAN [30] and based on auto-encoder.

Pix2Pix-based work is based on conditional GAN, where the generator exists in the form of encoder-decoder and requires paired data to train the auto-encoder. Related work includes AutoPainter [21], ScribblerGAN [24], and SchetchyGAN [8]. However, none of the above research works can control the style effect of the generated image through the exemplar image. Early CycleGAN-based image translation work is UNIT [19], which uses a pair of additional encoders to model an assumed domain-invariant feature space, and MUNIT [12] further implements multimodal image translation. Later U-GAT-IT [15] and US2P [20] were proposed to support exemplar-based sketch2image translation. U-GAT-IT includes an attention module to align visual features and style inputs of content; US2P first draws sketches and grayscale images via

CycleGAN, and then utilizes a separate model for example-based colorization. The CycleGAN-based method can accept unpaired data during training, but requires two GANs to learn and convert back and forth, which requires higher computing power. Liu Bingcheng et al. propose an S2I translation method based on self-supervised Auto-Encoder(AE) [18]. Firstly they propose an unsupervised model called TOM to synthesize sketches of different styles for a given RGB image. During the S2I translation process, the synthesized paired data are input to a self-supervised AE to decouple the style and content features from both sketches and RGB images, in order to synthesize images that are both content-faithful to the sketches and style-consistent to the RGB-images. At last, they utilize a GAN-based network to further refine the details of synthesized image and improve the synthesis quality.

Table 1. Fashion Datasets.

Name	Contents	Scale	Supported Task
FashionAI	Clothes images, landmarks	357K	attribute recognition
ModaNet	Clothes & Shoes images, masks	55K	item, attribute recognition
DeepFashion	Clothes images, landmarks	800K	attribute recognition, retrieval
DeepFashion2	Clothes images, landmarks & masks	491K	attribute recognition, retrieval
ShoesV2	Shoes images, sketches	2K, 6K	sketch2image translation

3   The ShoeMaster Benchmark

Shoes are an important part of human clothing culture. The production process and style of shoes are constantly changing with the advancement of technology. Nowadays, the shoes are of wide variety, and different organizations and online platforms adopt different shoes classification system. In order to cover complete daily shoes categories, we propose the shoe category knowledge hierarchy and construct the ShoeMaster dataset, which contains over 50,000 shoes images and corresponding sketches. Figure 2 shows some examples of the proposed dataset.

3.1   Shoes Category Knowledge Hierarchy

The existing shoes S2I dataset ShoesV2 contains five types of shoes, the classification is relatively coarse-grained. In order to improve the learning ability of S2I model, the training data should preferably cover the whole shoe category. However, the classification of shoes is very complex, the shoes can be divided into different categories according to different standards such as style, material, functions, craftsmanship, etc [6]. The e-commerce platforms and fashion community always classify the shoes based on market demands and consumer preferences. Take the classification of one shoes online selling site for example, high-heeled

real images amateur drawing fashion drawing WikiArt

Fig. 2. Shoe images and sketches in ShoeMaster.

shoes, leather shoes and Gommini belong to classifications of the same level, however, the shoes of these categories have overlaps, which may bring confusions to the dataset of a technical benchmark.

We carefully studied the Chinese shoe classification standard documents [3], which classify the shoes from several dimensions including functions, materials and structures. The shoe category during the standard is so comprehensive that it contains some shoes of special purposes, such as conductive footwear, antistatic footwear, electrically insulating footwear, etc. What's more, the shoes classification of the official standards is very professional, which is always difficult for most consumers and computer vision researchers to understand and discriminate. In this paper, we focus on usual shoes worn by people in daily life. After discussions with footwear designers about the shoes classification of Chinese shoe classification standard and the mainstream e-commerce platforms, we propose a knowledge system of daily shoe classification based on wearers, functions and styles, as shown in Figs. 3 and 4.

3.2 Dataset Construction

The S2I task belongs to cross-modal translation, and the model training requires both real images and sketches. Some S2I research work adopts manual sketches [23,25], whose cost is relatively high, so it is not suitable for large-scale dataset. Some research work extracts the edge map of real images as sketches, including Holistic Nested Edge Detection (HED), XDoG edge detector, FDoG filter, etc. The sketch details obtained by such methods depend on the thresholds, and the extracted edges are quite different from hand-drawn sketches. Image2sketch translation network is also used to generate sketches, such as Im2pencil [17], Photosketching [16]. The sketches generated by this kind of methods can capture the target contour well and even finely describe them, however, they cannot imitate the sparse and abstract hand-drawn sketches of ordinary users.

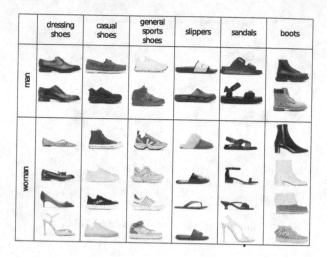

Fig. 3. Example images of shoes classification.

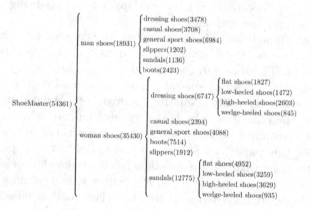

Fig. 4. Shoes category hierarchy.

The ShoeMaster dataset consists of real images and corresponding sketches. We collect the real shoe images from Farfetch [1], which is a global e-commerce platform specializing in fashion and luxury goods. Its products cover most luxury brands, and these luxury brands lead the global fashion trend to some extent. Therefore, the fashion items on Farfetch are representative. The resolution of each original image is 480 × 641, we adopt XnConvert [5] to convert the image resolution to 512 × 512 through batch processing. We manually remove the images that are irrelevant to shoes, and at last we collect 54,361 real shoe images. To realistically represent human hand-drawn style, we use TOM to generate three different styles of sketches for each image. TOM is a GAN-based domain transfer model that can generate multiple sketches for a single image [18]. Compared with other image2sketch translation networks, the sketches generated by TOM can imitate the characteristics of human hand-drawings such as randomness and incompleteness. It consists of three modules: a pre-trained VGG module, a sketch generator and a discriminator. By calculating the discriminative loss in the generator, it ensures that the generated sketch is both realistic and random. It requires only twenty unpaired images and sketches to get decent training results, and synthesizes out-domain sketches brilliantly. We collected a dataset of different styles from the internet to train TOM. The dataset includes fashion drawings, WikiArt paintings, and amateur drawings of shoes, these images can effectively represent three different hand-drawn styles: professional hand-painting, more abstract artistic hand-painting, and amateur hand-painting, as shown in Fig. 5. Through training on the dataset, TOM can generate sketches with different styles of strokes (shows in Fig. 6), which can contribute to multi-style shoes image generation and image retrieval. We generate three sketches of different styles for every shoe image in ShoeMaster, which includes 54,361 real shoe images and 163,083 sketches.

3.3 Evaluation Metric

Evaluating the performance of generating models is complex. The evaluation should not only consider the quality of generated image, but also how well the generated image matches the input condition and servers the intended application. The quantitative metrics lack consistency with human perception, it's

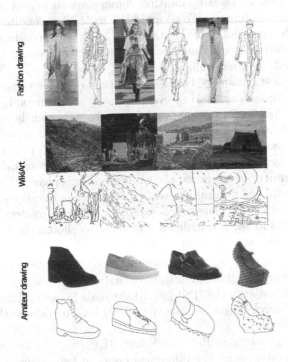

Fig. 5. Different styles to train TOM.

Fig. 6. Sketch generated by TOM.

not enough to use only one metric to demonstrate the effectiveness of models. ShoeMaster evaluates the S2I models based on both qualitative metrics and quantitative metrics.

Qualitative Metrics. Qualitative evaluation takes people's intuitive feelings as evaluation criteria, and sets up multiple dimensions to require respondents to evaluate the generated images. We adopted the method of sending out questionnaires through the community of questionnaire stars [4] to conduct a perception study of the generation effect. The questionnaire mainly focuses on three aspects: loyalty, authenticity and naturalness.

We design a questionnaire of 14 questions based on three tests. In the loyalty test we set three questions, during every question we randomly choose three similar shoe sketches and the generated image by the translation model, the respondents are asked to identify which sketch the image is translated from. In the authenticity test, there are six questions, each question is given the ground truth image and synthesized images generated by different translation models, and the respondents need to choose the generated image which is the closest to the ground truth. In the naturalness test, there are five questions. During each question, we give different images generated by different models based on the same shoe sketch, and the respondents are asked to choose the image which is the most natural and owns the best visual effect.

Quantitative Metrics. For quantitative analysis, we use Learning Perceptual Image Patch Similarity (LPIPS) [28], Multi-scale Structural Similarity (MS-SSIM) [26], and Fréchet Inception Distance (FID) [11] to evaluate the generation effect.

Learning Perceptual Image Patch Similarity (LPIPS), also known as "perceptual loss", is used to measure the difference between two images. LPIPS essentially computes the similarity between the activations of two image patches for some pre-defined network. Lower values of LPIPS indicate that the two images are more similar, and higher values indicate greater differences.

The FID score is used to measure the distance between the real image distribution and the generated image distribution based on the features extracted by the pre-trained network. Real images obey a distribution in space, and the features generated by GAN are also subject to a distribution. What the image generator does is to continuously train to make the two distributions as identical as possible. FID is to calculate the direct distance between these two distributions, and the distance algorithm used is called Fréchet distance. The smaller the distance, the closer the generated distribution is to the real distribution, so the smaller the FID, the better.

SSIM (Structural Similarity) is a method to measure the similarity of two images. Assuming an image has perfect quality, the SSIM index can be viewed as another measure of image quality. MS-SSIM (Multi-scale Structural Similarity) is a SSIM index based on multi-scale (pictures are scaled from large to small according to certain rules). The proposed method is more flexible than previous single-scale methods in considering changes in viewing conditions.

4   Experiments

We choose three representative models of S2I translation task, and train the models on a subset of 2,000 images and their corresponding sketches from Shoe-Master, another subset of 10000 sketches is used as test data. Meanwhile, we evaluate the quality of the generated images through the proposed metrics of ShoeMaster.

4.1   Approaches

As described in Sect. 2.2, the main solutions of GAN-based S2I translation include Pix2Pix-based methods, CycleGAN-based methods, and auto-encoder-based methods, so we conduct the experiments based on ShoeMaster on three models: Pix2Pix [14], CycleGAN [30], and Self-Supervised Sketch-to-Image Synthesis [18].

Pix2Pix. Pix2Pix [14] is a Conditional Generative Adversarial Network (cGAN) based model. It can not only learn the mapping relationship from the input image to the output image, but also learn the loss function used to train the mapping relationship. That is, we can get an ideal result without manually designing the loss function. Its generator uses a "U-net" structure and the discriminator uses a convolutional "PatchGAN" classifier, which only penalizes structure at the scale of image patches. Among the three models, Pix2Pix is the only one that requires image-sketch paired data during the training, it can also be seen from the experiments results that the generated images are closer to real images in color.

CycleGAN. CycleGAN [30] is a classic deep learning algorithm in the field of image translation, which is suitable for style transfer of unpaired images. The idea of this model is to form a universal mapping from data domain A to data domain B, and the learning goal is the transformation between the styles of data domain A and B, rather than the one-to-one mapping between specific data A and B. Unlike other models, CycleGAN retains the original input image information after image transfer by constructing two GAN networks and two cycle-consistency self-supervised loss functions. Image pairing is achieved indirectly while preventing mode collapse.

Self-Supervised Sketch-to-Image Synthesis. This model implements the S2I translation in a self-supervised learning manner, which also eliminates the requirements for paired image-sketch data [18]. This model consists of two parts. The first part is an auto-encoder (AE), which decoupled content and style from sketch and RGB image to synthesize an image with sketch content and RGB image style. The second part is a GAN network, which is used to refine the details of the synthesized image.

4.2   Methodology

We train the models over the online deep learning platform AutoDL, the training environment is constructed during one instance, which has exclusive access to the GPU. The hardware and software configurations are shown in Table 2. Due to our limited hardware configuration, we choose 2000 images of casual shoes and general sport shoes as training set, and 10000 sketches of different styles as the test set. The epoch of Pix2Pix and CycleGan is set to 200 and 180 respectively. The batch size of Pix2Pix is set to 4, and LR(Adam's initial learning rate) is 0.0001. The batch size of CycleGAN is set to 1, and LR is 0.0002. In the self-supervised method, the batch size of AE is 4, the iteration is 50000, and the batch size of GAN is 4. The training and image generation of CycleGAN requires higher computing power than the other two models, so we set the resolution of generated image based on CycleGAN to 256×256, while the resolution of generated images based on the other two models is set to 512×512.

Table 2. Hardware and software configuration.

name	configuration
CPU	Intel(R) Xeon(R) Gold 6330 CPU @ 2.00 GHz (14 cores)
GPU	Nvidia RTX 3090
Hard Disk	100G SSD
RAM	160G
Video Memory	24G
Operating System	Ubuntu 18.04
Language	Python 3.6
CUDA	11.3

4.3   Results and Analysis

Figure 7 shows some examples of S2I translation on the test set. It can be seen that the image synthesized by CycleGAN and self-supervised method are more closer to the real images in texture, but the color is relatively single. The images synthesized by Pix2Pix are more diverse in color but less realistic in texture. Figure 8 shows the images generated by the three models based on the real hand-drawn sketches, which are also more abstract than the sketches from the test set of ShoeMaster. It can be seen that the images generated by Pix2Pix is not faithful to the sketches in terms of both color range and texture, CycleGAN and the self-supervised method perform better, reflecting stronger generalization abilities.

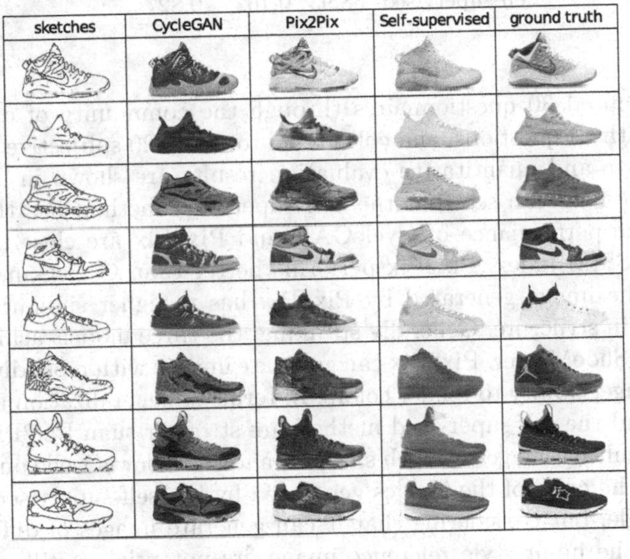

Fig. 7. S2I translation results.

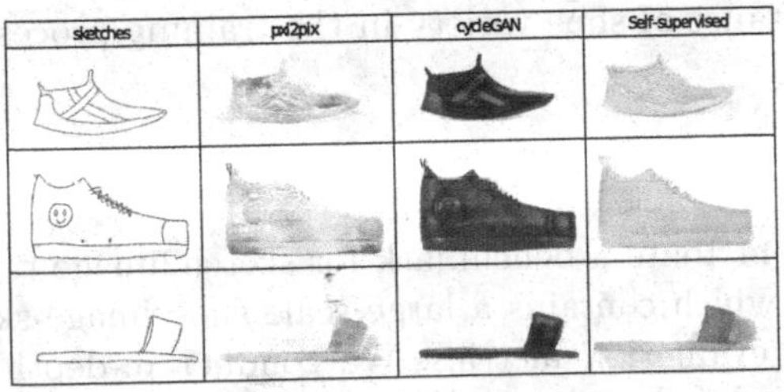

Fig. 8. Amateur hand-drawn translation results.

Table 3. Results of qualitative metrics.

	loyalty	authenticity	naturalness
Pix2Pix	30.00%	52	36
CycleGAN	33.33%	62	52
Self-supervised	60.00%	66	62

Table 4. Results of quantitative metrics.

	FID	LPIPS	MS-SSIM
Pix2Pix	49.85	0.193	0.785
CycleGAN	49.76	0.192	0.719
Self-supervised	38.93	0.162	0.827

We distributed 30 questionnaires through the community of questionnaire stars, each with 14 questions, and collected a total of 420 subjective evaluations. The qualitative and quantitative evaluation results are shown in Tables 3 and 4. From Table 4 we can see that the Self-supervised method has the best performance. The performance of CycleGAN and Pix2Pix are close. However, in terms of MS-SSIM index, Pix2Pix performs better than CycleGan, which may be because the image generated by Pix2Pix has a higher similarity with the ground truth in structure. Generally speaking, the three models achieve promising results on ShoeMaster. Pix2Pix can generate images with more diverse colors, so it has stronger ability to render colors. In terms of generalization ability, both CycleGAN and the self-supervised method are stronger than Pix2Pix. The texture of the resulting images is much sharper, and the color is well confined to the shoe image. The color of the images generated by the self-supervised method is relatively single, but considering that it can generate images of different styles according to the input style reference image, its potential is still greater than that of CycleGAN. During the experiment, we also found that the models have poor effect on the generation of high heel sketches. This may be because the training set contains only general sport shoes and casual shoes, which further confirms the importance of shoe variety in the training process.

5   Conclusion

In this paper, we contribute a benchmark for sketch2image translation of shoes called ShoeMaster, which contains a large-scale shoe image-sketch pair dataset and comprehensive evaluation metrics. We conduct in-depth study with shoe designers on professional classification standards of footwear, shoes category system of online fashion communities and online sales platforms, and propose the daily shoes category knowledge hierarchy. We construct a dataset covering the proposed shoes category hierarchy, which contains 54,361 real shoe images and

3 sketches of different drawing styles for every real image. In order to evaluate the shoes S2I models, we propose the evaluation metrics from both qualitative and quantitative aspects. In the qualitative aspect, perception research based on questionnaire is used to evaluate the loyalty, authenticity and naturalness of generated images. In terms of quantification, FID, LPIPS and MS-SSIM are adopted to measure the image generation effect. From extensive experimental validation on three representative S2I models, we show that ShoeMaster dataset enables the S2I tasks to achieve promising results, and can measure the performance of different models from different dimensions.

Acknowledgement. This research was supported by the grants from the 2022 Undergraduate Training Program for Innovation and Entrepreneurship of Beijing Institute of Fashion Technology (No. 20223060321), the 2022 Postgraduate Education Quality Improvement Special Project and General Teaching Reform Project Funding of Beijing Institute of Fashion Technology (No. 120301990132), the Natural Science Foundation of China (No. 62062058), the General Program of Science and Technology Development Project of Beijing Municipal Education Commission (No. KM202210012002), the Graduate Education Quality Improvement Project of Beijing Institute of Fashion Technology (No. NHFZ20220206).

References

1. FARFETCH. https://www.farfetch.cn/. Accessed 4 Oct 2022
2. FashionAI dataset. http://fashionai.alibaba.com/datasets/. Accessed 4 Oct 2022
3. Multilingual classification and named of cross-border E-commerce trading products-Footwear. https://openstd.samr.gov.cn/bzgk/gb/newGbInfo?hcno=D5D292658B6924EEA1E0D82313DB4EAC. Accessed 4 Oct 2022
4. Questionnaire stars. https://www.wjx.cn/. Accessed 4 Oct 2022
5. XnConvert. https://www.xnview.com/en/xnconvert/. Accessed 4 Oct 2022
6. Chen, S.: Brief talk of classification and nomenclature of footware products, vol. 12, pp. 100–102 (2016)
7. Chen, T., Cheng, M.M., Tan, P., Shamir, A., Hu, S.M.: Sketch2photo: internet image montage. ACM Trans. Graph. (TOG) **28**(5), 1–10 (2009)
8. Chen, W., Hays, J.: SketchyGAN: towards diverse and realistic sketch to image synthesis. In: Proceedings of the IEEE Conference on Computer Vision and Pattern Recognition, pp. 9416–9425. IEEE, Los Alamitos (2018)
9. Eitz, M., Richter, R., Hildebrand, K., Boubekeur, T., Alexa, M.: Photosketcher: interactive sketch-based image synthesis. IEEE Comput. Graph. Appl. **31**(6), 56–66 (2011)
10. Ge, Y., Zhang, R., Wang, X., Tang, X., Luo, P.: DeepFashion2: a versatile benchmark for detection, pose estimation, segmentation and re-identification of clothing images. In: Proceedings of the IEEE/CVF Conference on Computer Vision and Pattern Recognition, pp. 5337–5345. IEEE, Los Alamitos (2019)
11. Heusel, M., Ramsauer, H., Unterthiner, T., Nessler, B., Hochreiter, S.: GANs trained by a two time-scale update rule converge to a local Nash equilibrium. In: Advances in Neural Information Processing Systems, vol. 30 (2017)
12. Huang, X., Liu, M.-Y., Belongie, S., Kautz, J.: Multimodal unsupervised image-to-image translation. In: Ferrari, V., Hebert, M., Sminchisescu, C., Weiss, Y. (eds.)

ECCV 2018. LNCS, vol. 11207, pp. 179–196. Springer, Cham (2018). https://doi.org/10.1007/978-3-030-01219-9_11

13. Ian, J.G., et al.: Generative adversarial nets. In: Proceedings of Annual Conference on Neural Information Processing Systems, pp. 2672–2680 (2014)

14. Isola, P., Zhu, J.Y., Zhou, T., Efros, A.A.: Image-to-image translation with conditional adversarial networks. In: Proceedings of the IEEE Conference on Computer Vision and Pattern Recognition, pp. 1125–1134. IEEE, Los Alamitos (2017)

15. Kim, J., Kim, M., Kang, H., Lee, K.: U-GAT-IT: unsupervised generative attentional networks with adaptive layer-instance normalization for image-to-image translation. arXiv e-prints, p. arXiv-1907 (2019)

16. Li, M., Lin, Z., Mech, R., Yumer, E., Ramanan, D.: Photo-sketching: inferring contour drawings from images. In: 2019 IEEE Winter Conference on Applications of Computer Vision (WACV), pp. 1403–1412. IEEE, Los Alamitos (2019)

17. Li, Y., Fang, C., Hertzmann, A., Shechtman, E., Yang, M.H.: Im2pencil: controllable pencil illustration from photographs. In: Proceedings of the IEEE/CVF Conference on Computer Vision and Pattern Recognition, pp. 1525–1534. IEEE, Los Alamitos (2019)

18. Liu, B., Zhu, Y., Song, K., Elgammal, A.: Self-supervised sketch-to-image synthesis. In: Proceedings of the AAAI Conference on Artificial Intelligence, vol. 35, pp. 2073–2081. AAAI Press, Menlo Park (2021)

19. Liu, M.Y., Breuel, T., Kautz, J.: Unsupervised image-to-image translation networks. In: Proceedings of the 31st International Conference on Neural Information Processing Systems, pp. 700–708 (2017)

20. Liu, R., Yu, Q., Yu, S.: An unpaired sketch-to-photo translation model. arXiv preprint arXiv:1909.08313, vol. 1, no. 3, p. 6 (2019)

21. Liu, Y., Qin, Z., Wan, T., Luo, Z.: Auto-painter: cartoon image generation from sketch by using conditional Wasserstein generative adversarial networks. Neurocomputing **311**, 78–87 (2018)

22. Liu, Z., Luo, P., Qiu, S., Wang, X., Tang, X.: DeepFashion: powering robust clothes recognition and retrieval with rich annotations. In: Proceedings of the IEEE Conference on Computer Vision and Pattern Recognition, pp. 1096–1104. IEEE, Los Alamitos (2016)

23. Qiu, H., Wang, C., Zhu, H., Zhu, X., Gu, J., Han, X.: Two-phase hair image synthesis by self-enhancing generative model. In: Computer Graphics Forum, vol. 38, pp. 403–412. Wiley Online Library (2019)

24. Sangkloy, P., Lu, J., Fang, C., Yu, F., Hays, J.: Scribbler: controlling deep image synthesis with sketch and color. In: Proceedings of the IEEE Conference on Computer Vision and Pattern Recognition, pp. 5400–5409. IEEE, Los Alamitos (2017)

25. Shu-Yu, C., Wanchao, S., Lin, G., Shihong, X., Hongbo, F.: DeepFaceDrawing: deep generation of face images from sketches. ACM Trans. Graph. **39**(4), 72 (2020)

26. Wang, Z., Simoncelli, E.P., Bovik, A.C.: Multiscale structural similarity for image quality assessment. In: 2003 the Thrity-Seventh Asilomar Conference on Signals. Systems & Computers, vol. 2, pp. 1398–1402. IEEE, Los Alamitos (2003)

27. Yu, Q., Liu, F., Song, Y.Z., Xiang, T., Hospedales, T.M., Loy, C.C.: Sketch me that shoe. In: Proceedings of the IEEE Conference on Computer Vision and Pattern Recognition, pp. 799–807. IEEE, Los Alamitos (2016)

28. Zhang, R., Isola, P., Efros, A.A., Shechtman, E., Wang, O.: The unreasonable effectiveness of deep features as a perceptual metric. In: Proceedings of the IEEE Conference on Computer Vision and Pattern Recognition, pp. 586–595. IEEE, Los Alamitos (2018)

29. Zheng, S., Yang, F., Kiapour, M.H., Piramuthu, R.: ModaNet: a large-scale street fashion dataset with polygon annotations. In: Proceedings of the 26th ACM International Conference on Multimedia, pp. 1670–1678. ACM, New York (2018)
30. Zhu, J.Y., Park, T., Isola, P., Efros, A.A.: Unpaired image-to-image translation using cycle-consistent adversarial networks. In: Proceedings of the IEEE International Conference on Computer Vision, pp. 2223–2232. IEEE, Los Alamitos (2017)

Open Source Software Supply Chain Recommendation Based on Heterogeneous Information Network

HaiMing Lin[1,2], Guanyu Liang[1,3], Yanjun Wu[1,3], Bin Wu[1,3], Chunqi Tian[2(✉)], and Wei Wang[4]

[1] Nanjing Institute of Software Technology, Nanjing 211135, China
[2] School of Computer and Science, Tongji University, Shanghai 201804, China
`tianchunqi@163.com`
[3] Institude of Software Chinese Academy of Science, Beijing 100190, China
[4] School of Data Science and Engineering, East China Normal University, Shanghai 200062, China

Abstract. In the GitHub open-source collaborative development scenario, each entity type and the link relationship between them have natural heterogeneous attributes. In order to improve the accuracy of project recommendation, it is necessary to effectively integrate this multi-source information. Therefore, for the project recommendation scenario, this paper defines an open source weighted heterogeneous information network to represent the different entity types and link relationships in the GitHub open source collaborative development scenario, and effectively model the complex interaction among developers, projects and other entities. Using the weighted heterogeneous information network embedding method, extract and use the rich structural and semantic information in the weighted heterogeneous open source information network to learn the node representation of developers and projects, and fuse the personalized nonlinear fusion function into the matrix decomposition model for open source project recommendation. Finally, this paper makes a large number of comparative experiments based on the real GitHub open data set, and compares it with other project recommendation methods to verify the effectiveness of our proposed open source project recommendation model. At the same time, it also explores the impact of different metapaths on the effect of project recommendation. The experimental results show that the recommendation method based on heterogeneous information network can effectively improve the recommendation quality.

Keywords: Heterogeneous Information Network · Open source · GitHub project recommendation

With the rapid development of the open source ecosystem and the popularity of GitHub, a code hosting platform, more and more developers are choosing to build open source projects based on the GitHub platform in an open, shared,

A. Gainaru et al. (Eds.): Bench 2022, LNCS 13852, pp. 70–86, 2023.
https://doi.org/10.1007/978-3-031-31180-2_5

and collaborative software development model. According to the 2021 annual report published by GitHub, there are over 16 million new developers and 61 million newly-created repositories. The vast number of open source projects provides developers with tremendous opportunities to learn and gain experience [1], and developers can use the keyword-based project search function provided by GitHub to search for projects of interest in order to reuse their features or participate in open source contributions. However, due to the extremely large number of open source projects, active search often requires a lot of developer time and effort and is inefficient. The main purpose of the GitHub project recommendation system is to recommend open source projects of interest to developers and to establish more connections between the vast number of developers and open source projects distributed on the GitHub platform. On the one hand, it can help developers find projects of interest to them, on the one hand, and allowing it helps developers find projects that are of interest or value to them, and on the other hand, it exposes open source projects that match the interests and needs of developers to more developers, thus promoting the healthy development of the open source ecosystem. In the research on GitHub project recommendation system, an important problem is how to effectively characterize developers' interest preferences and open source project features. Traditional methods mainly use collaborative filtering-based approach to recommend open source projects for developers. However, different from traditional recommendation systems, the number of projects that developers contributed to is generally not large, especially for novice developers and low-active developers, there is less information available on historical interaction behavior, resulting in a sparse developer-project scoring matrix. To alleviate the cold start problem and data sparsity problem faced in traditional collaborative filtering-based methods, some scholars try to integrate techniques such as machine learning and deep learning to build a feature set of developers and use the historical behavior dataset to train to get a recommendation ranking model. To date, existing methods mainly mine isomorphic information and only consider a few types of developer behavior i.e., create, fork and star, ignoring various semantic information contained in other aspects of contributions such as issue and pull request. In the real GitHub open source collaboration scenario, developers often make extensive use of issue and pull request mechanisms to conduct distributed communication and collaborative development with other developers. In addition, as a typical large-scale distributed collaboration scenario, open source has special social properties, and the contribution behaviors and collaboration relationships among developers based on repositories constitute a complex open source collaboration network, and the types of objects and links in the network have naturally heterogeneous properties. Therefore, this paper proposes a personalized GitHub project recommendation framework based on heterogeneous information network. This framework is mainly composed of the following parts: first, this paper proposes an open source weighted heterogeneous information network (OSWHIN) to effectively integrate heterogeneous information in the field of open source; second, a series of semantically rich extension metapaths are defined to mine the structural and semantic information in the network; third, a graph embedding method is used to learn the representations of developers and projects; finally, personalized nonlinear fusion functions are fused into a matrix decomposition algorithm for open source project recommendation. The main contributions of this paper are as follows:

1. We propose a new OSWHIN structure, which fully consider the heterogeneity of different objects and their relations in GitHub historical behavior data. OSWHIN can naturally capture complex semantic information in the network.
2. We propose a new GitHub project recommendation framework using OSWHIN-based embedding method guided by extended metapaths to uncover the structural and semantic information of OSWHIN and learn a more effective embedding representation for nodes.
3. We conducted extensive experiments based on the real GitHub open data set containing 206823 developers and 54433 repositories. The results verified the effectiveness of our proposed method.

The rest of this paper is organized as follows. Section 1 presents related work. The framework for personalized recommendation is discussed in Sect. 2. The experiments and results are presented in Sect. 3. Section 4 concludes this paper.

1   Related Work

1.1   GitHub Open Source Data Collection and Mining

As the world's largest code hosting and social programming platform, GitHub has accumulated a large amount of repository and open source collaboration log data. These GitHub open source data have important practical value for the analysis and research of the open source ecosystem. Therefore, many researchers have done a lot of research work on the collection and mining of GitHub open source data. Part of the research effort is dedicated to collecting and making available GitHub open source datasets so that other researchers don't have to repeatedly collect and organize datasets. GH Archive is an early representative of this work, which uses a simple and straightforward but effective archiving approach to archive all of GitHub's event stream data by calling the GitHub REST API. It archives all of GitHub's event stream data in JSON format, organized by date. In order to provide scalable, queryable, and offline GitHub data mirroring, Gousios et al. [2] proposed and implemented the GHTorrent tool, which supports both structured and unstructured storage in MySQL databases Stored in a MongoDB database. World of Code [3] is an infrastructure project that mines open source version control system (such as GitHub) data. It currently contains 12 billion Git objects and updates the data once a month to support researchers in their research efforts related to the open source ecosystem. Another part of the work is dedicated to providing software repository mining (MSR) frameworks and tools to support the targeted collection of open source data from many open

source platforms, including GitHub, and quantitative analysis based on relevant
metrics. A representative work in this area is the CHAOSS project [4], a project
of the Linux Foundation to measure the health of open source communities,
which provides quantitative metrics to evaluate the development of open source
communities and projects, and offers two open source metrics data collection
and quantitative analysis tools, Augur [5] and GrimoireLab [6]. Augur is a tool
for collecting and evaluating structured data about free and open source communities, while GrimoireLab provides a one-stop solution for data acquisition,
data storage and analysis, and visualization.

1.2 GitHub Project Recommendation

In order to recommend projects to developers that match their interests and
expertise, most of the early research work generally used a collaborative filtering-
based approach. Guendouz et al. [7] used developers' Fork behavior data to
construct a developer-project scoring matrix based on whether developers fork
project repositories, and used project-based collaborative filtering to achieve
Top-N project recommendations. Zhang et al. [8] proposed a project similarity
measure using developer's star behavioral data to recommend relevant projects
for developers based on the similarity between projects. Xu et al. [9] proposed
the REPERSP model, which utilizes three behavioral data of developers, create, fork, and star, and assigns different weight values to these three behavioral
operations to construct a developer-project scoring matrix, while considering the
textual data of project descriptions and source code to calculate the similarity
between projects and projects using the TF-IDF method. He et al. [10] also used
the developer's create, fork, and watch behavioral data to construct a developer-
project scoring matrix, and combined the user-based and project-based collaborative filtering methods to propose a data-based personalized hybrid recommendation method for GitHub projects. To address the problem of highly sparse
developer-project scoring matrix and cold-start users, Yang et al. [11] calculated
the popularity of the project, the technical correlation between developers and
projects, and the social interaction between developers and projects. The feature
information of the three dimensions of relevance is used to conduct supervised
learning using the developer's historical behavior data set to build a ranking
recommendation model. Zhang et al. [12] proposed a FunkR-pDAE based on a
deep learning model that uses autoencoders to learn vector representations of
developers and open source projects. Liu et al. [13] designed NNLRank, a neural network for list ranking, to extract nine features related to project status
and developer history experience to recommend projects that developers may
contribute to.

1.3 Recommendation Methods Based on Heterogeneous
   Information Networks

Since heterogeneous information networks are able to comprehensively model
the rich structural and semantic information in complex systems and have sig-

nificant advantages in fusing multi-source information and capturing structural semantics [14], many works have introduced heterogeneous information networks into recommender systems and proposed many recommendation models based on heterogeneous information networks. Many previous works have focused on similarity measures for heterogeneous information networks, including random walk-based and metapath-based approaches. HeteLearn [15] based on random walking and Bayesian personalized ranking techniques to learn the weights of links in heterogeneous networks and applied them to personalized recommendation tasks. To leverage additional prior knowledge to capture high-level semantic information in the network, HeteRecom [16] calculates user similarity based on weighted meta-paths based on HeteSim [17] and uses a heuristic weight learning method to learn the weights of different metapaths. semRec [18] proposes a new similarity measure by distinguishing the attribute values on links and designed a new weight regularization to obtain personalized weight preferences on different paths. To better capture structural and attribute information in networks, researchers have introduced network representation learning techniques. Grover et al. [19] proposed a network representation learning framework with biased random walks. LINE [20] portrayed first-order proximity properties and second-order proximity properties on networks. Metapath2vec [21] proposed a meta-path based random walk approach to obtain the heterogeneous domain for each different type of vertex in the heterogeneous network, and then use the extended SkipGram [22] to predict the context nodes within the sliding window and finally learn the network embedding representation for each different type of vertex. HERec [23] also uses a metapath-based random wandering strategy to generate a sequence of objects, and then uses node2vec [19] to learn the object HueRec [24], on the other hand, learns embedding representations of users and items that are uniform across all meta-paths based on the assumption that users and items have common semantics under different metapaths.

2   Proposed Framework

In Fig. 1, it can be seen that the proposed framework consists of four stages: data preprocessing, OSWHIN construction, OSWHIN-based embedding and personalized recommendation.

– Data preprocessing: The data source comes from the GitHub Archive project. We designed the automated data integration program to manage the massive GitHub public event stream data;
– OSWHIN construction. The formal definition of the OSWHIN and OSWHIN schema is given. Based on the above definition, we present the practical algorithm for network instance generation and select multiple metapaths with different semantics;
– OSWHIN-based embedding. A random walk strategy based on unweighted metapaths and weighted metapaths constraints is proposed. We maximize the conditional probability of the local structure of the network according to the optimization objective function, and fuse the embedding representations

under multiple metapaths to obtain the final embedding representations of developers and projects;
– Personalized recommendation. We integrate the personalized nonlinear fusion function into a matrix factorization model for GitHub project recommendation.

2.1 Data Preprocessing

The data source we use is the GitHub public event stream data archived by GH Archive. This dataset records historical behavioral data generated by developers around open source projects across the GitHub platform. To meet the demand for high-speed queries on large-scale data, we parsed the GH Archive archived raw data image into structured data and imported it into ClickHouse, an open source column storage high-performance real-time analytics database, to facilitate subsequent log data aggregation calculations.

2.2 Oswhin Construction

In order to accurately model the weighted heterogeneous open source information network in the project recommendation scenario, we combed the open source collaborative development process based on the GitHub platform, and analyzed the GitHub public event stream data, and finally selected 4 types of nodes and abstract the link relationship between nodes and the attribute values on the relationship to derive the definition of OSWHIN and OSWHIN schema. The OSWHIN can be represented as $G = (V, E, w, A, R, W)$, where V is the object set E is the relation set, and w is the attribute value set on the relation. Each object belongs to one particular object type in the object type set $A : \varphi(\nu) \in A$, $A = U \cup R \cup I \cup P$ and U, R, I, P are the object set of four types: user, repo, issue and pull request, respectively. Each link $e \in \mathcal{E}$ belongs to a particular relation $\mathcal{R} : \psi(e) \in \mathcal{R}$, $\mathcal{R} = \mathcal{R}_{u-r} \cup \mathcal{R}_{u-i} \cup \mathcal{R}_{u-pr} \cup \mathcal{R}_{u-u} \cup \mathcal{R}_{i-r} \cup \mathcal{R}_{pr-r}$. $\mathcal{W}$ is the type set of attribute value on the link relationship, $\mathcal{W} = \mathcal{W}_{u-r} \cup \mathcal{W}_{u-i} \cup \mathcal{W}_{u-pr}$. Figure 2 gives the OSWHIN schema which contains 4 types of objects and various relationships between those objects. The 4 types of objects are user, repo, issue, and pull request. $\mathcal{R}*$ represents the interactions between two types of objects. The color identification in Fig. 2 indicates an attribute value constraint relationship, while black indicates a normal relationship. Based on the above network schema, we propose a OSWHIN generation algorithm shown in Algorithm 1. The algorithm consists of two stages. In the first stage, for each repository in the given set of open source projects, the developers, issues and pull requests associated with the repository are aggregated and filtered from the GitHub event stream data, and then add these nodes to the network instance. For each developer, the second stage filters the developers of interest and the associated issues and pull requests, and aggregates the attribute values of $\mathcal{R}_{u-r}$, $\mathcal{R}_{u-i}$ and $\mathcal{R}_{u-pr}$, and then add them to the network instance.

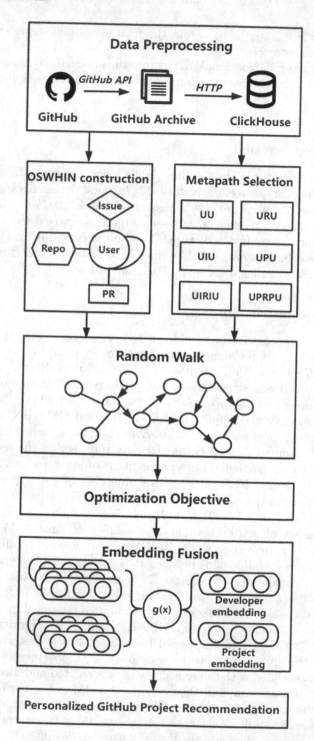

Fig. 1. GitHub project recommendation method based on heterogeneous information network.

Algorithm 1: OSWHIN instance generation

Input Time span t, Repositories set R , Events data D, Importance function W.

Output OSWHIN instance G.

FOREACH $r \in R$ DO

$U_r, ISSUE_r, PR_r = Extract(D, r, t)$

$AddToNetwork\,(G, U_r, I_r, PR_r)$

FOREACH $u \in U_r$ DO

$U_u, I_u^r, PR_u^r = GetActivity(D, u, r, t)$

$w_u = Aggreegate\,(D, u, r, I_u^r, PR_u^r, W)$

$AddToNetwork\,(G, U_u, w_u)$

END

END

RETURN G

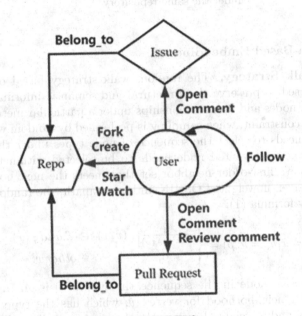

Fig. 2. OSWHIN schema.

2.3   Metapath Selection

The weighted metapath can be expressed as $\rho : A_1 \overset{\delta(R_1)}{\to} A_2 \overset{\delta(R_2)}{\to}$ ... $\overset{\delta_{l-1}(R_{l-1})}{\to}$ A_l , If there is an attribute value on the relation R, the attribute value function $\delta(R)$ represents the range of the attribute value; otherwise, it is an empty set. Table 1 lists the six selected metapaths, and these different metapaths represent different semantic information in OSWHIN.

Table 1. Metapath and its corresponding semantics.

ID	Metapath	Semantics
ρ_1	UU	Developer follows another developer
ρ_2	URU	Developers are associated with the same repository
ρ_3	UIU	Developers participate in the same issue
ρ_4	UPU	Developers participate in the same pull request
ρ_5	UIRIU	Developers participate in different issues under the same repository
ρ_6	UPRPU	Developers participate in different pull requests under the same repository

2.4 Oswhin-Based Embedding

Random Walk Strategy. The random walk strategy based on metapaths constraint is used to preserve the structural and semantic information implicit in the network nodes and link relationships under a particular metapath. Under the metapath, constraint, when sampling is performed by random walk, the next selected node needs to select the sequence of node types under that metapath definition, so the next visited node needs to be selected within the subset of the current node's first-order neighbor set that meets the next node type constraint. For a given unweighted OSHIN and a metapath, the random walk path is generated by formula (1):

$$P\left(n_{t+1} = x | n_t = v; \rho\right) = \begin{cases} \frac{1}{\left|\mathcal{N}^{A_{t+1}}(v)\right|}, & (v,x) \in \mathcal{E} \: and \: \varphi(x) = A_{t+1} \\ 0, & otherwise \end{cases} \quad (1)$$

where n_t is the t_{th} node in the sequence the type of v is A_t, and $N_{A_{t+1}}(n)$ is the first-order neighborhood for vertex v, which has the type A_{t+1}. For a given OSWHIN and a weighted metapath, the random walk path is generated by formula (1):

$$P\left(n_{t+1} = x | n_t = v; \rho\right) = \begin{cases} \frac{1}{\left|\mathcal{N}_{w_t}^{A_{t+1}}(v)\right|}, & \begin{array}{l} (v,x) \in E \: and \: \varphi(x) = A_{t+1}, \\ w_t = w_{l-t}, w_t \in \delta_t\left(R_t\right) \end{array} \\ 0, & otherwise \end{cases} \quad (2)$$

where $\delta_t\left(R_t\right)$ is the set of attribute values on the path that connects A_t and A_{t+1} .w_t and w_{l-t} represent an attribute value on two symmetric relations. $\mathcal{N}_{w_t}^{A_{t+1}}(v)$ is the first-order neighborhood for vertex v with the type A_{t+1}, and the attribute value of the relations between nodes in $\mathcal{N}_{w_t}^{A_{t+1}}(v)$ and vertex v is w_t. Based on the above rules, the random walk strategy used in this paper is as follows: if the attribute value constraint function $\delta\left(R\right)$ is an empty set, the weighted metapath degenerates to an unweighted metapath, and formula (1) is used to generate a random walk sequence of nodes; if the attribute value constraint function $\delta\left(R\right)$

is not empty, a random walk is performed on the weighted metapath based on the rules defined in formula (2).

Optimization Objective. According to metapath2vec [21], in order to learn the feature representation of a given node, we maximize the conditional probability of the local structure of the network by using the following formula.

$$argmax \sum_{v \in \mathcal{V}} \sum_{A_t \in \mathcal{A}} \sum_{c_{A_t} \in \mathcal{N}_{A_t}(v)} \log p\left(c_{A_t} | v; \theta\right) \tag{3}$$

$$\log p\left(c_{A_t} | v; \theta\right) = \frac{e^{x_{c_{A_t}} \bullet x_v}}{\sum_{u \in \mathcal{V}} e^{x_u \bullet x_v}} \tag{4}$$

where $\mathcal{N}_{A_t}(v)$ represents the node set of type A_t in the first-order neighborhood of vertex v . $\log p\left(c_{A_t}|v; \theta\right)$ is commonly defined as a softmax function. is the representation of vertex x_v. In each iteration of optimization, all nodes are traversed, which leads to low efficiency of the whole model. Therefore, we refer to word2vec and adopt the negative sampling method to update only a small part of the model weight in each sample training to reduce the calculation burden and improve the quality of node embeddings. Given a negative sample size M, the optimization objective can be updated to formula (6):

$$\log \sigma \left(X_{c_{A_t}} \bullet X_v\right) + \sum_{M}^{m=1} E_{u^m \sim P(u)} \left[\log \sigma \left(-X_{u^m} \bullet X_v\right)\right] \tag{5}$$

where $P(u)$ is a predefined distribution from which a negative node is extracted M times.

Embedding Fusion. After optimization, the same nodes in different input sequences are mapped to different vector spaces. In order to improve the effectiveness of the recommendation, we need to map these node representations into the appropriate space. For a given vertex v and selected metapath set P, we use e_v^l represents the embedding of vertex v on the lth metapath. Thus, $e_v^{(l)}{}_{l=1}^{|\mathcal{P}|}$ represents the set of embeddings on each metapath for vertex v. To make full use of these node embeddings to enhance the recommendation performance, a fusion function $g(x)$ is adopted to fuse the node embedding set into one representation:

$$e_v = g \left(\left\{e_v^{(l)}{}_{l=1}^{|\mathcal{P}|}\right\}\right) \tag{6}$$

where e_v is the final representation of vertex v, which contains much more information under multiple semantic metapaths. In the next section, a specific fusion function is defined.

2.5 Personalized Recommendation

Based on the matrix decomposition approach, the following formula is used to represent the developer's rating of the project by applying the embedding vector of nodes.

$$\hat{r_{u,i}} = x_u^T \cdot y_i + \alpha \cdot e_u^{(U)^T} \cdot \gamma_i^I + \beta \cdot \gamma_u^{U^T} \cdot e_i^{(I)} \tag{7}$$

where x_u and y_i represent the latent factors of developer u and project i, respectively, $e_u^{(U)}$ and $e_i^{(I)}$ represent the fused embedding of developer u and project i, respectively, g_i^I and g_u^U are the latent factors paired with embeddings $e_u^{(U)}$ and $e_i^{(I)}$, respectively, and are the parameters that can be adjusted to better integrate three polynomials. Then, a specific fusion function g(x) is given to realize personalized nonlinear fusion:

$$g\left(\left\{e_v^{(l)}\right\}\right) = \sigma\left(\sum_{l=1}^{|\mathcal{P}|} w_v^{(l)} \sigma\left(M^{(l)} e_v^{(l)} + b^{(l)}\right)\right) \tag{8}$$

where S is a sigmoid function. P is a metapath set containing vertex v, $M^{(l)}$ is a transformation matrix on the lth metapath, $b^{(l)}$ is a bias vector on the lth metapath, and $w_v^{(l)}$ is the weight of vertex v on the lth metapath. The above fusion function is integrated into the matrix decomposition framework and the stochastic gradient descent is used to train the parameters of the model with the following optimization objectives:

$$\mathcal{L} = \sum_{(u,i,r_{u,i})\in\mathcal{R}} (r_{u,i} - \hat{r_{u,i}})^2 + \lambda\sum_u (||x_u||_2+||y_i||_2)+\left|\left|\gamma_u^U\right|\right|_2+\left|\left|\gamma_i^I\right|\right|_2+\left|\left|\Theta^{(U)}\right|\right|_2+\left|\left|\Theta^{(I)}\right|\right|_2\right) \tag{9}$$

where $r_{u,i}$ is the calculated predictive value l is a regularization parameter, $\Theta^{(U)}$ and $\Theta^{(I)}$ are the parameters in embedding fusion functions corresponding to developer u and project i, respectively.

3 Experiment

To verify the effectiveness of the proposed method, we conduct experiments on the real GitHub full-domain public dataset and compare the analysis with other GitHub project recommendation methods, and finally analyze the impact of different metapaths on the recommendation effect through the experimental results.

3.1 Dataset

Based on the GitHub 2020 public dataset, we select 360 open source projects from the Cloud Native Computing Foundation (CNCF) to build the experimental dataset and generate a OSWHIN instance according to Algorithm 1. The data statistics are shown in Table 2.

Table 2. Data statistics of experimental dataset.

Type	name	name
node	User	206823
	Repo	54433
	Issue	788259
	PR	713564
Edge	User-Repo	962742
	User-Issue	1351137
	User-PR	1135677
	Repo-Issue	789909
	Repo-PR	816695

3.2 Evaluation Metrics

We use the precision, recall, F1-score and accuracy to measure the performance of the proposed method. Precision refers to the ratio of the number of correctly recommended items to the total number of recommended items. Recall refers to the ratio of the number of correctly recommended items to the total number of items. F1-score is used to evaluate the Precision and Recall together. accuracy is the percentage of all developers who actually participated in at least one of the recommended projects. The formulae for the four evaluation metrics are as follows.

$$Precision@K = \frac{1}{|U_{test}|} \sum_{i=1}^{|U_{test}|} \frac{\left| s_i \cap s_i^{TopK} \right|}{\left| s_i^{TopK} \right|} \tag{10}$$

$$Recall@K = \frac{1}{|U_{test}|} \sum_{i=1}^{|U_{test}|} \frac{\left| s_i \cap s_i^{TopK} \right|}{\left| s_i \right|} \tag{11}$$

$$F1@K = \frac{2 \times Precision@K \times Recall@K}{Precision@K + Recall@K} \tag{12}$$

$$Accuracy@K = \frac{1}{|U_{test}|} \sum_{i=1}^{|U_{test}|} \left| \left\{ s_i \cap s_i^{TopK} \neq \varnothing \phi \right\} \right| \tag{13}$$

where s_i represents the project set in which the target developer u_i actually participated, s_i^{TopK} represents the set of Top-K projects recommended to the target developers u_i, U_{test} represents the set of all developers in the test set.

3.3 Experimental Results and Analysis

Recommendation Performance. In order to verify the effectiveness of the method proposed in this paper, the following GitHub project recommended method was chosen as the baseline method for experimentation.

1. *ICF* The item-based collaborative filtering recommendation method, and the similarity of developers is calculated by the factor between the project sets stared by developers.
2. *UCF* The user-based collaborative filtering recommendation method and calculate the developer-project score matrix from the developer's create, fork, and star behavioral information
3. *RepoLike*: A multi-feature-based personalized recommendation approach with LTR algorithm to train recommendation models. The parameters of the algorithm in this paper are set as follows: the representation dimension of the nodes $d = 64$, the coefficients $a = b = 1.0$, the length of the random walk is set to 40, and the number of hidden factors of the matrix decomposition is set to 10. The experimental results are shown in Table 3.

Table 3. Comparison of the recommendation quality of different models.

Method	Precision	Recall	F1 score	Accuracy
ICF	0.053	0.041	0.046	0.218
UCF	0.136	0.129	0.132	0.309
RepoLike	0.273	0.255	0.264	0.428
Our Method	0.481	0.394	0.433	0.693

As is shown in Table 3, our method performs better than other traditional project recommendation models on the all four metrics. In contrast to the collaborative filtering-based approach, by introducing heterogeneous contextual information in the network, the problem of sparsity of the developer-project scoring matrix in the collaborative filtering-based approach is avoided, which is conducive to the improvement of recommendation quality. The RepoLike model constructs a social network and a project dependency network respectively, but does not fuse the multi-source information in the network. Our method takes into account the heterogeneous object types and relationships in the open source collaborative network, and extracts the rich semantic and structural information contained in the heterogeneous contexts of the network based on the constructed multiple metapaths, which can reflect the characteristic information of developers and projects more objectively and improve the performance of the recommendation model.

Metapaths. In order to measure the effectiveness of our constructed metapaths, we compare the performance of the recommendation method under different metapaths through several comparison experiments of different metapaths. Figure 3 shows the variation of precision, recall, F1-score and accuracy of the model when different metapaths are added sequentially. The metrics of the model gradually increase as metapaths are added. When the metapaths $\rho_3 : UIU, \rho_4 : UPU$ are added, we can see that the performance of the model is improved, which indicates that adding the issue and pull request contributions of developers can more comprehensively explore the interest preferences expressed by developers in the GitHub platform for open source collaborative development and ρ_4 brings a larger increase than ρ_3. An intuitive explanation is that since the cost of participating in the pull request is higher than the cost of participating in the issue, the interest relationship between developers implied in ρ_4 is stronger than that in ρ_3. Also, we note that with the addition of the metapath ρ_5, the recall and F1-score decreased instead. One possible explanation is that a project usually contains more issues (compared to pull request) with a larger number of participating developers, so that this metapath introduces some noise, which leads to a decrease in model recommendation accuracy. Therefore, the number of meta-paths is not as large as possible, and only a small number of high-quality meta-paths need to be fused, which can bring a large performance improvement to the model, and at the same time can effectively control the complexity of the model.

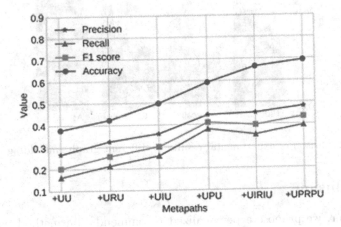

Fig. 3. Metapath effectiveness.

Graph Embedding Method. In recent years, graph representation learning methods have been well used in recommender systems. In this paper, we measure the performance of different graph representation learning methods in project recommendation scenarios. The comparison method is as follows.

1. DeepWalk A method of learning the representation of nodes in homogeneous information networks by random walks.

2. Node2vec Based on DeepWalk, this method control search preferences during random walks by hyperparameters p and q.
3. Metapath2vec A random walk sampling method based on metapath constraints, without distinguishing edge weights.

The experimental results show that the proposed OSWHIN-based embedding method is better than the recommendations of other benchmark methods in all metrics. DeepWalk and Node2vec are more suitable for homogeneous information network learning and cannot fully learn the structural and semantic information embedded in the heterogeneous nodes and relationships in OSWHIN. The Metapath2vec method cannot adequately characterize the developer and project feature information because it cannot learn different attribute value information on different metapaths. Therefore, compared with other graph representation learning methods, the proposed method is more suitable for the open source project recommendation scenario and can extract the rich structural and semantic information contained in different metapaths in the network, thus improving the recommendation accuracy (Fig. 4).

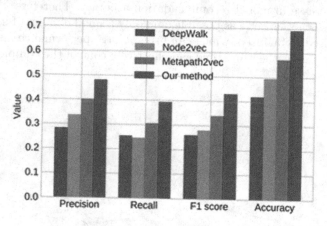

Fig. 4. Comparison of experimental results of different graph embedding methods.

4   Conclusion

In this paper, we propose a personalized recommendation method for GitHub projects based on heterogeneous information networks. First, we abstract the objects and the relationships between nodes based on the open source collaborative development process of the GitHub platform, derive the definition of a OSWHIN and its schema, and select metapaths that reflect the semantic information of developers' interests and preferences in the open source collaborative development process. Then, the OSWHIN-based embedding is used to learn the representation of developers and projects. Experimental results on real GitHub developers' historical behavioral data show that the GitHub project recommendation method based on heterogeneous information networks can effectively extract and exploit the rich structural and semantic information embedded in the open source collaborative development network, which helps to improve the recommendation effectiveness. In future work, we will consider applying large-scale network embedding algorithms to conduct efficient training on large-scale network instances to obtain real-time node representation vectors to improve recommendation performance in real-world scenarios.

References

1. Zhao, H., Li, N., Chen, Q., et al.: Projects and developers recommendation in open source ecosystem. J. Chin. Comput. Syst. **42**(11), 2259–2268 (2021)
2. Gousios, G., Spinellis, D.: GHTorrent: GitHub's data from a firehose. In: 2012 9th IEEE Working Conference on Mining Software Repositories (MSR), pp. 12–21 (2012)
3. Ma, Y., Bogart, C., Amreen, S., et al.: World of code: an infrastructure for mining the universe of open source VCS data. In: 2019 IEEE/ACM 16th International Conference on Mining Software Repositories (MSR), pp. 143–154 (2019)
4. Goggins, S.P., Germonprez, M., Lumbard, K.: Making open source project health transparent. Computer **54**(08), 104–111 (2021)
5. Peterson, J., Krug, J.: Augur: a decentralized, open-source platform for prediction markets. arXiv preprint arXiv:1501.01042, p. 507 (2015)
6. Dueñas, S., Cosentino, V., Gonzalez-Barahona, J.M., et al.: GrimoireLab: a toolset for software development analytics. Peer J. Comput. Sci. **7**, e601 (2021)
7. Guendouz, M., Amine, A., Hamou, R.M.: Recommending relevant open source projects on GitHub using a collaborative-filtering technique. Int. J. Open Source Softw. Process. (IJOSSP) **6**(1), 1–16 (2015)
8. Zhang, Y., Lo, D., Kochhar, P.S., et al.: Detecting similar repositories on GitHub. In: 2017 IEEE 24th International Conference on Software Analysis, Evolution and Reengineering (SANER), pp. 13–23. IEEE (2017)
9. Xu, W., Sun, X., Hu, J., et al.: REPERSP: recommending personalized software projects on GitHub. In: 2017 IEEE International Conference on Software Maintenance and Evolution (ICSME), pp. 648–652. IEEE (2017)
10. He, K., Ma, Y., Zhang, Y., Liu, H.: A data-based personalized mixed recommendation method for GitHub projects. J. Jilin Univ. Sci. Edn. **58**(6), 1399–1406 (2020)
11. Yang, C., Fan, Q., Wang, T., et al.: RepoLike: personal repositories recommendation in social coding communities. In: Proceedings of the 8th Asia-Pacific Symposium on Internetware, pp. 54–62 (2016)
12. Zhang, P., Xiong, F., Leung, H., et al.: FunkR-pDAE: personalized project recommendation using deep learning. IEEE Trans. Emerg. Top. Comput. **9**, 886–900 (2018)
13. Liu, C., Yang, D., Zhang, X., et al.: Recommending GitHub projects for developer onboarding. IEEE Access **6**, 52082–52094 (2018)
14. Sun, Y., Han, J.: Mining heterogeneous information net-works: a structural analysis approach. ACM SIGKDD Explor. Newsl. **14**(2), 20–28 (2013)
15. Jiang, Z., Liu, H., Fu, B., et al.: Recommendation in heterogeneous information networks based on generalized random walk model and Bayesian personalized ranking. In: Proceedings of the Eleventh ACM International Conference on Web Search and Data Mining, pp. 288–296 (2018)

16. Shi, C., Zhou, C., Kong, X., et al.: HeteRecom: a semantic-based recommendation system in heterogeneous networks. In: Proceedings of the 18th ACM SIGKDD International Conference on Knowledge Discovery and Data Mining, pp. 1552–1555 (2012)
17. Shi, C., Kong, X., Huang, Y., et al.: HeteSim: a general framework for relevance measure in heterogeneous networks. IEEE Trans. Knowl. Data Eng. 26(10), 2479–2492 (2014)
18. Shi, C., Zhang, Z., Luo, P., et al.: Semantic path based personalized recommendation on weighted heterogeneous information networks. In: Proceedings of the 24th ACM International on Conference on Information and Knowledge Management, pp. 453–462 (2015)
19. Grover, A., Leskovec, J.: node2vec: scalable feature learning for networks. In: Proceedings of the 22nd ACM SIGKDD International Conference on Knowledge Discovery and Data Mining, pp. 855–864 (2016)
20. Tang, J., Qu, M., Wang, M.: Large-scale information network embedding. In: Proceedings of the 24th International Conference on World Wide Web. International World Wide Web Conferences Steering Committee, pp. 1067–1077 (2015)
21. Dong, Y., Chawla, N.V., Swami, A.: metapath2vec: scalable representation learning for heterogeneous networks. In: Proceedings of the 23rd ACM SIGKDD International Conference on Knowledge Discovery and Data Mining, pp. 135–144 (2017)
22. Mikolov, T., Chen, K., Corrado, G., et al.: Efficient estimation of word representations in vector space [EB/OL]. arXiv preprint arXiv:1301.3781 (2013)
23. Shi, C., Hu, B., Zhao, W.X., et al.: Heterogeneous information network embedding for recommendation. IEEE Trans. Knowl. Data Eng. 31(2), 357–370 (2019)
24. Wang, Z., Liu, H., Du, Y., et al.: Unified embedding model over heterogeneous information network for personalized recommendation. In: IJCAI, pp. 3813–3819 (2019)

BasicTS: An Open Source Fair Multivariate Time Series Prediction Benchmark

Yubo Liang[1,2], Zezhi Shao[1,2], Fei Wang[1(✉)], Zhao Zhang[1], Tao Sun[1], and Yongjun Xu[1]

[1] Institute of Computing Technology, Chinese Academy of Sciences, Beijing, China
{liangyubo20g,shaozezhi19b,wangfei,zhangzhao2021,suntao,xyj}@ict.ac.cn
[2] University of Chinese Academy of Sciences, Beijing, China

Abstract. Multivariate Time Series (MTS) is ubiquitous in the real world, and its prediction plays a vital role in a wide range of applications. Recently, many researchers have made persistent efforts to design powerful models. For example, Spatial-Temporal Graph Neural Networks (STGNNs) have become increasingly popular MTS prediction methods due to their state-of-the-art performance. However, we found there exists much unfairness in the comparison of the performance of existing models, which may prevent researchers from making correct judgments. Meanwhile, researchers usually have to build training pipelines that are complex and error-prone when designing new models, which further obstacles the quick and deep innovation in the MTS prediction field. In this paper, we first analyze the sources of unfairness and then propose a fair and easy-to-use benchmark, BasicTS, to address the above two issues. On the one hand, for a given MTS prediction model, BasicTS evaluates its ability based on rich datasets and standard pipelines. On the other hand, BasicTS provides users with flexible and extensible interfaces to facilitate convenient designing and exhaustive evaluation of new models. In addition, based on BasicTS, we provide performance revisits of several popular MTS prediction models. The proposed benchmark is publicly available at https://github.com/zezhishao/BasicTS.

Keywords: Multivariate time series prediction · Unfairness · Benchmark

1 Introduction

Multivariate Time Series (MTS) contains time series from multiple correlated variables and exists in many real-world systems. Accurate MTS prediction fuels a wide range of services related to intelligent transportation, financial investment, and environmental protection. It helps people to make better decisions. Thus, MTS prediction has remained an enduring topic in both academia and industry.

Z. Shao—Project leader.

A. Gainaru et al. (Eds.): Bench 2022, LNCS 13852, pp. 87–101, 2023.
https://doi.org/10.1007/978-3-031-31180-2_6

Despite the significant progress, we find that the evaluation and comparison of existing models are not fair enough, which may lead researchers to make wrong judgments and thus hind innovation in the field of MTS prediction. Specifically, after an exhaustive technical review of existing works, we summarize the sources of unfairness into three levels: data level, model level, and evaluation level.

Data Level:

Unfairness caused by the lack of richness of the datasets. Different datasets are often heterogeneous, i.e., datasets have different physical characteristics, dynamics, and so on. Therefore, the same model may have different performances on different types of datasets. Thus, using only a specific type of dataset for comparison may lead to unfair results.

Unfairness caused by data pre-processing. Different normalization methods (e.g., max-min normalization, z-score normalization) may affect the model's performance. Therefore, if different models adopt different pre-processing approaches, the comparison of their performance results is unfair.

Model Level:

Unfairness caused by different pipelines. Pipeline controls many details of the training process. Since each researcher tends to construct their own model pipeline, it may bring an unfair comparison of results.

Unfairness caused by hyper-parameters settings. In deep learning-related prediction models, the hyper-parameters have a significant impact on the final performance, e.g., learning rate, weight decay, random seeds, etc. For example, we find that in some works [1,2], the performance of important baselines, such as DCRNN [3] and Graph WaveNet [4], is surprisingly poor, this may be caused by unreasonable hyper-parameter settings. Thus, different settings of hyper-parameters may lead to an unfair comparison of results.

Evaluation Level:

Unfairness caused by different ways of calculating the evaluation metrics. Common evaluation metrics for MTS prediction problems include MAE, MAPE, RMSE. Although they have strict mathematical definitions, the implementation details may vary, such as the way of handling outliers, and mini-batch computations [5]. These differences can cause significant deviations from test results and actual performance, thus leading to an unfair comparison of results.

Unfairness caused by different ways of evaluation. For example, in the field of MTS prediction, the metrics of **horizon x** denotes the error metrics **at** the x-th prediction time step, while many researchers make mistakes and calculate the average of the error metrics over 0-x prediction time step, which results in a significant reduction in error and thus significant unfairness.

In order to solve the above unfairness problems and fairly evaluate the performance of a given model, we propose a fair and easy-to-use open-source benchmark for MTS prediction, named BasicTS. Specifically, BasicTS provides an exhaustive and fair evaluation of a given model based on a unified pipeline and rich datasets. In addition, to make it easier for researchers to use, BasicTS provides a set of rich and extensible interfaces that allows users to focus on model design and ignore the building of the training and evaluating pipeline, enabling rapid development and comprehensive evaluation. Finally, based on BasicTS, we present a performance review of popular deep learning-based MTS predicting methods, to provide researchers with a solid reference.

Our contributions are summarized as follows:

- We designed a benchmark named BasicTS for solving the unfair comparison problem of MTS prediction models. For a given MTS prediction model, BasicTS utilizes a unified pipeline to perform an exhaustive evaluation of its capabilities based on rich datasets.
- We designed a set of rich and extensible interfaces in BasicTS, which can help researchers quickly design and evaluate their own models and be free from the hassle of building complex pipelines.
- Based on BasicTS, we provide a fair performance comparison of existing popular MTS prediction models to provide researchers with a solid reference and thus inspire innovations.

2   Related Works

In this section, we list the existing benchmarks related to time series prediction.

GluonTS [6] is an open-source benchmark designed by Amazon that focuses on time series prediction. However, it cannot handle datasets with pre-defined graphs, which limits its usability for STGNN-related models. FOST is a spatio-temporal prediction framework designed by MSRA. Compared to GluonTS, it adds a GNN model to ensure its ability to handle data with pre-defined graphs. However, FOST lacks interfaces for hyper-parameter settings, and it can only make predictions but cannot evaluate the prediction results, which makes it difficult to guarantee the fairness of this benchmark. In addition, FOST contains only three models (RNN, CNN, GNN) and has not designed interfaces to add new models. Also, its form of input data is fixed, which significantly limits its extensibility. LibCity [7] is a library specifically focused on traffic-related problems, which aims to provide experimental tools for researchers. However, it is not designed for benchmarking and only focuses on traffic-related data, ignoring many other real-world MTS prediction problems.

Compared with existing works, BasicTS is the first work that provides unified pipelines and rich datasets for benchmarking given MTS prediction models, and provides users with extensible and easy-to-use interfaces for quickly designing and evaluating new models.

3   Benchmark Building

In the Introduction, we analyze the factors that may lead to unfairness. In this section, we will explore our ideas to solve the above unfairness problems and propose the specific implementation of BasicTS.

3.1 Design Thoughts

In this part, we demonstrate the design thoughts of BasicTS, which aims to address the critical unfairness issues discussed in the Introduction and provide extensibility for users to enable users adding their models and datasets.

Unfairness. We propose the following solutions to the factors that lead to unfairness in the field of MTS prediction:

Data Level. For unfairness caused by the lack of richness of the datasets, we used rich and heterogeneous datasets. Specifically, BasicTS currently includes ten datasets, including traffic speed datasets (METR-LA, PEMS-BAY), traffic flow datasets (PEMS03, PEMS04, PEMS07, PEMS08), electricity, solar-energy, exchange-rate, and Beijing air quality. In particular, in addition to datasets that include a pre-defined graph indicating spatial dependency, the latter four datasets, which do not contain a pre-defined graph, can help to evaluate the model's capability more comprehensively. For unfairness caused by data pre-processing, we adopted a uniform data pre-processing process, which takes Z-Score normalization as default.

Model Level. For unfairness caused by different pipelines, we use an identical, standard, extensible pipeline to avoid the unfairness problem caused by different training pipelines. For unfairness caused by hyper-parameter settings, we have provided interfaces that allow flexible parameter settings and carefully tuned the parameters of all existing models in BasicTS.

Evaluation Level. We use unified evaluation metrics and pipelines to ensure the fairness of the evaluation. In addition, to measure the model's performance at different prediction lengths, users can evaluate the performance of the model at any time step less than the length of the prediction.

Extensibility. BasicTS provides researchers with rich, easy-to-use, and extensible interfaces to configure the standard Pipeline and functions built in BasicTS. Specifically, for the convenience of researchers, a unified configuration file is designed to allow users to configure all parameters, such as dataloader, environment, and parameters to be optimized. Users can configure it by simply editing them at the string level as if they were filling out a form. In addition, the unified configuration file imports the model to be evaluated and its runner (optional), which can be designed at will by simply following the standard input and output interfaces designed by BasicTS.

The unified configuration profile and extensible interface design allow users to ignore the construction of the training process and focus on the design of the model, enabling rapid iteration and effective innovation.

3.2 Implementation of BasicTS

The specific implementation of BasicTS is shown in Fig. 1. Among them, users communicate with BasicTS through a unified configuration file. In this part, we will describe the implementation of each module in detail.

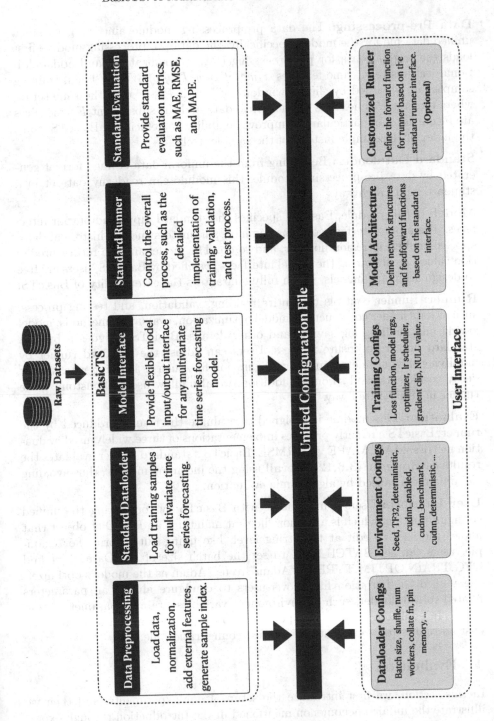

Fig. 1. BasicTS components.

Data Pre-processing: The data pre-processing module aims to generate a unified data file for the model. Specifically, the data pre-processing module first loads the original data for pre-processing (e.g., normalization) and adds additional features (e.g., time features *Time of Day, Day of Week*). Then, training samples are obtained by sliding windows of length $P + F$ over the time series, where the first P time slices are historical data and the subsequent F time slices are future data. In particular, to improve flexibility and efficiency, BasicTS stores the index of the sample instead of the sample itself.

Standard Dataloader: Benefiting from the uniform data storage format generated by data pre-processing module, this module can read any dataset in a standard mini-batch way.

Model: In this module, BasicTS specifies the standard input and output interfaces. The input interface contains common parameters such as historical data, epochs number, iteration number, and so on. The model aims to return prediction values. By following the model interfaces specified by BasicTS, users are free to design arbitrary models, which fully guarantees the extensibility of BasicTS.

Runner: Runner controls the entire training, validation, and testing process, such as data loader construction, model optimization, evaluation methods, model saving and loading, log saving, and other details. BasicTS includes a built-in standard runner to ensure fairness. Users can adjust the standard runner by modifying the parameters in the configuration file, such as learning rate, weight decay coefficients, and so on. In addition, we also allow users to customize the runner in an inherited way.

Evaluation: This module is designed to evaluate the results produced by the runner. BasicTS currently provides implementations of three widely-used evaluation metrics, MAE, MAPE, and RMSE. BasicTS's standard runner evaluates the results on **Horizon@3,6,12, overall** using the incoming metrics, thus avoiding the unfairness caused by algorithmic evaluation.

User Interface: Users communicate with BasicTS by configuring the unified configuration file, which is a python file that maintains an EasyDict object that allows the user to edit at the string level, like filling out a form. For example, users can set BATCH_SIZE to set the batch size of the Dataloader and CFG.TRAIN.OPTIM.TYPE to "Adam" to use Adam as the model's optimizer. the unified configuration file allows users to configure almost all parameters related to Dataloader, such as environment variables, training parameters, and so on. In addition, users can import their own designed model structure and custom runner (optional) into the unified configuration file.

4 Evaluation

In this section, we first introduce the setup of our experiments, and then we illustrate the unfair phenomenon mentioned in the Introduction through experiments. Finally, we provide a fair performance revisit of existing popular MTS prediction models.

4.1 Experimental Setup

Datasets: We conducted experiments on ten commonly used MTS prediction datasets: PEMS03, PEMS04, PEMS07, PEMS08, PEMS-BAY, METR-LA, Electricity, solar-energy, exchange-rate, and Beijing air quality.

The information of these datasets is shown in Table 1. Traffic-related predictions, such as traffic flow prediction and traffic speed prediction, are the most common issues of MTS prediction. Among them, PEMS03, PEMS04, PEMS07, and PEMS08 are traffic flow datasets, while PEMS-BAY and METR-LA are traffic speed datasets. These datasets contain a pre-defined graph indicating the spatial dependency between traffic sensors.

However, the MTS problem has a wide range of applications in many fields. Therefore, we also include four datasets from different areas. They are electricity and solar-energy for energy, exchange-rate for economics, and Beijing air quality dataset for environmental protection. Since there are no spatial dependencies among multiple time series in the applications of these domains, none of these four datasets contain pre-defined graphs.

Table 1. Information of datasets used in BasicTS.

Dataset	Length	Variants	Sample Rate	Time Span	Application
PEMS03	26208	358	5 min	3 months	traffic flow
PEMS04	16992	307	5 min	2 months	traffic flow
PEMS07	28224	883	5 min	3 months	traffic flow
PEMS08	17856	170	5 min	6 months	traffic flow
PEMS-BAY	52116	325	5 min	6 months	traffic speed
METR-LA	6850	207	5 min	4 months	traffic speed
Electricity	2208	336	60 min	3 months	electricity
solar-energy	52560	137	10 min	1 year	energy
exchange-rate	7588	8	1 day	20 years	economics
Beijing air quality	6000	7	6 h	1500 days	environment

Models: In this part, we briefly introduce the MTS prediction baselines included in BasicTS. Particularly, we choose MTS prediction models that contain official public code, which helps researchers to make a quick and accurate comparison and reproduction.

- HI [8]: Historical Inertia (HI) model adopts the most recent historical data points in input time series as the prediction results.
- LSTM [9]: Long Short-Term Memory (LSTM) network with fully connected hidden units is a well-known network architecture that is powerful in capturing sequential dependency.
- DCRNN [3]: Diffusion Convolutional Recurrent Neural Network (DCRNN) models the traffic flow as a diffusion process. It replaces the fully connected layer in GRU with a diffusion convolutional layer to form a new Diffusion Convolutional Gated Recurrent Unit (DCGRU).

- Graph WaveNet [4]: Graph WaveNet stacks Gated TCN and GCN layer by layer to jointly capture the spatial and temporal dependencies.
- STGCN [10]: Spatial-Temporal Graph Convolutional Network (STGCN) integrate graph convolution (spatial dimension) and 2D gated temporal convolution (temporal dimension) to model the correlations in MTS data.
- StemGNN [1]: Spectral Temporal Graph Neural Network (StemGNN) takes the advantage of both inter-series correlations and temporal dependencies by modeling them jointly in the spectral domain.
- MTGNN [11]: MTGNN extends Graph WaveNet through the mix-hop propagation layer in the spatial module, the dilated inception layer in the temporal module, and a more delicate graph learning layer.
- DGCRN [12]: DGCRN models the dynamic graph and designs a novel Dynamic Graph Convolutional Recurrent Module (DGCRM) to capture the spatial-temporal pattern in a seq2seq architecture.
- GTS [5]: GTS learns a graph structure among multiple time series and forecasts them simultaneously with DCRNN.
- AGCRN [13]: Adaptive Graph Convolutional Recurrent Network (AGCRN) captures node-specific spatial and temporal correlations in MTS based on two modules, i.e., node adaptive parameter learning and data-adaptive graph generation modules.
- STNorm [14]: STNorm refines the high-frequency component and the local component from the MTS data based on the proposed temporal normalization and spatial normalization, respectively.
- D^2STGNN [15]: D^2STGNN decouples the diffusion and inherent signals built in MTS data to achieve more precise modeling, and features a dynamic graph learning module for the dynamic characteristics of traffic networks.

Metrics: We evaluated all models by three most widely used metrics in MTS prediction, including Mean Absolute Error (MAE), Root Mean Squared Error (RMSE), and Mean Absolute Squared Error (MSE). In addition, we compared the performance of these methods on the error metrics at the 3, 6, 12, and overall prediction time steps, which is shown in the Horizon@3, @6, @12, and overall, respectively.

Experimental Environment: All models are trained on Intel(R) Xeon(R) Gold 5217 CPU @ 3.00 GHz, 128G RAM computing server, equipped with NVIDIA RTX 3090 graphics cards.

4.2   Experimental Results

In this section, we will experimentally demonstrate the unfairnesses mentioned in the Introduction.

Unfairness Caused by Lack of Richness of the Datasets. Different datasets often have different properties, e.g., different distributions, different dynamics, etc. Therefore, even the same model tends to show different performances on different datasets. Here, we select two typical models, GTS and

Table 2. Comparison of DCRNN and GTS performance on different datasets.

Datasets	Models	@Horizon 3			@Horizon 6			@Horizon 12			Overall (12 Horizon)		
		MAE	RMSE	MAPE	MAE	RMSE	MAPE	MAE	RMSE	MAPE	MAE	RMSE	MAPE
METR-LA	DCRNN	2.67	5.16	6.86%	3.07	6.29	8.42%	3.57	7.56	10.37%	3.04	6.26	8.33%
	GTS	2.75	5.28	7.13%	3.14	6.33	8.70%	3.60	7.46	10.42%	3.10	6.29	8.54%
PEMS-BAY	DCRNN	1.31	2.80	2.73%	1.66	3.81	3.75%	1.98	4.64	4.73%	1.60	3.74	3.61%
	GTS	1.36	2.91	2.85%	1.72	3.86	3.88%	2.05	4.62	4.87%	1.65	3.77	3.73%
PEMS03	DCRNN	14.16	24.61	14.21%	15.41	27.01	15.07%	17.31	30.05	16.71%	15.37	26.92	15.10%
	GTS	13.93	23.96	14.02%	15.27	26.12	15.35%	17.35	29.11	17.23%	15.24	26.08	15.24%
PEMS04	DCRNN	18.53	29.61	12.71%	19.65	31.37	13.45%	21.67	34.19	15.03%	19.71	31.43	13.54%
	GTS	19.27	30.46	13.33%	20.86	32.78	14.68%	23.52	36.31	17.03%	20.91	32.86	14.77%
PEMS07	DCRNN	19.45	31.39	8.29%	21.18	34.42	9.01%	24.14	38.84	10.42%	21.20	34.43	9.06%
	GTS	20.00	31.87	8.45%	22.11	35.02	9.39%	25.49	39.77	10.96%	22.08	35.07	9.40%
PEMS08	DCRNN	14.16	22.20	9.31%	15.24	24.26	9.90%	17.70	27.14	11.13%	15.26	24.28	9.96%
	GTS	14.50	22.97	9.23%	15.77	25.08	10.00%	18.02	28.25	11.74%	15.82	25.13	10.18%

DCRNN, for performance comparison on six different traffic-related datasets we mentioned above.

As shown in Table 2, The two models have different performances on different datasets. DCRNN performs better on METR-LA, PEMS-BAY, PEMS04, PEMS07, and PEMS08; however, GTS performs better on PEMS03. Therefore, we introduce 10 datasets in multiple domains to comprehensively measure the performance of a model on each dataset. In particular, six traffic datasets contain a predefined graph to describe spatial associations; the other four datasets do not contain predefined graphs. This helps to comprehensively measure the ability of the model to handle different datasets.

Unfairness Caused by Data Pre-processing. For most machine-learning-related models, it is essential to perform data pre-processing on the raw data. Among the pre-processing methods, normalization is the most common means, which helps to improve the efficiency of gradient descent and enables models to obtain better results. Common normalization methods include Z-score normalization and max-min normalization. Here, we choose three models, Graph WaveNet, STGCN, AGCRN to compare the effects of different data pre-processing methods on the results. The experiments were conducted on the PEMS-BAY dataset.

Table 3. Effect of different data pre-processing methods on MTS prediction.

Methods	Min-max Normailization			Z-score Normalization		
	MAE	RMSE	MAPE	MAE	RMSE	MAPE
GraphWaveNet	1.56	3.57	3.49%	1.59	3.69	3.52%
STGCN	1.66	3.72	3.70%	1.63	3.73	3.69%
AGCRN	1.69	3.91	3.81%	1.63	3.78	3.73%

As shown in Table 3, The same model may show very different results when using different data pre-processing methods. Therefore, when comparing results, it is crucial to ensure that all models use the same data pre-processing methods. We provide a convenient normalization processing interface in the data preparation stage mentioned above, which can fully guarantee fairness in this aspect.

Unfairness Caused by Different Pipelines. Different model pipelines may likewise lead to an unfair comparison of results. For example, Whether or not to add gradient clipping to the training pipeline will have a great impact on the result. Here, we tested the effect of adding gradient clipping to the MTGNN and STNorm's training pipeline on the exchange-rate dataset, shown in Table 4.

Table 4. Effect of different pipeline on MTS prediction.

Methods	Add Gradient clipping			Not Add Gradient clipping		
	MAE	RMSE	MAPE	MAE	RMSE	MAPE
MTGNN	0.0133	0.0227	7.05%	0.0130	0.0205	5.45%
STNorm	0.0068	0.0116	1.81%	0.0070	0.0118	2.63%

As shown in Table 4, adding gradient clipping to the training pipeline has a huge impact on the results. Furthermore, there are also many other details about pipeline construction, which can also affect the results. Therefore, different pipelines often bring significant unfairnesses. As described in the Benchmark Building, we use the same pipeline for all models to circumvent the possible unfair comparison of results.

Unfairness Caused by Hyper-Parameters Setting. Hyper-parameters setting is an integral part of determining a model's effect, and there are considerable works on this.

There is a wide variety of hyper-parameters, including optimizer [16,17], weight-decay [18], batch_size [19,20], and so on. Many of them can significantly impact the algorithm's performance. Here, we set up two experiments to show the effect of the hyper-parameter settings on the model.

Optimizer. Optimizer is one of the most important hyper-parameters in deep learning models. It refers to the method of finding the optimal deep neural network parameters through gradient descent, which determines the efficiency and stability of gradient learning optimization methods. Here, we test the effects of Adam [16], Adagrad [17], and SGD [21] optimizers on the performance of model STGCN on PEMS-BAY. The result is shown in Table 5.

Weight Decay. The strong fitting ability of neural networks may lead to overfitting. Therefore, it is often necessary to take measures to improve the generalization ability of neural networks. Weight decay is one of the most common regularization methods, which improves the generalization ability of neural networks by introducing a discount factor when the parameters are updated. Therefore, the coefficient of weight decay is one of the most important hyper-parameters of the deep learning model. Here, we set the weight decay coefficients

Table 5. Effect of different optimizers on the performance of STGCN on PEMS-BAY.

Optimizer	@Horizon 3			@Horizon 6			@Horizon 12			Overall (12 Horizon)		
	MAE	RMSE	MAPE	MAE	RMSE	MAPE	MAE	RMSE	MAPE	MAE	RMSE	MAPE
Adam	1.35	2.86	2.86%	1.69	3.83	3.85%	2.00	4.56	4.74%	1.63	3.73	3.69%
Adagrad	1.46	3.09	3.07%	1.88	1.98	4.78%	2.41	5.51	5.93%	1.86	4.26	4.26%
SGD	1.67	3.35	3.56%	2.10	4.63	4.57%	2.79	6.33	6.45%	2.12	4.78	4.70%

to 0.00001,0.0001,0.001 to test the effect of the weight decay coefficient on the performance of model STGCN on PEMS-BAY. The result is shown in Table 7.

Table 6. Effect of different weight-decay coefficients on the performance of STGCN on PEMS-BAY.

Coefficient	@Horizon 3			@Horizon 6			@Horizon 12			Overall (12 Horizon)		
	MAE	RMSE	MAPE	MAE	RMSE	MAPE	MAE	RMSE	MAPE	MAE	RMSE	MAPE
0.00001	1.37	2.70	2.88%	1.71	3.92	3.83%	2.03	4.70	4.66%	1.65	3.83	3.67%
0.0001	1.35	2.86	2.86%	1.69	3.83	3.85%	2.00	4.56	4.74%	1.63	3.73	3.69%
0.001	1.59	3.35	3.63%	1.92	4.24	4.54%	2.29	5.17	5.47%	1.88	4.21	4.44%

As shown above, hyper-parameters show a considerable impact on the performance of the model. Therefore, reasonable parameter adjustment is an important part of ensuring the fairness of the comparison of the performance of models. However, the optimal hyper-parameters of different models are often different, and the adjustment of hyper-parameters still depends largely on artificial experience. To this end, we provided interfaces that allows flexible parameter settings. Also, we have carefully tuned the parameters of all existing models in BasicTS to make them optimal (Table 6).

4.3 Review

In this subsection, we review 11 models on METR-LA, PEMS-BAY, PEMS03, PEMS04, PEMS07, PEMS08, and Electricity, solar-energy, exchange-rate, and Beijing air quality. In particular, some models require a pre-defined adjacency matrix as input, thus these models will not work on the latter four datasets. We divide reviews into three categories: traffic speed datasets, traffic flow datasets, and datasets that does not contain pre-defined graph.

For a fair comparison, we follow the dataset division in previous works. The ratio of training, validation, and test sets for the PEMS-BAY dataset is 7 : 1 : 2, while the ratio for other datasets is 6 : 2 : 2. We aim to predict the future time series with a length of 12, i.e., $F = 12$, on all datasets. We compared the performance of these methods on the 3rd, 6th, and 12th time slots and the average 12 time slots, which are shown in the **@3**, **@6**, **@12**, and **@overall** columns, respectively. The results of the review are shown in Table 7, Table 8, Table 9.

Table 7. Review of MTS prediction methods on dataset which doesn't contain predefined graph.

Datasets	Methods	@Horizon 3			@Horizon 6			@Horizon 12			Overall (12 Horizon)		
		MAE	RMSE	MAPE	MAE	RMSE	MAPE	MAE	RMSE	MAPE	MAE	RMSE	MAPE
Electricity	HI	92.42	167.00	70.16%	92.58	167.05	70.46%	92.79	167.21	70.91%	92.58	167.07	70.43%
	AGCRN	22.88	50.02	41.30%	24.49	54.16	48.90%	27.25	59.80	52.57%	23.87	53.00	10.16%
	StemGNN	21.43	46.80	35.08%	22.02	49.87	40.00%	26.06	56.99	47.59%	22.75	49.80	39.52%
	MTGNN	16.78	36.91	48.17%	18.43	42.61	51.32%	20.51	48.34	56.27%	18.19	42.04	50.77%
	STNorm	18.94	40.77	39.10%	21.73	47.70	51.66%	24.62	55.04	66.98%	21.32	47.46	49.49%
Solar Energy	HI	7.20	9.65	376.10%	7.20	9.65	376.10%	7.20	9.65	376.10%	7.20	9.65	376.10%
	AGCRN	1.48	2.61	101.08%	2.02	3.39	136.36%	2.76	4.50	158.56%	1.98	3.45	125.68%
	StemGNN	1.74	2.83	128.85%	2.26	3.62	161.17%	2.88	4.58	183.25%	2.21	3.63	151.21%
	MTGNN	1.35	2.41	70.70%	1.81	3.06	107.07%	2.56	4.09	178.68%	1.80	3.13	109.25%
	STNorm	0.56	1.58	59.70%	0.77	2.10	101.69%	1.13	2.84	169.64%	0.77	2.14	96.57%
Exchange Rate	HI	0.0092	0.0151	1.18%	0.0092	0.0151	1.18%	0.0092	0.0151	1.18%	0.0092	0.0151	1.18%
	AGCRN	0.0060	0.0088	4.83%	0.0082	0.0127	2.29%	0.0106	0.0168	2.05%	0.0082	0.0130	3.33%
	StemGNN	0.1521	0.1991	179.07%	0.1511	0.1974	199.18%	0.1534	0.1998	192.41 %	0.1549	0.2022	169.47%
	MTGNN	0.0133	0.0227	7.05%	0.0167	0.0273	8.30%	0.0184	0.0300	7.34%	0.0164	0.0273	7.70%
	STNorm	0.0048	0.0081	0.69%	0.0068	0.0112	1.01%	0.0098	0.0156	2.77%	0.0068	0.0116	1.81%
Beijing Air Quality	HI	30.20	57.99	99.54%	30.27	58.03	99.60%	30.24	58.02	99.43%	30.23	58.01	99.47%
	AGCRN	30.16	53.60	119.24%	31.41	55.53	130.92%	32.63	58.77	139.12%	30.20	54.14	126.12%
	StemGNN	27.02	48.07	143.93%	27.09	48.55	211.92%	26.64	48.55	129.88%	26.65	48.48	151.80%
	MTGNN	21.68	42.02	78.52%	25.66	46.39	129.62%	26.24	47.83	120.64%	23.66	44.39	100.39%
	STNorm	20.69	39.07	92.66%	23.64	42.63	102.89%	24.26	44.65	99.14%	21.99	41.05	100.28%

Table 8. Review of MTS prediction methods on traffic speed datasets.

Datasets	Methods	@Horizon 3			@Horizon 6			@Horizon 12			Overall (12 Horizon)		
		MAE	RMSE	MAPE	MAE	RMSE	MAPE	MAE	RMSE	MAPE	MAE	RMSE	MAPE
METR-LA	HI	6.80	14.21	16.72%	6.80	14.21	16.72%	6.80	14.20	10.15%	6.80	14.21	16.72%
	Graph WaveNet	2.69	5.15	6.96%	3.08	6.21	8.47%	3.53	7.30	10.15%	3.04	6.15	8.31%
	DCRNN	2.67	5.16	6.86%	3.07	6.29	8.42%	3.57	7.56	10.37%	3.04	6.26	8.33%
	AGCRN	2.88	5.57	7.72%	3.26	6.61	9.17%	3.67	7.60	10.74%	3.20	6.50	9.00%
	STGCN	2.76	5.31	7.20%	3.16	6.36	8.72%	3.62	7.45	10.43%	3.12	6.30	8.58%
	StemGNN	2.96	5.77	7.90%	3.46	6.96	9.79%	4.11	8.32	12.25%	3.43	6.93	9.70%
	GTS	2.75	5.28	7.13%	3.14	6.33	8.70%	3.60	7.46	10.42%	3.10	6.29	8.54%
	MTGNN	2.71	5.22	6.89%	3.07	6.23	8.27%	3.51	7.28	9.90%	3.04	6.17	8.15%
	STNorm	2.82	5.55	7.48%	3.19	6.59	9.00%	3.56	7.47	10.51%	3.12	6.45	8.77%
	STID	2.79	5.53	7.64%	3.16	6.57	9.30%	3.53	7.51	10.78 %	3.10	6.45	9.01%
	DGCRN	2.61	5.02	6.57%	2.99	6.07	7.90%	3.45	7.27	9.49%	2.96	6.05	7.79%
	D²STGNN	2.56	4.90	6.52%	2.90	5.90	7.88%	3.34	7.02	9.63%	2.87	5.88	7.79%
PEMS-BAY	HI	3.06	7.05	6.85%	3.06	7.04	6.84%	3.05	7.03	6.83%	3.05	7.05	6.84%
	Graph WaveNet	1.30	2.80	2.69%	1.65	3.75	3.65%	1.97	4.58	4.63%	1.59	3.69	3.52%
	DCRNN	1.31	2.80	2.73%	1.66	3.81	3.75%	1.98	4.64	4.73%	1.60	3.74	3.61%
	AGCRN	1.37	2.93	2.95%	1.70	3.89	3.88%	1.99	4.64	4.72%	1.63	3.78	3.73%
	STGCN	1.35	2.86	2.86%	1.69	3.83	3.85%	2.00	4.56	4.74%	1.63	3.73	3.69%
	StemGNN	1.44	3.12	3.08%	1.93	4.38	4.54%	2.57	5.88	6.55%	1.91	4.46	4.54%
	GTS	1.36	2.91	2.85%	1.72	3.86	3.88%	2.05	4.62	4.87%	1.65	3.77	3.73%
	MTGNN	1.34	2.84	2.80%	1.67	3.79	3.74%	1.97	4.55	4.57%	1.60	3.70	3.57%
	STNorm	1.34	2.88	2.82%	1.67	3.83	3.75%	1.96	4.52	4.62%	1.60	3.71	3.60%
	STID	1.30	2.81	2.73%	1.62	3.72	3.68%	1.89	4.40	4.47%	1.55	3.62	3.51%
	DGCRN	1.29	2.80	2.74%	1.63	3.80	3.75%	1.95	4.58	4.64%	1.58	3.71	3.61%
	D²STGNN	1.25	2.65	2.62%	1.58	3.63	3.57%	1.86	4.37	4.44%	1.52	3.55	3.50%

Table 9. Review of MTS prediction methods on traffic flow datasets.

Datasets	Methods	@Horizon 3			@Horizon 6			@Horizon 12			Overall (12 Horizon)		
		MAE	RMSE	MAPE	MAE	RMSE	MAPE	MAE	RMSE	MAPE	MAE	RMSE	MAPE
PEMS03	HI	32.46	49.78	30.58%	32.45	49.76	30.59%	32.44	49.75	30.63%	32.45	49.76	30.60%
	Graph WaveNet	13.37	23.04	13.90%	14.51	25.29	14.85%	16.16	27.91	16.12%	14.48	25.19	14.67%
	DCRNN	14.16	24.61	14.21%	15.41	27.01	15.07%	17.31	30.05	16.71%	15.37	26.92	15.10%
	AGCRN	14.22	25.02	13.40%	15.47	27.28	14.43%	17.09	28.78	16.43%	15.41	27.15	14.76%
	STGCN	14.71	25.19	14.41%	15.66	26.99	15.38%	17.47	29.80	17.55%	15.73	27.03	15.44%
	StemGNN	14.16	24.33	14.40%	15.76	26.98	15.32%	18.50	30.94	18.10%	15.24	26.08	15.60%
	GTS	13.93	23.96	14.02%	15.27	26.12	15.35%	17.35	29.11	17.23%	14.80	25.65	15.24%
	MTGNN	13.71	23.04	14.84%	14.87	25.94	15.12%	16.50	28.76	16.88%	15.34	26.33	15.04%
	STNorm	14.23	24.05	13.98%	15.45	26.54	14.49%	17.08	29.42	15.73%	15.34	26.33	14.56%
	STID	17.51	28.48	12.00%	18.29	29.86	12.46%	19.58	31.79	13.38%	18.29	29.82	12.49%
	DGCRN	13.46	23.92	14.23%	14.67	26.36	15.13%	16.41	29.02	16.71%	14.61	26.15	15.10%
	D²STGNN	13.42	23.11	13.71%	14.71	25.61	14.73%	16.62	28.69	16.64%	14.72	25.61	14.70%
PEMS04	HI	42.33	61.64	29.90%	42.35	61.66	29.92%	42.38	61.67	29.96%	42.35	61.66	29.92%
	Graph WaveNet	18.00	28.83	13.64%	18.96	30.33	14.23%	20.53	32.54	15.41%	18.97	30.32	14.26%
	DCRNN	18.53	29.61	12.71%	19.65	31.37	13.45%	21.67	34.19	15.03%	19.71	31.43	13.54%
	AGCRN	18.52	29.79	12.31%	19.45	31.45	12.82%	20.64	33.31	13.74%	19.36	31.28	12.81%
	STGCN	18.74	29.84	12.93%	19.04	31.34	13.27%	21.12	33.53	14.22%	19.63	31.32	13.32%
	StemGNN	19.48	30.74	13.84%	21.40	33.46	15.85%	24.90	38.29	19.50%	21.61	33.80	16.10%
	GTS	19.27	30.46	13.33%	20.86	32.78	14.68%	23.52	36.31	17.03%	20.91	32.86	14.77%
	MTGNN	18.65	30.13	13.32%	19.48	32.02	14.08%	20.96	34.66	14.96%	19.50	32.00	14.04%
	STNorm	18.28	29.70	12.28%	18.92	31.12	12.71%	20.20	32.91	13.43%	18.96	30.98	12.69%
	STID	17.51	28.48	12.00%	18.29	29.86	12.46%	19.58	31.79	13.38%	18.29	29.82	12.49%
	DGCRN	17.88	29.12	12.25%	18.86	30.92	12.85%	20.20	33.20	13.80%	18.81	30.82	12.80%
	D²STGNN	17.44	28.48	11.91%	18.20	29.91	12.29%	19.31	31.68	12.99%	18.15	29.80	12.25%
PEMS07	HI	49.02	71.15	22.73%	49.04	71.18	22.75%	49.06	71.21	22.79%	49.03	71.18	22.75%
	Graph WaveNet	18.69	30.69	8.02%	20.26	33.37	8.56%	22.79	37.11	9.73%	20.25	33.32	8.63%
	DCRNN	19.45	31.39	8.29%	21.18	34.42	9.01%	24.14	38.84	10.42%	21.20	34.43	9.06%
	AGCRN	19.31	31.68	8.18%	20.70	34.52	8.66%	22.74	37.94	9.71%	20.64	34.39	8.74%
	STGCN	20.33	32.73	8.68%	21.66	35.35	9.16%	24.16	39.48	10.26%	21.71	35.41	9.25%
	StemGNN	19.74	32.32	8.27%	22.07	36.16	9.20%	26.20	42.32	11.00%	22.23	36.46	9.20%
	GTS	20.00	31.87	8.45%	22.11	35.02	9.39%	25.49	39.77	10.96%	22.08	35.07	9.40%
	MTGNN	19.23	31.15	8.55%	20.83	33.93	9.30%	23.60	38.10	10.10%	20.94	34.03	9.10%
	STNorm	19.15	31.70	8.26%	20.63	35.10	8.84%	22.60	38.65	9.60%	20.52	34.85	8.77%
	STID	18.31	30.39	7.72%	19.59	32.90	8.30%	21.52	36.29	9.15%	19.54	32.85	8.25%
	DGCRN	18.57	30.49	7.82%	20.12	33.43	8.45%	22.31	37.04	9.44%	20.05	33.32	8.45%
	D²STGNN	18.56	30.52	7.79%	20.10	33.15	8.41%	22.30	36.73	9.40%	20.05	33.08	8.42%
PEMS08	HI	36.65	50.44	21.60%	36.66	50.45	21.63%	36.68	50.46	21.68%	36.66	50.45	21.63%
	Graph WaveNet	13.72	21.71	8.80%	14.67	23.50	9.49%	16.15	25.85	10.74%	14.67	23.47	9.52%
	DCRNN	14.16	22.20	9.31%	15.24	24.26	9.90%	17.70	27.14	11.13%	15.26	24.28	9.96%
	AGCRN	14.51	22.87	9.34%	15.66	25.00	10.34%	17.49	27.93	11.72%	15.65	24.99	10.17%
	STGCN	14.95	23.48	9.87%	15.92	25.36	10.42%	17.65	28.03	11.34%	15.98	25.37	10.43%
	StemGNN	14.49	23.02	9.73%	15.84	25.38	10.78%	18.10	28.77	12.50%	15.91	25.44	10.90%
	GTS	14.50	22.97	9.23%	15.77	25.08	10.09%	18.02	28.25	11.74%	15.82	25.13	10.18%
	MTGNN	14.30	22.55	10.56%	15.25	24.41	10.54%	16.80	26.96	10.90%	15.31	24.42	10.70%
	STNorm	14.44	22.68	9.22%	15.53	25.07	9.94%	17.20	27.86	11.30%	15.54	25.01	10.00%
	STID	13.28	21.66	8.62%	14.21	23.57	9.24%	15.58	25.89	10.33%	14.20	23.49	9.28%
	DGCRN	13.47	21.87	8.85%	14.44	23.77	9.44%	15.90	26.35	10.50%	14.43	23.75	9.40%
	D²STGNN	13.24	21.83	8.47%	14.19	23.98	9.09%	15.50	26.43	9.90%	14.20	23.95	9.10%

5 Conclusion

In this paper, we propose a fair, standard, and open-source benchmark for multivariate time series prediction, named BasicTS, to address the unfairnesses in the comparison of MTS prediction models. Given a model, BasicTS evaluates it based on rich datasets, standard training pipeline, and standard evaluation, to give a fair performance validation. Furthermore, BasicTS provides users with flexible and extensible interfaces to facilitate quick designing and fair evaluation of new MTS prediction models. Last but not least, we also provide a fair performance review of several popular MTS prediction models based on BasicTS.

6 Future Works

This paper explores and evaluates the unfairness of the MTS prediction and proposes a framework dedicated to the MTS prediction problem. In the future, we will continue this research in three aspects:

1. MTS prediction problems contain a wide variety of methods and data forms. We plan to add more datasets and models into BasicTS. We will also conduct more experiments on these datasets.
2. The MTS prediction models also include some long-time prediction models. We plan to add more long-time prediction models into BasicTS.
3. With the development of machine learning, auto hyperparameter optimization techniques are beginning to be used more and more abundantly. We plan to add auto hyperparameter optimization technology into our benchmark, which can help researchers to find optimal parameters for deep learning models conveniently.

References

1. Cao, D., et al.: Spectral temporal graph neural network for multivariate time-series forecasting. In: Advances in Neural Information Processing Systems, vol. 33, pp. 17766–17778 (2020)
2. Li, M., Zhu, Z.: Spatial-temporal fusion graph neural networks for traffic flow forecasting. In: Proceedings of the AAAI Conference on Artificial Intelligence, vol. 35, pp. 4189–4196 (2021)
3. Li, Y., Yu, R., Shahabi, C., Liu, Y.: Diffusion convolutional recurrent neural network: data-driven traffic forecasting. arXiv preprint arXiv:1707.01926 (2017)
4. Wu, Z., Pan, S., Long, G., Jiang, J., Zhang, C.: Graph wavenet for deep spatial-temporal graph modeling. arXiv preprint arXiv:1906.00121 (2019)
5. Shang, C., Chen, J., Bi, J.: Discrete graph structure learning for forecasting multiple time series. arXiv preprint arXiv:2101.06861 (2021)
6. Alexandrov, A., et al.: GluonTS: probabilistic and neural time series modeling in Python. J. Mach. Learn. Res. 21(116), 1–6 (2020)
7. Wang, J., Jiang, J., Jiang, W., Li, C., Zhao, W.X.: Libcity: an open library for traffic prediction. In: Proceedings of the 29th International Conference on Advances in Geographic Information Systems, pp. 145–148 (2021)

8. Cui, Y., Xie, J., Zheng, K.: Historical inertia: a neglected but powerful baseline for long sequence time-series forecasting. In: Proceedings of the 30th ACM International Conference on Information & Knowledge Management, pp. 2965–2969 (2021)
9. Hochreiter, S., Schmidhuber, J.: Long short-term memory. Neural Comput. **9**(8), 1735–1780 (1997)
10. Yu, B., Yin, H., Zhu, Z.: Spatio-temporal graph convolutional networks: a deep learning framework for traffic forecasting. arXiv preprint arXiv:1709.04875 (2017)
11. Gao, J., et al.: MTGNN: multi-task graph neural network based few-shot learning for disease similarity measurement. Methods **198**, 88–95 (2022)
12. Li, F., et al.: Dynamic graph convolutional recurrent network for traffic prediction: Benchmark and solution. ACM Trans. Knowl. Discov. Data (TKDD) **17**, 1–21 (2021)
13. Bai, L., Yao, L., Li, C., Wang, X., Wang, C.: Adaptive graph convolutional recurrent network for traffic forecasting. In: Advances in Neural Information Processing Systems, vol. 33, pp. 17804–17815 (2020)
14. Deng, J., Chen, X., Jiang, R., Song, X., Tsang, I.W.: ST-Norm: spatial and temporal normalization for multi-variate time series forecasting. In: Proceedings of the 27th ACM SIGKDD Conference on Knowledge Discovery & Data Mining, pp. 269–278 (2021)
15. Shao, Z., et al.: Decoupled dynamic spatial-temporal graph neural network for traffic forecasting. arXiv e-prints, pp. arXiv-2206 (2022)
16. Kingma, D.P., Ba, J.: Adam: a method for stochastic optimization. arXiv preprint arXiv:1412.6980 (2014)
17. Lydia, A., Francis, S.: Adagrad-an optimizer for stochastic gradient descent. Int. J. Inf. Comput. Sci. **6**(5), 566–568 (2019)
18. Loshchilov, I., Hutter, F.: Decoupled weight decay regularization. arXiv preprint arXiv:1711.05101 (2017)
19. Smith, S.L., Kindermans, P.-J., Ying, C., Le, Q.V.: Don't decay the learning rate, increase the batch size. arXiv preprint arXiv:1711.00489 (2017)
20. Radiuk, P.M.: Impact of training set batch size on the performance of convolutional neural networks for diverse datasets (2017)
21. Amari, S.-I.: Backpropagation and stochastic gradient descent method. Neurocomputing **5**(4–5), 185–196 (1993)

Benchmarking Object Detection Models with Mummy Nuts Datasets

Darren Ng[1], Colin Schmierer[1], Andrew Lin[1], Zeyu Liu[2], Falin Yu[3],
Shawn Newsam[1], Reza Ehsani[1], and Xiaoyi Lu[1(✉)]

[1] University of California Merced, Merced, USA
{dng350,cschmierer,alin85,snewsam,rehsani,xiaoyi.lu}@ucmerced.edu
[2] Valley Christian High School, San Jose, USA
[3] Santa Margarita Catholic High School, Rancho Santa Margarita, USA
falin.yu@smhsstudents.org

Abstract. Agriculture presents challenges in automation, especially so
in vision systems. Varying lighting conditions, sporadic diversity, and
large amounts of noise create difficulty in detecting target objects. Our
Mummy Nuts datasets present these challenges in tiny scale, camouflaged, dark, or even hidden target objects. However, the most recent
advancements in Convolutional Neural Networks (CNN) in the object
detection task have become increasingly accurate and robust. As there
are many different CNNs, selecting which CNN will perform the best
may become challenging. This paper proposes a two-dimensional benchmarking methodology to evaluate five popular CNN models (YOLOv3,
YOLOv5, CenterNet, Faster R-CNN, and MobileNet SSD) on two
NVIDIA GPUs (Tesla T4 and A100). Our benchmarking methodology
evaluates accuracy across all models and performance among models on
each GPU. Our results show the benefits of selecting models using our
Augmented dataset over the Original dataset. CNN Models overall see
an increase in recall values during inference by an average of 2.77X (with
the highest increase as YOLOv3 by 6.5X). For performance, over both
Original and Augmented datasets, the model training time reduces by
an average of 4.45X when using A100 over Tesla T4.

Keywords: Benchmarking · Object Detection · Mummy Nuts

1 Introduction

Object detection using Convolutional Neural Networks (CNN) has become
increasingly popular. CNNs appear in an ever-growing field of applications and
are crucial in precision agriculture automation tasks such as yield estimation,
disease detection, and robotic harvesting. Agricultural object detection proves
to be a complex engineering problem due to many unseen variables that come
as a trait of agriculture.

This work was supported in part by the NSF research grants CCF #2132049, EEC
#1941529, and a COR grant from University of California, Merced.

Pest control is a challenging problem in agriculture and, if not performed correctly, will damage farmer crop yield significantly. Almond growers are a prime target as orchards may take permanent damage from pests known as Navel Orangeworm (NOW), which nestle and feed on off-season almond nuts (Mummy Nuts). Growers must adequately monitor and track NOW disease to prevent spreading [1]. Furthermore, Mummy Nuts have diverse appearances and prove difficult for manual inspection. Due to this, Mummy Nut object detection has been an under-researched topic in precision agriculture.

CNNs can be applied to an environment that may contain erratic behaviors. For Mummy Nut detections, this is in the endless variations of the appearance in the target object. Furthermore, agriculture relies heavily on the season and restricts necessary data collection to a particular time frame each year. In the case of Mummy Nuts, image data can only be taken during the winter. This window would limit the data available to train CNNs.

In CNN training, the most critical component would be the dataset used. A robust CNN model must be trained with a carefully curated dataset. High-quality datasets should include thousands of images, with each class containing images of similar features, respectively. For example, the Microsoft Common Objects in COntext (MS COCO) dataset contains 2,500,000 labeled instances in 328,000 images standing among the richest datasets [2]. Other popular, large-scale datasets include ImageNet [3], Pascal VOC [4], SUN Database [5], and Pedestrian Database [6]. Due to the necessity of large datasets, there is little work on training CNNs with insufficient data.

For Mummy Nut detection problems, we face numerous issues with dataset curation. Most existing datasets are easy to annotate and can be considered a simple task for human workflow. MS COCO deployed an annotation pipeline to richly annotate each image using Amazon Mechanical Turk workers [2]. This workflow assumes each image contains objects easily identifiable by non-expert annotators. However, our proposed datasets are difficult to annotate, showing varying results in recall values between each annotator. Multiple expert annotators reviewed each image to ensure the highest annotation recall and precision. A large amount of noise contributes to the complication of annotation and detection of target objects within an image, though it allows for model robustness. Lastly, there is a significant underrepresentation of the variety of nuts. Each nut classifies for a different difficulty class (e.g., Noisy, Dark, Tiny, etc.) we assigned that will tell us how complex a particular detection may be. Difficulty classes are not equally represented in the training set, which may decrease the recall value per underrepresented class.

Another factor that predominantly affects CNN performance is the type of object detection model used. Multiple popular CNN models are in use, and each has a very different structure in training and inference computations. Lately, quick one-stage detectors have been utilized in systems and show high accuracy, such as You Only Look Once (YOLO) [7], Regions with CNN features (R-CNN) [8], Fast R-CNN [9], and Faster R-CNN [10]. These models create spaced boxes across the input image called anchor boxes, each individually responsible for determining if a target object is within that box. Models like CenterNet [11] take a different approach, using heatmaps to determine peak points where a target object may appear. MobileNet [12] prioritizes a smaller network with significantly lower parameters to run well on mobile devices.

With the Mummy Nuts dataset, deciding which CNN model may provide the best results for each possible vision solution can become challenging. Only a few benchmark studies in the community can aid the selection of CNN models for the Mummy Nuts problem. Each model provides varying results depending on the proposed solution. We design tools to richly annotate and enhance our dataset to tackle its challenges. Our Data Augmentation tool expands the original dataset by performing image transformations on each annotation, artificially generating more diversity in our dataset. Our Difficulty Classification Annotator (DCA) tool is a notation tool that marks each annotation in our dataset with flags. These flags provide much more informative annotations denoting what difficulty class each annotation falls within.

To help guide the community in selecting the proper CNN model, this paper proposes a two-dimensional benchmarking methodology (e.g., accuracy and performance) on different CNN models. Each image is large in resolution and complexity, so performance latency during training and inference is evaluated on different hardware accelerations.

We deploy five different CNN models (e.g., YOLOv3, YOLOv5, CenterNet, Faster R-CNN, and MobileNet SSD) on two NVIDIA GPUs (e.g., A100 and Tesla T4). Throughout our experiments, our significant observations include: 1) All models saw an increase in recall value by an average of 2.77X (@IoU50) when using the Augmented dataset compared to the Original dataset; 2) The recall value of YOLOv3 increases by 6.5X (@IoU50) when using the Augmented dataset compared to the Original dataset; 3) All models except for MobileNet SSD suffer localization precision issues when using the Original dataset; 4) CenterNet, Faster R-CNN, and MobileNet SSD all decrease precision by an average of 10.53X (@IoU50) using Augmented over Original; 5) For performance, over both Original and Augmented datasets, the model training time reduces by an average of 4.45X when using A100 over Tesla T4; 6) Faster R-CNN sees a considerable speed up when running computations on A100 over Tesla T4 by about 5.76X; and 7) YOLO models have the fastest overall inference speed.

This paper makes the following contributions: 1) We create real-world datasets for the Mummy Nuts problem, which can help the community to perform in-depth interdisciplinary research between computer science and precision agriculture areas; 2) We design easy-to-use benchmarking tools (e.g., Data Augmentation Tool, DCA Tool, etc.) and integrate representative deep learning models into tools for agriculture scientists to investigate the Mummy Nuts problems conveniently; and 3) Through our benchmarking methodology and results, we provide guidance on which models may be ideal for different proposed solutions.

2   Background and Motivation

Mummy Nuts and NOW Disease: Leaving Mummy Nuts on trees can attract Navel Orangeworm pests (NOW) that will feed off of the nutmeat, leaving behind aflatoxins, a food safety contaminate linked to cancers [1]. Due to this, managing the spread of NOW is crucial and requires several steps. Firstly, monitoring the number of NOW pests and their mating growth is vital for planning the timing of pesticide applications. NOW capture and mating disruption methods also effectively reduce the population growth throughout NOW generations. Lastly, winter sanitation by removing remaining Mummy Nuts from orchards helps to remove the attractive food source for NOW pests. We tackle an early experience in automating the monitoring process of the spread. By detecting Mummy Nuts, we can monitor the food supply of NOW pests, produce a concentration heatmap of Mummy Nuts, and target and sanitize areas with high concentrations. We observe the task of object detection to implement this monitoring system. However, we notice that CNN model selection is essential as not all models can provide similar results. The dataset provided to each model also must be rich in features and carefully curated.

Object Detection and Inference: Object detection is an essential application for CNNs, and many models can perform this differently. It takes both localization and classification tasks into account by creating a spatially aware bounding box labeled with the name of the class detected. Training a CNN requires millions of parameter updates, equating to a large number of computations. Inference is the compression of those millions of parameters into a model that can quickly run and make detections. Thus CNN training requires high throughput while inference requires low latency [13]. As newer versions of object detection systems have been built, each has continued to speed up the inference process using different detection methods. There are multiple methods currently in use to perform detections. One popular method is employing anchor boxes and region proposals. This method creates anchor boxes spaced throughout input images in which each anchor box is responsible for making a detection. Other models eliminate the need for anchor boxes by converting the input image into a heatmap where the maxima are assumed to be a detection. We will go into more detail about each model in Sect. 3.

3   Requirements of Detecting Mummy Nuts with CNNs

This section presents an overview of selected object detection CNNs. We then review the requirements of detecting Mummy Nuts on our datasets with CNNs.

3.1   Overview of Object Detection Models

You Only Look Once (YOLO) is based on spatially set anchor boxes on input images that can observe if an object classification is within the boxes [7]. These anchor boxes will then produce a large number of bounding boxes around each instance of the object that is detected. The algorithm uses Non-Maximum Suppression (NMS) to reduce bounding boxes within the Intersection over Union (IoU) of another box with a higher confidence rate than the other boxes. In Fig. 1a, NMS is performed during the dense layer after making detections.

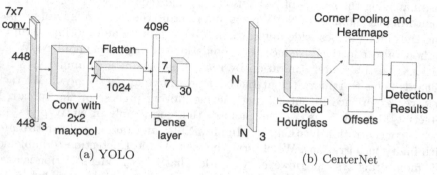

(a) YOLO   (b) CenterNet

Fig. 1. (a) shows the design of YOLO, which contains 24 convolutional layers with two fully connected layers at the end. (b) shows the design of CenterNet, which uses an hourglass backbone where the convolutional layers are structured with input and output layers at the largest sizes and the middle at the smallest, mimicking an hourglass shape.

CenterNet focuses on the center points of each box detection rather than the box dimensions. A heatmap of the detection is created, and the maxima of the heatmap produce the detected center points [11]. CenterNet was proposed to eliminate the need for anchor-based detectors. Removing the chances that an anchor box would not be in range to make a detection. In Fig. 1b, we see that CenterNet uses the Stacked Hourglass network as its backbone, which is 104 layers deep [14].

Faster R-CNN is a two-stage detector with a region proposal stage and Region of Interest (RoI) pooling stage [10]. Its post-processing stage, which includes the RoI pooling, puts this model behind YOLO and other single-stage detectors in speed. However, R-CNN has been a good baseline in previous years to compare to other speed-centered models in precision. The newer versions (e.g., Fast R-CNN and Faster R-CNN) also have increased in speed and now compete with YOLO models.

Faster R-CNN can run with multiple backbone networks (e.g., VGG [15], ResNet [16]) which in our results we use ResNet-101. In Fig. 2a, the Conv layers denote the section where different backbone networks may be used. The original network that Faster R-CNN runs on (VGG-16) has high memory usage compared to other networks. VGG-16 has between 95–125 million operations compared to ResNet-101 at 35–65 million [17]. Though ResNet uses less memory, it is also a significantly deeper network. ResNet is 101 layers deep which is 8X deeper than VGG [16].

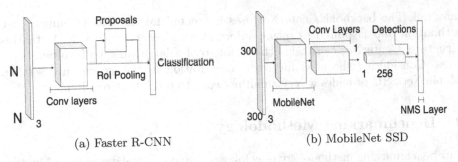

(a) Faster R-CNN   (b) MobileNet SSD

Fig. 2. (a) shows the network of Faster R-CNN. We can observe the region proposal stage (Proposals) and the Region of Interest (RoI) pooling as the first detection stage. (b) shows the network of MobileNet SSD. It uses MobileNet as its backbone before entering convolutional layers.

MobileNet Single Shot Multibox Detector (MobileNet SSD) is a single stage detector. It provides competitive results in accuracy and computation speeds compared to other single-stage detectors like YOLO. MobileNet SSD makes more detections per class than YOLO, 8732 to 98 detections, respectively [18]. In our experiments, we use MobileNet SSD to observe a model that can operate on a mobile device. In Fig. 2b, we can see MobileNet SSD uses the MobileNet backbone. Should edge computing be necessary, this model can provide satisfactory results alongside the small network size of MobileNet. The MobileNet backbone significantly decreases the number of parameters in the network. MobileNet lowers the number of parameters on COCO object detection results from 138 million (VGG) to 4.2 million [12], making it ideal for mobile computations.

3.2 Requirements of Benchmarking Models

To properly benchmark our models, each must tackle a different challenge in our Mummy Nut datasets. YOLO outperforms R-CNN when trained on artwork and natural images. This high generalizability makes YOLO less likely to break down when applied to new domains or unexpected inputs [7]. Given our dataset's vast appearance diversity, high generalizability may increase recall value. Faster R-CNN may also create more detection errors on background content compared to YOLO [19]. Considering the amount of noise in our Original dataset, Faster R-CNN may be more suitable for our Augmented dataset, presenting less noise within images.

In our experiments, we use modern versions of YOLO, including YOLOV3 [19] and V5 [20]. YOLOv3 runs on the DarkNet-53 backbone network, which is 53 convolutional layers deep [21]. This is nearly half the size of the ResNet-101 network that Faster R-CNN uses. Considering the tiny objects in our dataset, the chances of missing a target object with anchor-based detectors (e.g., YOLO, Faster R-CNN, or MobileNet SSD) are relatively high. Thus CenterNet provides a different approach for problems where typical anchor boxes may fail. The backbone CenterNet uses is created for the task of human pose estimation and is built to capture information at every scale [14]. With this structure, CenterNet can tackle the problem of a large variety of Mummy Nut sizes. Considering the need for edge computation in the agricultural setting, MobileNet SSD provides a very small network to fulfill that requirement.

4 Benchmarking Methodology

Our benchmarking methodology is as follows: we collect real datasets on Mummy Nuts, analyze object detection results with popular CNN models, propose our Augmented dataset, and redo our object detection analysis until we achieve adequate numbers with our chosen metrics.

4.1 Proposed Datasets: Original and Augmented

A carefully curated dataset must be used during training to build a robust model. Underrepresentation in different values within the dataset should be avoided whenever possible. However, when data can only be collected during a specific time of the year, it would significantly limit the amount of data and improvements to the data (e.g., better lighting, more angles, etc.). In collaboration with agriculture scientists, we have curated two datasets (Original and Augmented) for the task of Mummy Nut object detection. In our Original dataset, we observe a large amount of underrepresentation in specific shapes and sizes of the nuts. Due to the sporadic diversity in agriculture, a rich dataset is challenging to produce. Hence, we propose a new Augmented dataset that derives from the Original and includes data augmentation methods to artificially increase the size of annotations. Our Original dataset contains 33 images (4032×3024) and about 267 annotated nuts, while our Augmented dataset contains 294 images (200×200), each containing a modified or original annotated nut.

The proposed datasets pose many challenges for deep neural networks: **Noise**: Most training datasets should include noise to a certain degree to create a more robust model. However, our original dataset contains a significantly larger object-to-noise ratio that most models can not understand well. Approximately 75% of each image include noise that severely hinders the visual features of our objects. **Small Scale**: Our dataset contains tiny annotation boxes (smallest at an area of 121 pixels), which may cause difficulty for anchor-based object detection systems. We observe which models may be affected by this difficulty. **Large Data**: To preserve as many visual features as possible, we use the full-size image (3024 by 4032). However, this requires much larger training times between models and larger memory space for computations. We experiment with different models' training and inference times. **Diversity**: There is a large variety in the appearance of our objects in shapes, sizes, and coloration. Due to unpredictable exposure to light, target objects within our dataset may lose all surface textures or appear overwhelmingly rich in features.

Fig. 3. Four sample pictures of the Mummy Nut dataset. Hanging on the branches of these trees are the target objects (Mummy Nuts).

In Fig. 3, we can observe the variety of difficult detections in our dataset. These nuts account for 71.8% of all annotated nuts throughout our dataset, affecting a large portion of our accuracy. Within our difficult detections, we also classified tiny nuts as about 9% of the total dataset.

Figure 4 shows a close-up collage to display examples of difficult Mummy Nuts detections. Frames (a) and (f) contain dark nuts that lack visual features and are further surrounded by a noisy background, causing models to miss these nuts as detections. Frames (b) and (d) contain bundles of nuts that, conversely to frames (a) and (f), are rich in visual features. However, they are overly rich and feature a rare trait in coloration. Frames (c) and (e) contain camouflaged nuts, which cause trouble even for the human eye to spot.

Fig. 4. Six examples of difficult detections. Each frame contains a red box that denotes where the Mummy Nuts appear. (Color figure online)

Without tuning the anchor boxes of a CNN, the chances of missing detections increase. This raises the question of whether to resize anchors for small or large objects. In Fig. 5, most annotations are tiny, though many outliers exist. Resizing anchors for small target objects would make detecting larger target objects more difficult and vice versa. Models that remove the need for anchor boxes can altogether avoid this problem (e.g., CenterNet).

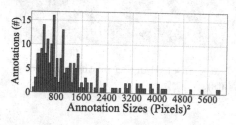

Fig. 5. The area (in pixels) of each annotation box across the entire dataset. We can see a majority of annotation boxes are smaller than 2000px in size.

We also introduce our second dataset (Augmented), which expands our Original training dataset by 8.9X. The Augmented dataset contains cropped data augmented annotations from the Original dataset. Networks that rely heavily on anchor boxes may see a change in performance from this dataset. To create this dataset, we first used the original fully annotated dataset and produced a crop window per annotation centered on each annotation. The crop window (200×200) is larger than the largest annotation in the training set. Cutoff annotations or multiple annotations within one crop were excluded. Each annotation was subject to a random number of image transformations (up to 6), including stretching and rotations. These augments are done to each cropped image, effectively enlarging our input dataset.

4.2 Metrics

In the evaluation of the accuracy of each model, we observe the following metrics: precision (Prec), recall (Rec), and average precision (AP). These are evaluated based on the true positives, true negatives, false positives, and false negatives we observe after a model has run its predictions. IoU tells us if a detection will classify as one of the four prediction categories. For performance, we evaluate latency between models and GPUs. These values give us the four evaluation metrics we will focus on, which are as follows: **Precision**: is the proportion that the target object in an image will be detected correctly over all attempts. **Recall**: tells us the proportion of target objects captured over all attempts. In other words, it represents the target objects overlooked by the detection model. **Average Precision (AP)**: is the precision with respect to recall. AP is calculated by the area under the curve (AUC) of a precision-recall graph based on each model's precision and recall values. In the MS COCO object detection challenge, a 101-point interpolation is used to evaluate models [2]. While for ImageNet, AUC method is used [3]. We used AUC rather than 11 or 101-point interpolation to evaluate lower accuracy values better, as n-point interpolation may be prone to drops in precision in between interpolations and lead to less evaluation accuracy [22]. In our datasets, we observe that 101-point interpolation leads to less sensitive accuracy, where AUC evaluation calculates the area each time there is a drop in precision. For this reason, we evaluate AUC. The equation is provided below:

$$AP = \sum (r_{n+1} - r_n) P_{interp}(r_{n+1}) \tag{1}$$

Performance: Performance represents how long it takes for models to perform computations on our dataset. The time it takes to perform required computations will be vital in determining which model is most suitable for specific agriculture applications. We measure two different processing phases. 1) Training results observe the time it takes to train a model to the point where the loss converges. 2) Inference measures the total time (including pre-processing time of convolutional layers) to perform inference on a single image.

4.3 Proposed Tools

We propose tools to ease the workflow with our Mummy Nuts dataset. In Table 1, we list all tools we have created for the object detection task of Mummy Nuts. **Difficulty Class Annotation (DCA)** is a tool that allows the user to input an annotated dataset and receive a richer annotation set that includes one or more difficulty class flags per annotation. For example, we can create a specific set of flags (e.g., Camouflaged, Dark, Overlap, etc.) and mark each annotation with as many difficulty flags that apply. **Metric Evaluation (Metric Eval)** computes all evaluation metrics on input detection results from any of the 5 models. This tool is flexible to multiple model annotation formats. If the input contains DCA flags, the evaluation will also include results for each difficulty class. **Data Augmentation (Data Aug)** tool takes an annotated dataset, crops windows (200 × 200 px) centering on each annotation, and produces new images with image transformations. The complete output creates an enlarged dataset. This tool is used to create our Augmented dataset.

   Annotation Plot (APlot) plots all annotations on an image, which allows us to visualize annotation box concentrations, scale sizes, and empty areas. Annotation Plot tool can also provide data on all annotation box sizes, similar to Fig. 5. **Noise Isolation (Noise Iso)** helps reduce the amount of noise in a Mummy Nut tree image. Pixels that classify as the grass gets lowered, allowing focus on pixels that are the tree or Mummy Nut. This tool can aid in the annotation pipeline to increase annotation recall. **Annotation View (Anno View)** creates a temporary viewing window during the tool's runtime that shows the target nut and the annotation bounding box. The tool can cycle through all annotations in a dataset, aiding the annotation pipeline when peer-reviewing annotations. **Annotation Reformat (Anno Reformat)** allows reformatting of an annotation to a different format. This is especially useful when using multiple models requiring different annotation formats.

5   Experiments

This section provides our experimental setups and benchmarking results.

Table 1. All proposed tools and their functions. These tools require two types of inputs: Annotated Dataset (AD) and Detection Box (DT) Results.

Tool	Input(s)	Output(s)
DCA	AD	AD w/difficulty class flags per annotation
Metric Eval	AD+DT	metrics based on detection box positions w/DCA
Data Aug	AD	enlarged AD via image augments per annotation
APlot	AD	all annotation boxes plotted + data of all box sizes
Noise Iso	AD	AD w/all noise values lowered
Anno View	AD	viewing window of each annotation
Anno Reformat	AD	reformatted annotations for different model formats

5.1   Platform Selection

We use two different GPU hardware to run our computations. The first is an in-home cluster with an NVIDIA A100 40 GB PCIe GPU. The NVIDIA A100 GPU is capable of 156 TFLOPS on dense 32-bit float tensors [23]. Model training benefits significantly from the GPU's high 1555 GB/s bandwidth and 40 GB of GPU memory. The cluster's CPU is an Intel(R) Xeon(R) Gold 6336Y with 24 cores, 36 MB of cache, and a base frequency of 2.40 GHz [24]. The second GPU is a Tesla T4 which is more easily accessible via Google Colab. The Tesla T4 contains 2560 NVIDIA CUDA cores and is capable of 65 trillion mixed-precision floating point operations [25]. The Colab CPU is a virtual CPU with two cores with a clock speed of 2.2GHz. We use these two platforms to test each model's performance throughput and speed.

5.2   Results

Our results are categorized into two subsections, as shown below. **Overall Accuracy**: An overview of how each model performs on our dataset. Due to the small size of our dataset, our numbers are preliminary. However, we may still make some significant distinctions. We observe the number of predictions a model makes on background pixels, quantifying the robustness of each model to noise. Localization performance can be observed between IoU results from 0.50 and 0.10. IoU becomes very sensitive with small-scale objects and scales disproportional to normal-sized boxes [26]. For this reason, we acknowledge the results of an IoU at 0.10. Recall also provides valuable data in a complex dataset where collecting maximum true positives is essential. **Performance**: We have observed each model's performance in training and inference. We quantify differences in those numbers with our Original dataset, our Augmented dataset, and different GPU platforms. For the Original dataset, we record the time for one inference. For the Augmented dataset we split input images evenly into 64 crops to match training inputs. We then record the total time of performing 64 inferences, equivalent to one Original dataset image.

Overall Accuracy: With a very noisy dataset, models will generate excessive detections on background pixels. Models that do not have a high threshold NMS may not properly filter out duplicate detections on the same true positive. In Table 2, MobileNet SSD suffers from this as it produces 2X the number of ground truths in the test set. We observe that this is due to the size of the MobileNet convolutional network. Since the network is much smaller than other modern networks, MobileNet SSD may need a deeper network to learn complex features properly. However, the lowest AP score comes from YOLOv3. YOLOv5's precision and recall increase by about 2X and AP by about 5X when the IoU threshold is set to 0.10. This tells us that YOLOv5 struggles with localization issues for detections on our dataset. The highest values overall are in Faster R-CNN with low localization error and high precision. The lowest amount of background detections is made from Faster R-CNN, which gives this model 100.0 precision at an IoU of 0.10. This may be due to Faster R-CNN running on the ResNet network, as it is a very deep network (101 layers), which provides higher confidence in detections and fewer false positives.

Table 2. Inference accuracy with our Original dataset (4032 by 3024 images). The predictions (Pred) show how many predictions each model has made. The true positives (TP) show the number of those predictions classified as correct according to the IoU threshold. Precision (Prec), Recall (Rec), and Average Precision (AP) are shown with corresponding IoU thresholds. The test partition has 15 ground truths.

Model	Pred	TP@.5	Prec@.5	Rec@.5	AP@.5	TP@.1	Prec@.1	Rec@.1	AP@.1
YOLOV3	11	2	18.18	13.3	2.87	3	27.2	20.0	7.33
YOLOV5	25	4	16.0	26.6	4.31	8	32.0	53.3	21.9
CenterNet	12	4	33.3	26.6	13.7	6	50.0	40.0	30.0
Faster R-CNN	9	7	**77.7**	**46.6**	**41.6**	9	**100.0**	**60.0**	**60.0**
MobileNet SSD	30	6	20.0	40.0	10.0	6	20.0	40.0	12.0

In Table 3, we notice our Augmented dataset causes each model to increase background detection errors. Since our Augmented test set contains much smaller input images, we notice higher number of detections. However, we see a significant increase in recall in the YOLO models compared to the Original dataset. For YOLOv3, We observed a 6.5X increase in the recall at IoU 0.50 from the Original dataset to the Augmented dataset. While for YOLOv5, we saw a 2.5X increase. While the YOLO models do not decrease in precision, each of the three other models does. This is due to the large number of background errors that these models now produce. CenterNet increases the most at about 29.6X more background detections. Since CenterNet uses heatmaps rather than anchor boxes, these background errors are likely due to a large amount of noise, as the maxima of the heatmaps may become lower when there are fewer distinctions in coloration. MobileNet SSD is ranked second, producing about 24X more background detections. As with the Original dataset, this is likely due to the small size of the backbone network. YOLO models are more robust to background errors, with the most significant increase in errors at 2.6X. Since they use anchor boxes rather than heatmaps and a larger backbone network than MobileNet SSD, they get better results using the Augmented dataset.

Table 3. Inference accuracy with our Augmented dataset (200 by 200 images).

Model	Pred	TP@.5	Prec@.5	Rec@.5	AP@.5	TP@.1	Prec@.1	Rec@.1	AP@.1
YOLOV3	37	13	35.1	**86.6**	38.5	13	35.1	**86.6**	38.5
YOLOV5	32	10	31.2	66.6	26.2	10	31.2	66.6	26.2
CenterNet	245	8	3.26	53.3	3.27	9	3.67	60.0	5.17
Faster R-CNN	30	13	**43.3**	**86.6**	**51.0**	13	**43.3**	**86.6**	**51.0**
MobileNet SSD	583	6	1.02	40.0	0.57	7	1.20	46.6	0.78

Performance: We can observe in Fig. 6 that on the Tesla T4, Faster R-CNN has a significantly longer training time than the rest of the models, likely due to the large depth of the backbone network and a large number of computations. On the A100, we see a significant decrease in latency due to the larger network benefiting greatly from the considerable upgrade in bandwidth, up to a 5.85X speedup for Faster R-CNN.

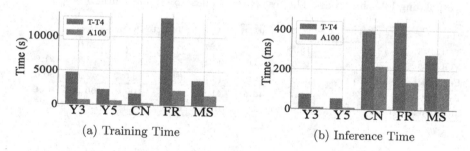

(a) Training Time   (b) Inference Time

Fig. 6. Computation times of each model using Original dataset on both GPUs. We compare the performance speed of our five models, YOLOv3 (Y3), YOLOv5 (Y5), CenterNet (CN), Faster R-CNN (FR), and MobileNet SSD (MS) on the Tesla T4 (T-T4) and A100 (A100).

In Fig. 7, we can observe that Faster R-CNN still takes the longest to run training on the Augmented dataset on the Tesla T4 and speedup of 5.68X with A100. YOLOv5 has faster training and inference times on the Original dataset, while YOLOv3 performs slightly better on the Augmented dataset. This is likely due to optimizations for larger image sizes of successive versions of YOLO. We also notice that YOLO has the fastest overall inference time on both datasets. MobileNet SSD can perform much quicker on the Augmented dataset than the Original dataset since it is a tiny network and benefits from smaller inputs, as provided by the Augmented dataset.

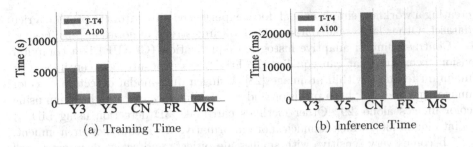

(a) Training Time   (b) Inference Time

Fig. 7. Computation times of each model using Augmented dataset.

5.3   Observations and Discussion

We evaluate our two-dimensional benchmarking methodology of accuracy and performance with all the results. We observe accuracy with a heavier emphasis on recall values rather than precision due to the small scale of our annotations which aids in compensating for the difficulty within our Mummy Nut dataset. For performance, we evaluate two different GPUs to observe computation latency. We collect the computation time of model training and inference.

From these results, we notice several key observations, and we make a note of their significance. Firstly, all models saw an average recall value increase of 2.77X, with YOLOv3 at the most significant increase of 6.5X, when using our Augmented dataset over the Original. This observation implies that our method can further improve the model recall. We notice that all models except MobileNet SSD face localization precision issues with the Original dataset. These localization issues tell us that most models create bounding boxes that may not enclose the Mummy Nut well, though MobileNet SSD performs more precisely. CenterNet, Faster R-CNN, and MobileNet SSD decrease precision by an average of 10.53X using the Augmented dataset over the Original. If an Augmented dataset approach is desired, YOLO models may provide better results in precision than the other three models. For performance, the overall model training time over both Original and Augmented datasets can be reduced by an average of 4.45X when using A100 over Tesla T4. Though we notice Faster R-CNN sees the most significant benefit from this speedup by 5.76X over both datasets. This would be due to larger CNNs being able to take full advantage of the increased computation capacity of A100. YOLO models have the fastest overall inference speed and prove useful for quick inference applications.

6   Related Work

A survey on popular precision agriculture datasets overviews 34 different datasets for deep learning workloads that include multimodal data [27].

Other highly rich datasets create an annotation pipeline to ensure the highest possible annotation precision and recall. MS COCO splits the pipeline into three sections: Category Labeling, Instance Spotting, and Instance Segmentation [2], creating a workflow simple enough for inexperienced annotators to provide a rich dataset. Other large-scale datasets [3–6] outline strong annotation pipelines.

Contrast limited adaptive histogram equalization (CLAHE) is a computer vision technique that can equalize the brightness exposure between images to maintain features within an image [28]. Using a dual-modal detection of color images and thermal, both precision and recall values are much higher than using color images alone [29]. Other methods can make 3D detection using LiDAR point clouds [30], which is much more informative for a complex environment. IoU becomes very sensitive with small-scale objects and scales disproportional to normal-sized boxes, lowering model accuracy. Normalized Wasserstein Distance (NWD) creates a new metric for IoU that can be implemented into Faster R-CNN [26]. Most models also struggle to make rotation-invariant detections. Multiple different models have been proposed [31–34] which tackles the challenges in oriented target objects.

Other proposed methods tackle accelerating EdgeAI inference systems for object detection, improving performance and accuracy with modern EdgeAI platforms [13,35]. There is also a study on the performance of mobile GPUs [36]. A benchmark of multiple Deep Learning models on different edge devices evaluates the performance latency of object detection tasks [37]. Work that lists and surveys multiple popular Deep Learning benchmarks provides insightful observations on each type of benchmark [38].

Our work is different than all of these existing studies since we aim to provide valuable benchmarking datasets and tools for an engaging, meaningful, and challenging research problem in the precision agriculture area (i.e., Mummy Nuts).

7   Conclusion and Future Work

We propose a benchmarking methodology to evaluate five different CNN models using two dimensions of measurement, which include accuracy and performance. Our results show that using our Augmented dataset can drastically change the CNN model's overall performance. All models increase recall with our Augmented dataset, with YOLO models as the most significant increase. Faster R-CNN and YOLOv3 can achieve the highest recall of all models when using data from the Augmented dataset. However, if it is desired that the Original dataset is used, we find that Faster R-CNN performs very well in both precision and recall values. YOLO models do well in speed, with the overall fastest inference speed. However, the Augmented dataset is significantly more sensitive to noise for each model, though less for YOLO models and Faster R-CNN. To sum up, YOLO and MobileNet SSD models may be more suitable for an Augmented dataset method, whereas CenterNet may perform better on the Original dataset. Faster R-CNN is the most versatile and may be well applicable to both datasets. For future work, we will enrich our datasets further.

References

1. Almonds, C.: Navel Orangeworm (2022). https://www.almonds.com/almond-industry/industry-news/mummy-nut-removal-ready-set
2. Lin, T.-Y., et al.: Microsoft COCO: common objects in context. In: Fleet, D., Pajdla, T., Schiele, B., Tuytelaars, T. (eds.) ECCV 2014. LNCS, vol. 8693, pp. 740–755. Springer, Cham (2014). https://doi.org/10.1007/978-3-319-10602-1_48
3. Deng, J., Dong, W., Socher, R., Li, L.-J., Li, K., Fei-Fei, L.: ImageNet: a large-scale hierarchical image database. In: 2009 IEEE Conference on Computer Vision and Pattern Recognition, pp. 248–255 (2009)
4. Everingham, M., Gool, L.V., Williams, C.K.I., Winn, J.M., Zisserman, A.: The pascal visual object classes (VOC) challenge. Int. J. Comput. Vis. **88**, 303–338 (2009)
5. Xiao, J., Hays, J., Ehinger, K.A., Oliva, A., Torralba, A.: SUN database: large-scale scene recognition from abbey to zoo. In: 2010 IEEE Computer Society Conference on Computer Vision and Pattern Recognition, pp. 3485–3492 (2010)
6. Dollár, P., Wojek, C., Schiele, B., Perona, P.: Pedestrian detection: an evaluation of the state of the art. IEEE Trans. Pattern Anal. Mach. Intell. **34**, 743–761 (2012)
7. Redmon, J., Divvala, S., Girshick, R., Farhadi, A.: You only look once: unified, real-time object detection. In: Proceedings of the IEEE Conference on Computer Vision and Pattern Recognition, pp. 779–788 (2016)
8. Girshick, R., Donahue, J., Darrell, T., Malik, J.: Rich feature hierarchies for accurate object detection and semantic segmentation. In: Proceedings of the IEEE Conference on Computer Vision and Pattern Recognition, pp. 580–587 (2014)
9. Girshick, R.: Fast R-CNN. In: 2015 IEEE International Conference on Computer Vision (ICCV), pp. 1440–1448 (2015)
10. Ren, S., He, K., Girshick, R., Sun, J.: Faster R-CNN: towards real-time object detection with region proposal networks. In: Advances in Neural Information Processing Systems, vol. 28 (2015)
11. Duan, K., Bai, S., Xie, L., Qi, H., Huang, Q., Tian, Q.: Centernet: keypoint triplets for object detection. In: Proceedings of the IEEE/CVF International Conference on Computer Vision, pp. 6569–6578 (2019)
12. Howard, A.G., et al.: MobileNets: efficient convolutional neural networks for mobile vision applications. arXiv preprint arXiv:1704.04861 (2017)
13. Hui, Y., Lien, J., Lu, X.: Early experience in benchmarking edge AI processors with object detection workloads. In: Gao, W., Zhan, J., Fox, G., Lu, X., Stanzione, D. (eds.) Bench 2019. LNCS, vol. 12093, pp. 32–48. Springer, Cham (2020). https://doi.org/10.1007/978-3-030-49556-5_3
14. Newell, A., Yang, K., Deng, J.: Stacked hourglass networks for human pose estimation. In: Leibe, B., Matas, J., Sebe, N., Welling, M. (eds.) ECCV 2016. LNCS, vol. 9912, pp. 483–499. Springer, Cham (2016). https://doi.org/10.1007/978-3-319-46484-8_29
15. Simonyan, K., Zisserman, A.: Very deep convolutional networks for large-scale image recognition. arXiv preprint arXiv:1409.1556 (2014)
16. He, K., Zhang, X., Ren, S., Sun, J.: Deep residual learning for image recognition. In: Proceedings of the IEEE Conference on Computer Vision and Pattern Recognition, pp. 770–778 (2016)
17. Canziani, A., Paszke, A., Culurciello, E.: An analysis of deep neural network models for practical applications. arXiv preprint arXiv:1605.07678 (2016)

18. Liu, W., et al.: SSD: single shot multibox detector. In: Leibe, B., Matas, J., Sebe, N., Welling, M. (eds.) ECCV 2016. LNCS, vol. 9905, pp. 21–37. Springer, Cham (2016). https://doi.org/10.1007/978-3-319-46448-0_2

19. Redmon, J., Farhadi, A.: YOLOv3: an incremental improvement. arXiv preprint arXiv:1804.02767 (2018)

20. Jocher, G., et al.: Ultralytics/YOLOv5: v6.1 - TensorRT, TensorFlow Edge TPU and OpenVINO Export and Inference (2022)

21. Redmon, J.: Darknet: Open Source Neural Networks in C (2013/2016). http://pjreddie.com/darknet/

22. Hui, J.: mAP (mean Average Precision) for Object Detection (2022). https://medium.com/p/45c121a31173

23. NVIDIA. NVIDIA A100 Tensor Core GPU Datasheet (2022). https://www.nvidia.com/content/dam/en-zz/Solutions/Data-Center/a100/pdf/nvidia-a100-datasheet-us-nvidia-1758950-r4-web.pdf

24. Intel: Intel Xeon Gold 6336Y Processor Datasheet (2022). https://www.intel.com/content/www/us/en/products/sku/215280/intel-xeon-gold-6336y-processor-36m-cache-2-40-ghz/specifications.html

25. NVIDIA: NVIDIA Tesla T4 Tensor Core GPU Datasheet (2022). https://www.nvidia.com/content/dam/en-zz/Solutions/Data-Center/tesla-t4/t4-tensor-core-datasheet-951643.pdf

26. Wang, J., Xu, C., Yang, W., Yu, L.: A normalized Gaussian Wasserstein distance for tiny object detection. arXiv preprint arXiv:2110.13389 (2021)

27. Lu, Y., Young, S.: A survey of public datasets for computer vision tasks in precision agriculture. Comput. Electron. Agric. **178**, 105760 (2020)

28. Choi, D., Lee, W., Ehsani, R., Schueller, J., Roka, F.: Detection of dropped citrus fruit on the ground and evaluation of decay stages in varying illumination conditions. Comput. Electron. Agric. **127**, 109–119 (2016)

29. Gan, H., Lee, W., Alchanatis, V., Ehsani, R., Schueller, J.: Immature green citrus fruit detection using color and thermal images. Comput. Electron. Agric. **152**, 117–125 (2018)

30. Qi, C.R., Su, H., Mo, K., Guibas, L.J.: PointNet: deep learning on point sets for 3D classification and segmentation. In: Proceedings of the IEEE Conference on Computer Vision and Pattern Recognition (CVPR) (2017)

31. Qin, R., Liu, Q., Gao, G., Huang, D., Wang, Y.: MRDET: a multi-head network for accurate oriented object detection in aerial images. arXiv preprint arXiv:2012.13135 (2020)

32. Yi, J., Wu, P., Liu, B., Huang, Q., Qu, H., Metaxas, D.: Oriented object detection in aerial images with box boundary-aware vectors. In: Proceedings of the IEEE/CVF Winter Conference on Applications of Computer Vision, pp. 2150–2159 (2021)

33. Zand, M., Etemad, A., Greenspan, M.: Oriented bounding boxes for small and freely rotated objects. IEEE Trans. Geosci. Remote Sens. **60**, 1–15 (2022)

34. Han, J., Ding, J., Xue, N., Xia, G.-S.: ReDet: a rotation-equivariant detector for aerial object detection. In: Proceedings of the IEEE/CVF Conference on Computer Vision and Pattern Recognition, pp. 2786–2795 (2021)

35. Hui, Y., Lien, J., Lu, X.: Characterizing and accelerating end-to-end EdgeAI inference systems for object detection applications. In: 2021 IEEE/ACM Symposium on Edge Computing (SEC), pp. 01–12 (2021)

36. Gao, C., Gutierrez, A., Rajan, M., Dreslinski, R.G., Mudge, T., Wu, C.-J.: A study of mobile device utilization. In: 2015 IEEE International Symposium on Performance Analysis of Systems and Software (ISPASS), pp. 225–234 (2015)

37. Allan, A.: Benchmarking Edge Computing (2022). https://aallan.medium.com/benchmarking-edge-computing-ce3f13942245
38. Zhang, Q., et al.: A survey on deep learning benchmarks: do we still need new ones? In: Zheng, C., Zhan, J. (eds.) Bench 2018. LNCS, vol. 11459, pp. 36–49. Springer, Cham (2019). https://doi.org/10.1007/978-3-030-32813-9_5

Network and Memory

An Analysis of Long-Tailed Network Latency Distribution and Background Traffic on Dragonfly+

Majid Salimi Beni(✉) and Biagio Cosenza

Department of Computer Science, University of Salerno, Salerno, Italy
{msalimibeni,bcosenza}@unisa.it

Abstract. Modern computing systems are highly affected by large performance variability, resulting in a long tail in the distribution of the network latency. For communication-intensive applications, the variability comes from several factors such as the communication pattern, job placement strategies, routing algorithms, and most importantly, the network background traffic. Although recent high-performance interconnects such as Dragonfly+ try to mitigate this variability by employing advanced techniques such as adaptive routing or topological improvements, the long tail is still there.

This paper analyzes the sources of performance variability on a large-scale computing system with a Dragonfly+ network. Our quantitative study investigates the impact of several sources, including the locality of job placement, the communication pattern, the message size, and the network background traffic. To tackle the difficulty in measuring the network background traffic, we propose a novel heuristic that accurately estimates the network traffic and helps to identify those highly-varying communications that contribute to the long tail. We have experimentally validated our proposed background traffic heuristic on a collection of pattern-based microbenchmarks as well as two real-world applications, HACC and miniAMR. Results show that the heuristic can successfully predict most of those runs in long-tail at job submission time on both microbenchmarks and real-world applications.

Keywords: MPI · Interconnect · Congestion · Dragonfly+ · Topology

1 Introduction

The growing gap between communication and computation in high-performance computing emphasizes the importance of optimized data communication. It is today well-understood that, to reach the Exascale, computing systems should provide high-performance network interconnects that deliver both high bandwidth and low latency.

The Dragonfly+ topology [47] is a modern hierarchical interconnect that has been recently introduced as an extended implementation of Dragonfly [30]. Such

© The Author(s), under exclusive license to Springer Nature Switzerland AG 2023
A. Gainaru et al. (Eds.): Bench 2022, LNCS 13852, pp. 123–142, 2023.
https://doi.org/10.1007/978-3-031-31180-2_8

interconnect not only provides better network utilization and scalability in comparison to Dragonfly but also improves router buffer utilization [47]. However, despite Dragonfly+'s improvements compared to its predecessor, it still suffers from performance variability, especially with higher network congestion. Performance variability affects both system and applications' performance, and the batch scheduler must have a more precise estimation of applications' runtime to make accurate scheduling decisions [53,67].

Several users use large-scale compute clusters simultaneously, with different utilization patterns regarding program workflow, number of nodes, and data communication. While single-node computes units are typically not shared between users, the network is a shared resource. Network elements such as routers and links, shared among several jobs, are subject to contention. They negatively impact users' program performance by degrading I/O and slowing communication time. To address these issues, recent work has focused on monitoring, predicting, and balancing network traffic [12,32,33,58], as well as taking topological and network designing aspects into account [7,9,22,52]. In fact, the network has been identified as the main reason for performance variability [5,10,11,48].

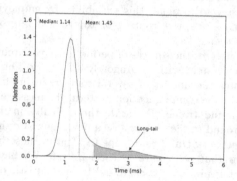

Fig. 1. Long-tail of the latency distribution on Dragonfly+.

1.1 Motivations

As performance variability is affected mainly by the network, it is essential to understand how network latency behaves on modern large-scale compute clusters. Figure 1 shows the frequency distribution of 1000 iterations of a latency test (MPI_Reduce in this case) on 16 nodes of the Marconi100 compute cluster with a Dragonfly+ topology. Interestingly, the results show a so-called *long-tailed* distribution. While a majority of the communication latencies are distributed around the median, more than 15% of the runs' latencies are larger than the 85th percentile (1.92 ms). The presence of such a long tail in the distribution also indicates that the distribution is not symmetric (e.g., not Gaussian), and there is a large gap between the mean and median. Also, the long tail negatively impacts the overall network performance by making the job execution highly unpredictable. While such performance variability is related to several network-related factors, our work aims to analyze the main reasons behind such performance degradation, from the application's communication patterns to the external network traffic involving all users.

At the topology level, our work focuses on the Dragonfly+, which has better network utilization [47] than Dragonfly (known to suffer from performance variability [37,50]) and it is becoming a common topology in newly developed supercomputers [34,42].

1.2   Contributions

This paper conducts a performance variability study on a large-scale compute cluster with Dragonfly+ topology. The study comprises the analysis of several known sources of performance variability, in particular network-related aspects, including: different communications patterns, the impact of message size, the locality of job placement, and the effect of network background traffic generated by other users. The latter, in particular, is difficult to measure; to this end, we propose an easy-to-measure heuristic that estimates such traffic. As a part of the study, we further point out the effect of the adaptive routing strategy on the communication performance of Dragonfly+.

To the best of our knowledge, this is the first work that analyzes Dragonfly+ performance variability on a real supercomputer. While most related work relies on simulating background traffic [28,57], our approach is based on real-world data of background traffic extracted from a large-scale compute cluster. Insights from this analysis provide valuable feedback for job placement policy implementations on Dragonfly+ as well as network design for large-scale clusters.

The main contributions of this paper are:

- The first detailed **analysis of communication performance on a large-scale Dragonfly+ network based on real-world data:** We analyze different inter-node communication scenarios and show the performance variability of microbenchmarks with varying job placements.
- A **novel heuristics for background traffic estimation**, which is easy to measure and based on information known at job submission time.
- A comprehensive **correlation analysis between estimated background traffic and the communication performance**, with different communication patterns and message sizes.
- An **evaluation of the background traffic's impact on the long-tail of the latency distribution**.
- Further extension of the evaluation on **two communication-intensive real-world applications:** HACC[1] and miniAMR.

The rest of the paper is organized as follows: Sect. 2 and 3 introduce, respectively, related work and experimental setup. Section 4 presents our analysis of latency distribution, and Sect. 5 describes our background traffic measurement approach and its analysis. Section 6 is the discussion, and Sect. 7 concludes the paper.

---

[1] Hardware Accelerated Cosmology Code.

2 Related Work

A large part of the execution time of HPC applications is spent on transferring data between nodes; for this reason, considerable research efforts have been paid to investigating network topologies [4,20,26,39] and, on the application side, studying, analyzing, and optimizing communication on top of existing topologies [2,16,18,46,51,54,55].

Performance variability is often correlated with heavy-tailed distributions, which are probability distributions whose tails are not exponentially bounded [3]. In fact, when scaling up and increasing the complexity of a computing system, the tail of the latency distribution, which is not long in small systems, becomes more dominant at the large scale [14].

Bhatele et al. [5] analyzed the performance variability of Dragonfly with periodic system profiling of mini-applications; based on this analysis, they trained a machine learning model that predicts future executions. Groves et al. [19] studied the performance variability of the MPI_Allreduce collective in the Aries Dragonfly network and considered the relationship between different metrics such as process count, Aries counters, and message size with communication time, and showed the impact of background traffic on the performance.

Research on performance variability has investigated locality aspects and studied how topological locality and communication patterns affect different applications' performance [63]. Other research, however, considered other metrics such as network designs [13,44,60], routing strategies [8,15,27,38,40,50], congestion control [35,45] and background traffic [65]. Wilke et al. [61] discuss and compare existing challenges of Dragonfly and Fat-tree and show how different configurations and routing algorithms may affect QoS. They further illustrate the performance variability of Dragonfly while having various background traffic and different routing strategies. Alzaid et al. [1] have explored the Dragonfly network and measured the impact of different link arrangements between nodes and routing strategies on communication between nodes. They showed how data transfer through different links might be affected while the links tolerate different bandwidths.

Job allocation strategies have been recognized as a determinant factor in communication performance [29,36]. Level-Spread proposed by Zhang et al. [66] is a job allocation policy on Dragonfly that puts jobs in the minor network level that the current job can fit in to not only benefit from the node adjacency but also balance link congestion. Brown et al. [6] analyzed the relation between MPI communications and I/O traffic in Fat-tree networks; their analysis considers different parameters such as job allocation policies, message sizes, communication intervals, and job sizes. Wang et al. [59] have performed a comparative analysis of network interference on applications with nearest-neighbor communication patterns, considering various job placement strategies on Dragonfly. They show that having a trade-off between localized communication and a balanced network in job placement can reduce network interference and alleviate performance variability. In another work [58], they carried out an in-depth performance analysis on Dragonfly and demonstrated how balanced network traffic and localized communication could impact different workloads.

Although related work has studied performance variability in Dragonfly, to the best of our knowledge, none of them have deeply investigated this variability in Dragonfly+. Moreover, we specifically show how background traffic affects different communication patterns, i.e., which collectives are more vulnerable to background traffic. Unlike most related work on background traffic, our analysis is based on real-world data (experiments have been conducted during a three-month time span at different times in order to have different background traffic) rather than simulations. Hence, the background traffic is generated by other users we have no control over, and we are not producing such traffic artificially.

3 Experimental Setup

Our analyses have been performed on a large-scale compute cluster, Marconi100 [34], available at the CINECA supercomputing center, which is currently ranked 18th in the TOP500 ranking [56].

3.1 Computing

The Marconi 100 cluster is an IBM Power System AC922 [43] consisting of 980 nodes, each of which is equipped with two IBM POWER9 AC922 multicore processors with 16 cores at 2.6 (3.1 turbo) GHz and four NVIDIA Volta V100 GPUs with 16GB, and 256 GB of per-node memory. All in all, the total number of CPU cores is 347,776, and it provides 347776 GB of memory.

3.2 Network

The internal interconnect of Marconi100 is a Mellanox InfiniBand EDR Dragonfly+. Figure 2 presents the Dragonfly+ topology implemented in this supercomputer. As shown, there are four large groups of nodes, each of which is called an

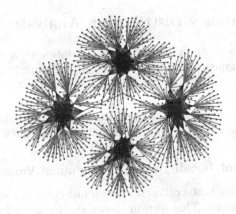

Fig. 2. The Dragonfly+ topology in Marconi100.

island. Within islands, there are smaller groups of nodes connected to one switch called *groups.* The main topological difference between Dragonfly and Dragonfly+ is that in Dragonfly+, intra-island routers are connected as a bipartite graph to improve the scalability.

It is worth mentioning that the Operating System is Red Hat Enterprise 7.6, IBM Spectrum-MPI 10.4 [25] is installed on the cluster, and SLURM [62] has the duty of resource management on this system. In addition, Adaptive Routing [17] is the default routing strategy used to prevent contention of the links and handle failures on the hardware.

3.3 Microbenchmarks and Applications

The main analysis and evaluation are done based on the OSU collection of microbenchmarks [41], which consists of three collectives, to which we added two real-world applications as summarized in Table 1. Moreover, to show the performance variability, each experiment is repeated in 1-millisecond intervals 1000 times in a loop (as suggested by [24] to perform at least 300 iterations), and, in all experiments, 1 MPI process is assigned to each physical node to leave other cores for the OS. Also, 16 physical nodes are allocated to the cluster in collective communications and application evaluations to partially involve all the islands in the communication.

Table 1. Benchmarks and applications used for the analysis.

Benchmark/App	Description	Evaluated sizes
Broadcast	Program calling Spectrum MPI_Bcast	$2^2, 2^{10}, 2^{15}, 2^{20}$(bytes)
Reduce	Program calling Spectrum MPI_Reduce	$2^2, 2^{10}, 2^{15}, 2^{20}$(bytes)
All-to-All	Representative of Spectrum MPI_Alltoall	$2^2, 2^{10}, 2^{15}, 2^{20}$(bytes)
HACC [21]	Includes various communication patterns	10M particles
miniAMR [23]	Includes various communication patterns	4K 3D blocks

4   Network Latency Distribution Analysis

This section provides an analysis of the network latency on a Dragonfly+. First, we show the performance variability considering different locality levels for node allocation. Then, we show how the performance of microbenchmarks is affected when having different job allocation scenarios. Note that to make sure we are using the best-fitting distribution with minimum error in distribution plots, more than 100 different distributions have been fitted to the data.

4.1   Job Placement Locality and Performance Variability

Performance variability is the difference in an individual program's performance in consecutive executions. This section shows the impact of different job placement (node allocation) strategies on performance variability.

In our analysis, we consider three locality levels according to the Dragonfly+ topology and analyze the performance variability when having the following three node allocation scenarios:

a) **Same Group:** In this case, all required nodes are allocated in a single group. Therefore, only one network switch is involved in the communication between every two nodes.

b) **Same Island:** Nodes are allocated on one island, but they are distributed across different groups of that island. Hence, there is less locality than in the previous scenario.

c) **Different Islands:** Nodes are distributed on different islands. In this case, there is no limitation on allocating nodes; they are allocated everywhere on different islands and groups. In doing so, less locality is imposed.

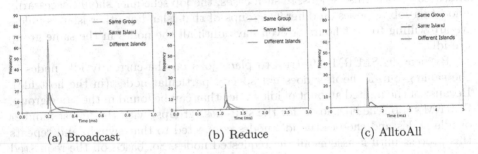

(a) Broadcast   (b) Reduce   (c) AlltoAll

Fig. 3. Communication time frequency distribution of collective communications for 1000 iterations, with different allocation locality scenarios.

According to the defined locality levels, we focus on the role of both communication patterns and job placement on the performance variability and long-tail. In fact, we analyze different communication patterns to understand how they affect performance variability. The selected microbenchmarks include *one-to-all* (MPI Broadcast), *all-to-one* (MPI Reduce), and *all-to-all* (MPI AlltoAll).

We refined the analysis with a by-pattern study as shown in Fig. 3. This figure shows the frequency distribution of under-study collectives with different allocations on 16 nodes. For the *same group* job placement, all 16 nodes are allocated on the *same group* and connected through a single switch. For *different islands* mode, four nodes are allocated on each island in different groups. As illustrated, Broadcast (Fig. 3a) shows the best performance and shortest tail for all three allocation strategies; in fact, it benefits local communications more than other patterns, especially for the *same group*: it is not only faster than others (average time= 0.2), but also its peak is higher, which means that communication times of different iterations are very similar and there is a low performance variability. In Fig. 3a, the peaks of *different islands* and *same island* are 19 and 6, respectively, and they possess a peak much lower than the *same group* (68). However, they still show higher peaks than the correspondings in Reduce and

AlltoAll. For the Reduce (Fig. 3b), the average communication times of the *same group* and *same island* are almost the same (1.17 and 1.18 ms, respectively). However, with *different islands* we observe a slower average communication time (1.4 ms) and a much longer tail, reaching 10 ms. Finally, AlltoAll (Fig. 3c) is the slowest and most variable collective when all the nodes are on *different islands*. Its frequency distribution shows a very long tail (notice that the end of its tail is not shown in the figure), with a maximum observed communication time reaching 13 ms and a peak of 2.

Although allocating all nodes on the *same group* has been beneficial for collective communications, the number of nodes in each group of Dragonfly+ is limited (up to 20 nodes in Marconi 100), and the job scheduler cannot exclusively allocate to the *same group* more than the existing physical nodes. Even worse, large-scale compute clusters are typically used by several users that submit multiple jobs; in fact, very often, other nodes in the same group are already allocated by other users' jobs. In such cases, the job scheduler should necessarily allocate a job to nodes on different groups of that island or other islands unless we are willing to wait hours or even days until all the nodes in the same group are idle.

By default, SLURM [49] tries to place jobs on the currently idle nodes in the same group if the user does not specify particular nodes (in the host file). Because of the limited amount of idle nodes that can be found in the same group, SLURM's job scheduler looks for the switches (groups) with the fewest number of idle nodes and chooses the idle nodes connected to that switch, and repeats this process until it assigns all the requested nodes. So, based on the requested number of nodes by the user and the availability of cluster nodes, it may decide to assign jobs to nodes on different groups of the same island, or it spans over different islands, which the latter is the more probable scenario according to our observations.

5   Background Traffic Analysis

In real-world supercomputers, a single user does not operate on a dedicated system; instead, it submits jobs concurrently with other users. While resources such as computing nodes are typically allocated so that they are not shared between users at the same time, unfortunately, there is a resource for which some degree of contention is unavoidable: the network.

Intuitively, the larger the number of active jobs, the more probable the network congestion. More precisely, network congestion is more probable when users' jobs involve a larger number of nodes.

This section analyzes how the background traffic generated by other users' jobs affects the performance variability. In particular, we first define a simple heuristic that approximates the amount of network activity generated by other users' jobs. Successively, the analysis focuses on the correlation between background traffic with several communication patterns and message sizes.

5.1   Background Traffic Heuristic

The network congestion due to other users' activity is an essential cause of high-latency runs when using a large-scale compute cluster. We indicate with network background traffic: the external network traffic made by other users who are running their job simultaneously. To quantify how much such network activities impact the latency of our program communications, we have monitored the SLURM job queue before executing our jobs (i.e., we queried the *squeue* command before program execution).

In this way, we obtained information regarding the number of running and pending jobs, running jobs' runtime, as well as the number of nodes allocated by each job. Since we have no information about pending jobs and it is unclear when they will be running, they are not considered in our background traffic analysis. Besides, the running jobs that allocate only one node are excluded from our calculations because they have no communication with other nodes and, therefore, no effect on the background traffic (we experimentally observed many jobs that only allocate one node). Therefore, only jobs with the running status that allocate at least two nodes have been taken into account.

To better understand the background traffic with a simple and countable metric, we define a simple heuristic named *background network utilization* (*b*), which is defined as the number of unique nodes allocated by the running jobs and whose allocation includes at least two nodes over all the available nodes of the cluster. In other words, it shows the ratio of nodes contributing to communication to all the physical cluster nodes.

Formally, the background network utilization *b* ratio is defined as follows:

$$b = \frac{N_c}{N_t} \tag{1}$$

where:

N_c: number of unique nodes contributing to communication
N_t: total number of cluster physical nodes

In some cases, one node may be shared among different jobs by the scheduler in order to fully utilize its resources, e.g., each job takes a computation resource; which means that the node is being utilized by more than one communicating job, and we cannot count this node in our heuristic only once since the node produces higher background traffic. In order to take such cases into account, we count the shared node as many times it appears in the jobs' node lists that allocate more than two nodes. Hence, considering the appearance of some nodes more than once in the nodes list, the number of all running nodes can become larger than the cluster's physical nodes (N_t), which is a constant number. In an effort to resolve the problem and refine the heuristic, we consider the overhead of shared nodes by multiplying *b* by a new ratio which is: the number of nodes contributing to communication (consider some nodes might be counted more than once) to all the allocated running nodes (Similarly, we count each node as many times they appear in the jobs' nodes list). By doing so, we ensure that we consider nodes contributing to different jobs and having communication with other nodes. Therefore, the refined version of the *background network utilization*, which will be considered in the rest of the paper, is defined as follows:

$$b = \frac{N_c}{N_t} * \frac{N_c'}{N_a} \tag{2}$$

where:

N_c': the number of nodes contributing to communication (containing duplication)
N_a: all allocated running nodes (containing duplication)

Ideally, the value of b is 1 (or 100, if the percentage is taken into account) if running jobs allocate all the nodes and all of them are actively involved in communication, while b is 0 if non of the nodes are communicating or there is no active job at that moment. In order to make sure the measured b is showing a more accurate background network utilization and it has not changed during the microbenchmark's execution, we perform the *squeue* query also after the execution of each test and capture the b value only if the difference between two b values calculated is less than a threshold (5% in our experiments).

Note that some other network-related metrics, such as vendor-provided counters, can be also measured in some clusters to make precise network congestion measurement. However, not in all compute clusters are these counters available or accessible by non-admin users. Moreover, using such counters, the proposed method would not be portable to other clusters with different network infrastructure vendors. Therefore, we rely on data provided by SLURM, which is available on most clusters.

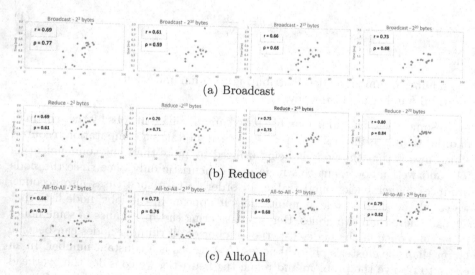

Fig. 4. The relation between background traffic (b) and the average communication time of different collectives with different message sizes.

5.2 Correlation Analysis

To evaluate how much the communication time is affected by the background traffic, we analyzed the correlation between the previously introduced b metric and the communication time over many runs with different workloads in terms of data sizes and communication patterns. In the evaluation, we used the Pearson Correlation Coefficient (r) [31] and Spearman Rank Correlation (ρ) [64] to analyze the relation between the two metrics. While Pearson's correlation shows if there is a linear relationship between data, Spearman's correlation evaluates the monotonic relationships in the data. In both, r, ρ: $r = +1$ or $\rho = +1$ means that there is a strong positive correlation between the variables, while $r = 0$ or $\rho = 0$ means independent variables. Figure 4 shows the correlation between background network utilization b and communication time for Broadcast (Fig. 4a), Reduce (Fig. 4b), and All-to-All (Fig. 4c) pattern, with different data sizes on 16 nodes allocated on *different islands*. We do not explore point-to-point communication here since it is not significantly affected by the background traffic. There are 22 points on each plot, and each point represents the average time of 1000 iterations. Experiments are performed in a three months time frame and represent experiments under different cluster utilization, i.e., different recorded background network utilization.

As shown in Fig. 4, the message transmission time is correlated with the *background network utilization* metric (b) and, overall, with increasing traffic, the communication time increases. In addition, as a general trend, with growing message size from 2^2, 2^{10}, and 2^{15} to 2^{20} bytes, the correlation between *background network utilization* and communication time becomes stronger, which means: the larger the data size is, the more the collective communication is affected by background traffic. Further, the correlations in Reduce collective for larger data (2^{15} and 2^{20} bytes) are higher than in others, meaning that in this collective, the communication time is highly dependent on the background traffic. Also, comparing the Pearson and Spearman correlations, Spearman shows a better fit for our use cases since it usually shows a more strong correlation.

It is worth mentioning that although background traffic is an essential factor that affects performance variability in communication-intensive jobs running on supercomputers, it is not the only player. Other reasons come from MPI itself, system activities, background daemons, garbage collection, queuing activities in intermediate servers and network switches, etc. [14,48]. Having said that, our *background network utilization* ratio is also an estimation relying on the obtainable information from other users. Hence, there might be possible errors in the measured runtimes, which is why some communications with smaller *background network utilization* have larger communication times, and the correlations are not +1.0 in Fig. 4.

5.3 The Impact of Background Traffic on Long-Tail

We have seen how performance variability is affected by the network background traffic for specific input sizes and communication patterns. In this section, we

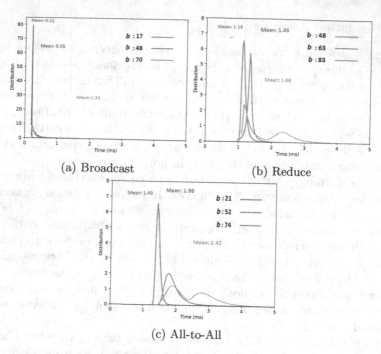

(a) Broadcast   (b) Reduce

(c) All-to-All

Fig. 5. Frequency distribution of communication times of 1000 iterations of Broadcast, Reduce, and All-to-All with different background network utilization.

go back to the motivation example and focus our analysis on the background traffic contribution to the long-tail effect. Figure 5 shows the frequency distribution of the execution time of 1000 iterations of 3 collectives on 16 nodes with message size 2^{20} bytes, with nodes allocated on *different islands*. For all three collectives, the higher the background network utilization, the lower the peak, and the longer the tail. For the Broadcast (Fig. 5a) and $b = 0.17$ (17%), the peak is very high, and there is a significant gap in the distribution of the higher and lower traffics; with higher background network utilization ($b = 0.70$), the tail of its corresponding distribution line is so long, which indicates that the communication performance is highly variable, ranging from 0.2 ms to 8 ms. Moreover, our experimental result reveals that the average execution time of 1000 iterations of Broadcast for $b = 0.70$ can be up to 6.4x larger than $b = 0.17$. Therefore, the Broadcast is highly affected by the background traffic, and, even if all the nodes are distributed on *different islands*, lower background traffic's performance can be as good as allocating all the nodes on the *same island*.

Similarly, in Figs. 5b and 5c, we observe that the distribution spreads at larger intervals with increasing background network utilization, and the tail becomes longer. For AlltoAll, especially when there is high background network utilization, the tail of the distribution is longer, the peak is lower, and the average communication time is larger than Broadcast and Reduce. Also, the mean of distribution with $b = 0.74$ is around $1.6x$ larger than $b = 0.21$. In addition, unlike others, in AlltoAll, a significant shift in the peak of the charts (Median) of different background network utilizations is observed. In fact, this shift in the peak of different traffics is because of the All-to-All's inherent communication intensity: in this pattern, all nodes send their data to the others, and more data is sent through the network, making the network links more congested.

Besides, for higher background network utilization of Reduce and AlltoAll, the frequency distribution becomes dual (bimodal), which means that the higher amounts of iterations mainly happen at two different times instead of one. This behavior is related to the adaptive routing algorithm employed in this Dragonfly+ network. In adaptive routing, the router has multiple paths to choose from for each packet. In this way, some packets traverse on the shortest (minimal) path, and some go through an alternative, longer (non-minimal) one. Hence, some communications happen slower than the majority due to the penalty of selecting the non-minimal path. As demonstrated in Figs. 5b and 5c, when the network tolerates higher background network utilization, going through the non-minimal path becomes more probable that this either causes the distribution tail longer or makes it dual. Note that we cannot change the routing strategy since we are performing our experiments on a real compute cluster. Overall, it is clear how the background traffic pushes the tail. While the adaptive routing strategy helps mitigate the problem, there are cases where the problem still exists, particularly when there is very high background traffic.

5.4   Application Analysis

So far, we have shown the impact of network background traffic and routing strategy on micro-benchmarks. In this section, we investigate the impact of background network utilization on two communication-intensive real-world applications that have shown to be affected by network congestion:

- HACC: a cosmology framework that performs n-body simulation to simulate the formation of structure in an expanding space.
- miniAMR: a mini-application that performs a stencil calculation on a unit cube computational domain.

Figure 6 shows the network latency distribution for HACC and miniAMR with both histogram and the frequency distribution. As shown in Fig. 6a for HACC, the average execution time and the peaks of $b = 34$ (the orange distribution) are 1.37 and 8.9, respectively. In contrast, for $b = 58$ (the blue distribution), the average time and peak reach 1.43 and 5.2, respectively. In other words, with a 24 percent increase in b, the average execution time increases by 4.4 percent. Moreover, both distributions in Fig. 6a are single and bell-shaped. However, the blue line is broadly distributed, and its tail reaches 2.5, while the orange line's tail is 2.1.

On the other hand, in Fig. 6b, when b changes from 51% to 64% and changes by 13, the average goes from 7.71 to 7.86 (2% increase). In contrast to all the

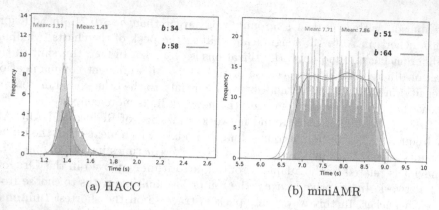

(a) HACC   (b) miniAMR

Fig. 6. Frequency distribution of 1000 iterations of HACC and miniAMR applications with two different background network utilization.

observations, in this figure, both plots have multiple peaks, and a different behavior has been observed. Regarding the previous analysis on the two applications [65], in HACC, around 67% of the overall execution time of the application belongs to MPI operations. However, a tiny fraction (0.1%) is related to blocking collective communications. On the contrary, in miniAMR, 27% of total time belongs to MPI operations, in which 9.2% of the overall execution time belongs to only MPI_Allreduce, which means miniAMR performs more collective communications with the All-to-All pattern.

As we have demonstrated in Figs. 3 and 5, the All-to-All pattern is more prone to be affected by the network background traffic, and it has shown the flattest distribution when it is exposed to higher network background traffic in comparison to others. Moreover, the routing's effect can make its distribution bimodal. Looking over miniAMR's code, there are more than 10000 MPI_Allreduce operations which make the All-to-All pattern dominant. In Fig. 6b, the distribution becomes flat-topped that the main reason is because of its dominant All-to-All pattern, and its distribution is an aggregation of all of its dominant MPI_Allreduce communication latencies. Having said that, the routing algorithm will also play a role here because of the communication intensity of the All-to-All pattern, and we could expect a multi-modal distribution because of mixing many MPI_Allreduce distribution patterns.

6 Discussion

Our analysis of network latency distribution on a large-scale compute cluster with Dragonfly+ topology led to several insights. In terms of node allocation, there is a remarkable discrepancy between the *same group* and the two other allocation policies. When all the nodes are allocated to a single group, there is only one hop between every two nodes, which makes the communication minimally affected by the global background traffic. For the same reasons, in this case, the minimal and non-minimal paths are the same for the adaptive routing (in contrast with the two other cases). So, it exhibits a latency distribution with the shortest tail and the higher peak. Hence, if there are enough available idle nodes on the *same group*, it is worth allocating all the required nodes there.

When analyzing the latency distribution according to the communication patterns, the Broadcast is the pattern that has significant benefit from the locality of the job allocation; in fact, results show that Broadcast has the shortest tail and higher peak and is faster than Reduce and All-to-All for both *same group* and *same island* allocations. However, when nodes are allocated on *different islands*, Broadcast is highly affected by the background traffic, showing a very long tail compared to the cases with lower background traffic. Moreover, when the background traffic is very low, Broadcast's allocation performance on *different islands* can be as variable as allocation on the *same group*. Nevertheless, since the introduced background network utilization has been between 0.40 and 0.70 most of the time, there is very little chance of being in this situation. On the other hand, All-to-All is the pattern with the most extended tail when the job placement expresses little locality on Dragonfly+. Although its distribution when allocating on the *same group* is similar to the Reduce on the *same group*, when performing All-to-All on *different islands*, the distribution tail becomes very long due to the higher amount of communication in All-to-All.

Among all possible sources of performance variability, it has been shown that the background traffic is the key factor in the performance variability of different collectives on Dragonfly+. Usually, with the increase in background traffic, the communication time of collectives takes longer. Additionally, collective communication increases with higher background traffic and larger message sizes.

On top of that, we have experimentally observed a two-peak distribution of the communication latency typically due to the adaptive routing algorithm, which offloads some packets to an alternative, longer path under congestion. Finally, when analyzing the latency distribution of a real-world communication-intensive application, the distribution is mostly affected by its dominant communication pattern, and the overall average execution time increases with an increment in the network background traffic.

7   Conclusion

In this paper, we showed the performance variability of Dragonfly+ and analyzed the impact of background traffic on the long-tailed distribution for different communication patterns. We proposed a novel network background traffic estimation method that relies on the data gathered from the job scheduler's execution queue. We further showed the relation between performance variability and message size and demonstrated how the adaptive routing algorithm impacts the distribution. Overall, this study considers different metrics, including communication patterns, message sizes, job placement locality, and background traffic, to show how they contribute to performance variability and long-tail. We have experimentally validated our proposed background traffic heuristic on a large-scale cluster, a collection of pattern-based microbenchmarks, and two real-world applications.

The insights coming of this paper can help either the user or the scheduler to make more optimal decisions by first, estimating the network congestion according to the user-level information, and second, submitting the job at an appropriate time to have the minimum network interference.

Acknowledgments. This research has been partially funded by the European High-Performance Computing Joint Undertaking (JU) under grant agreement No. 956137 (LIGATE project).

References

1. Alzaid, Z.S.A., Bhowmik, S., Yuan, X., Lang, M.: Global link arrangement for practical dragonfly. In: Proceedings of the 34th ACM International Conference on Supercomputing, pp. 1–11 (2020)
2. Aseeri, S.A., Chatterjee, A.G., Verma, M.K., Keyes, D.E.: A scheduling policy to save 10% of communication time in parallel fast Fourier transform. Concurr. Comput. Pract. Exp. e6508 (2021)
3. Beni, M.S., Cosenza, B.: An analysis of performance variability on dragonfly+topology. In: 2022 IEEE International Conference on Cluster Computing (CLUSTER), pp. 500–501 (2022). https://doi.org/10.1109/CLUSTER51413.2022.00061
4. Besta, M., et al.: Fatpaths: routing in supercomputers and data centers when shortest paths fall short. In: International Conference for High Performance Computing, Networking, Storage and Analysis, SC 2020, pp. 1–18. IEEE (2020)
5. Bhatele, A., et al.: The case of performance variability on dragonfly-based systems. In: 2020 IEEE International Parallel and Distributed Processing Symposium (IPDPS), pp. 896–905. IEEE (2020)
6. Brown, K.A., Jain, N., Matsuoka, S., Schulz, M., Bhatele, A.: Interference between I/O and MPI traffic on fat-tree networks. In: Proceedings of the 47th International Conference on Parallel Processing, pp. 1–10 (2018)
7. Brown, K.A., et al.: A tunable implementation of quality-of-service classes for HPC networks. In: Chamberlain, B.L., Varbanescu, A.-L., Ltaief, H., Luszczek, P. (eds.) ISC High Performance 2021. LNCS, vol. 12728, pp. 137–156. Springer, Cham (2021). https://doi.org/10.1007/978-3-030-78713-4_8
8. Chaulagain, R.S., Liza, F.T., Chunduri, S., Yuan, X., Lang, M.: Achieving the performance of global adaptive routing using local information on dragonfly through deep learning. In: ACM/IEEE SC Tech Poster (2020)
9. Cheng, Q., Huang, Y., Bahadori, M., Glick, M., Rumley, S., Bergman, K.: Advanced routing strategy with highly-efficient fabric-wide characterization for optical integrated switches. In: 2018 20th International Conference on Transparent Optical Networks (ICTON), pp. 1–4. IEEE (2018)
10. Chester, D., et al.: StressBench: a configurable full system network and I/O benchmark framework. In: IEEE High Performance Extreme Computing Conference, York (2021)
11. Chunduri, S., et al.: Run-to-run variability on Xeon Phi based cray XC systems. In: Proceedings of the International Conference for High Performance Computing, Networking, Storage and Analysis, pp. 1–13 (2017)

12. De Sensi, D., Di Girolamo, S., Hoefler, T.: Mitigating network noise on dragonfly networks through application-aware routing. In: Proceedings of the International Conference for High Performance Computing, Networking, Storage and Analysis, pp. 1–32 (2019)
13. De Sensi, D., Di Girolamo, S., McMahon, K.H., Roweth, D., Hoefler, T.: An in-depth analysis of the slingshot interconnect. In: International Conference for High Performance Computing, Networking, Storage and Analysis, SC 2020, pp. 1–14. IEEE (2020)
14. Dean, J., Barroso, L.A.: The tail at scale. Commun. ACM **56**, 74–80 (2013). http://cacm.acm.org/magazines/2013/2/160173-the-tail-at-scale/fulltext
15. Faizian, P., et al.: TPR: traffic pattern-based adaptive routing for dragonfly networks. IEEE Trans. Multi-Scale Comput. Syst. **4**(4), 931–943 (2018)
16. Farmer, S., Skjellum, A., Grant, R.E., Brightwell, R.: MPI performance characterization on infiniband with fine-grain multithreaded communication. In: 2016 IEEE 18th International Conference on High Performance Computing and Communications; IEEE 14th International Conference on Smart City; IEEE 2nd International Conference on Data Science and Systems (HPCC), pp. 1102–1106. IEEE (2016)
17. Glass, C.J., Ni, L.M.: The turn model for adaptive routing. ACM SIGARCH Comput. Archit. News **20**(2), 278–287 (1992)
18. Grant, R.E., Dosanjh, M.G.F., Levenhagen, M.J., Brightwell, R., Skjellum, A.: Finepoints: partitioned multithreaded MPI communication. In: Weiland, M., Juckeland, G., Trinitis, C., Sadayappan, P. (eds.) ISC High Performance 2019. LNCS, vol. 11501, pp. 330–350. Springer, Cham (2019). https://doi.org/10.1007/978-3-030-20656-7_17
19. Groves, T., Gu, Y., Wright, N.J.: Understanding performance variability on the Aries dragonfly network. In: 2017 IEEE International Conference on Cluster Computing (CLUSTER), pp. 809–813. IEEE (2017)
20. Hashmi, J.M., Xu, S., Ramesh, B., Bayatpour, M., Subramoni, H., Panda, D.K.D.K.: Machine-agnostic and communication-aware designs for MPI on emerging architectures. In: 2020 IEEE International Parallel and Distributed Processing Symposium (IPDPS), pp. 32–41. IEEE (2020)
21. Heitmann, K., et al.: The outer rim simulation: a path to many-core supercomputers. Astrophys. J. Suppl. Ser. **245**(1), 16 (2019)
22. Hemmert, K.S., et al.: Evaluating trade-offs in potential exascale interconnect technologies (2020)
23. Heroux, M.A., et al.: Improving performance via mini-applications. Sandia National Laboratories, Technical report. SAND2009-5574, vol. 3 (2009)
24. Hunold, S., Carpen-Amarie, A.: Reproducible MPI benchmarking is still not as easy as you think. IEEE Trans. Parallel Distrib. Syst. **27**(12), 3617–3630 (2016)
25. IBM Spectrum MPI, accelerating high-performance application parallelization. https://www.ibm.com/products/spectrum-mpi. Accessed 01 May 2022
26. Jeannot, E., Mansouri, F., Mercier, G.: A hierarchical model to manage hardware topology in MPI applications. In: Proceedings of the 24th European MPI Users' Group Meeting, pp. 1–11 (2017)
27. Kang, Y., Wang, X., Lan, Z.: Q-adaptive: a multi-agent reinforcement learning based routing on dragonfly network. In: Proceedings of the 30th International Symposium on High-Performance Parallel and Distributed Computing, pp. 189–200 (2020)
28. Kang, Y., Wang, X., McGlohon, N., Mubarak, M., Chunduri, S., Lan, Z.: Modeling and analysis of application interference on dragonfly+. In: Proceedings of the 2019

ACM SIGSIM Conference on Principles of Advanced Discrete Simulation, pp. 161–172 (2019). ISBN 9781450367233

29. Kaplan, F., Tuncer, O., Leung, V.J., Hemmert, S.K., Coskun, A.K.: Unveiling the interplay between global link arrangements and network management algorithms on dragonfly networks. In: 2017 17th IEEE/ACM International Symposium on Cluster, Cloud and Grid Computing (CCGRID), pp. 325–334. IEEE (2017)

30. Kim, J., Dally, W.J., Scott, S., Abts, D.: Technology-driven, highly-scalable dragonfly topology. In: 2008 International Symposium on Computer Architecture, pp. 77–88. IEEE (2008)

31. Kirch, W.: Pearson's correlation coefficient. In: Encyclopedia of Public Health, pp. 1090–1091 (2008)

32. Kousha, P., et al.: INAM: cross-stack profiling and analysis of communication in MPI-based applications. In: Practice and Experience in Advanced Research Computing, pp. 1–11 (2021)

33. Liu, Y., Liu, Z., Kettimuthu, R., Rao, N., Chen, Z., Foster, I.: Data transfer between scientific facilities - bottleneck analysis, insights and optimizations. In: 2019 19th IEEE/ACM International Symposium on Cluster, Cloud and Grid Computing (CCGRID), pp. 122–131 (2019)

34. Marconi100, the new accelerated system. https://www.hpc.cineca.it/hardware/marconi100

35. McGlohon, N., et al.: Exploration of congestion control techniques on dragonfly-class HPC networks through simulation. In: 2021 International Workshop on Performance Modeling, Benchmarking and Simulation of High Performance Computer Systems (PMBS), pp. 40–50. IEEE (2021)

36. Michelogiannakis, G., Ibrahim, K.Z., Shalf, J., Wilke, J.J., Knight, S., Kenny, J.P.: Aphid: hierarchical task placement to enable a tapered fat tree topology for lower power and cost in HPC networks. In: 2017 17th IEEE/ACM International Symposium on Cluster, Cloud and Grid Computing (CCGRID), pp. 228–237. IEEE (2017)

37. Mollah, Md.A., Faizian, P., Rahman, Md.S., Yuan, X., Pakin, S., Lang, M.: A comparative study of topology design approaches for HPC interconnects. In: 2018 18th IEEE/ACM International Symposium on Cluster, Cloud and Grid Computing (CCGRID), pp. 392–401. IEEE (2018)

38. Mollah, Md.A., et al.: Modeling universal globally adaptive load-balanced routing. ACM Trans. Parallel Comput. 6(2) (2019)

39. Navaridas, J., Lant, J., Pascual, J.A., Lujan, M., Goodacre, J.: Design exploration of multi-tier interconnection networks for exascale systems. In: Proceedings of the 48th International Conference on Parallel Processing, pp. 1–10 (2019)

40. Newaz, Md.N., Mollah, Md.A., Faizian, P., Tong, Z.: Improving adaptive routing performance on large scale Megafly topology. In: 2021 IEEE/ACM 21st International Symposium on Cluster, Cloud and Internet Computing (CCGrid), pp. 406–416. IEEE (2021)

41. OSU micro-benchmarks 5.8 (2021). https://mvapich.cse.ohio-state.edu/benchmarks/

42. Ponce, M., et al.: Deploying a top-100 supercomputer for large parallel workloads: the Niagara supercomputer. In: Proceedings of the Practice and Experience in Advanced Research Computing on Rise of the Machines (Learning), pp. 1–8 (2019)

43. POWER9 processor chip. https://www.ibm.com/it-infrastructure/power/power9

44. Rahman, Md.S., Bhowmik, S., Ryasnianskiy, Y., Yuan, X., Lang, M.: Topology-custom UGAL routing on dragonfly. In: Proceedings of the International Confer-

ence for High Performance Computing, Networking, Storage and Analysis, SC 2019. Association for Computing Machinery, New York (2019). ISBN 9781450362290

45. Rocher-Gonzalez, J., Escudero-Sahuquillo, J., Garcia, P.J., Quiles, F.J., Mora, G.: Efficient congestion management for high-speed interconnects using adaptive routing. In: 2019 19th IEEE/ACM International Symposium on Cluster, Cloud and Grid Computing (CCGRID), pp. 221–230. IEEE (2019)

46. Ruhela, A., Xu, S., Manian, K.V., Subramoni, H., Panda, D.K.: Analyzing and understanding the impact of interconnect performance on HPC, big data, and deep learning applications: a case study with infiniband EDR and HDR. In: 2020 IEEE International Parallel and Distributed Processing Symposium Workshops (IPDPSW), pp. 869–878. IEEE (2020)

47. Shpiner, A., Haramaty, Z., Eliad, S., Zdornov, V., Gafni, B., Zahavi, E.: Dragonfly+: low cost topology for scaling datacenters. In: 2017 IEEE 3rd International Workshop on High-Performance Interconnection Networks in the Exascale and Big-Data Era (HiPINEB), pp. 1–8. IEEE (2017)

48. Skinner, D., Kramer, W.: Understanding the causes of performance variability in HPC workloads. In: IEEE International 2005 Proceedings of the IEEE Workload Characterization Symposium, pp. 137–149. IEEE (2005)

49. Slurm, Slurm's job allocation policy for dragonfly network (2021). https://github. com/SchedMD/slurm/blob/master/src/plugins/select/linear/select_linear.c

50. Smith, S.A., et al.: Mitigating inter-job interference using adaptive flow-aware routing. In: International Conference for High Performance Computing, Networking, Storage and Analysis, SC 2018, pp. 346–360. IEEE (2018)

51. Subramoni, H., Lu, X., Panda, D.K.: A scalable network-based performance analysis tool for MPI on large-scale HPC systems. In: 2017 IEEE International Conference on Cluster Computing (CLUSTER), pp. 354–358. IEEE (2017)

52. Suresh, K.K., Ramesh, B., Ghazimirsaeed, S.M., Bayatpour, M., Hashmi, J., Panda, D.K.: Performance characterization of network mechanisms for non-contiguous data transfers in MPI. In: 2020 IEEE International Parallel and Distributed Processing Symposium Workshops (IPDPSW), pp. 896–905. IEEE (2020)

53. Tang, W., Desai, N., Buettner, D., Lan, Z.: Analyzing and adjusting user runtime estimates to improve job scheduling on the Blue Gene/P. In: 2010 IEEE International Symposium on Parallel & Distributed Processing (IPDPS), pp. 1–11. IEEE (2010)

54. Teh, M.Y., Wilke, J.J., Bergman, K., Rumley, S.: Design space exploration of the dragonfly topology. In: Kunkel, J.M., Yokota, R., Taufer, M., Shalf, J. (eds.) ISC High Performance 2017. LNCS, vol. 10524, pp. 57–74. Springer, Cham (2017). https://doi.org/10.1007/978-3-319-67630-2_5

55. Temuçin, Y.H., Sojoodi, A.H., Alizadeh, P., Kitor, B., Afsahi, A.: Accelerating deep learning using interconnect-aware UCX communication for MPI collectives. IEEE Micro **42**(2), 68–76 (2022)

56. Top500, MARCONI-100. https://www.top500.org/system/179845/. Accessed 01 May 2022

57. Wang, X., Mubarak, M., Kang, Y., Ross, R.B., Lan, Z.: Union: an automatic workload manager for accelerating network simulation. In: 2020 IEEE International Parallel and Distributed Processing Symposium (IPDPS), pp. 821–830 (2020)

58. Wang, X., Mubarak, M., Yang, X., Ross, R.B., Lan, Z.: Trade-off study of localizing communication and balancing network traffic on a dragonfly system. In: 2018 IEEE International Parallel and Distributed Processing Symposium (IPDPS), pp. 1113–1122. IEEE (2018)

59. Wang, X., Yang, X., Mubarak, M., Ross, R.B., Lan, Z.: A preliminary study of intra-application interference on dragonfly network. In: 2017 IEEE International Conference on Cluster Computing (CLUSTER), pp. 643–644. IEEE (2017)
60. Wen, K., et al.: Flexfly: enabling a reconfigurable dragonfly through silicon photonics. In: Proceedings of the International Conference for High Performance Computing, Networking, Storage and Analysis, SC 2016, pp. 166–177. IEEE (2016)
61. Wilke, J.J., Kenny, J.P.: Opportunities and limitations of quality-of-service in message passing applications on adaptively routed dragonfly and fat tree networks. In: 2020 IEEE International Conference on Cluster Computing (CLUSTER), pp. 109–118. IEEE (2020)
62. Yoo, A.B., Jette, M.A., Grondona, M.: SLURM: simple Linux utility for resource management. In: Feitelson, D., Rudolph, L., Schwiegelshohn, U. (eds.) JSSPP 2003. LNCS, vol. 2862, pp. 44–60. Springer, Heidelberg (2003). https://doi.org/10.1007/10968987_3
63. Zahn, F., Fröning, H.: On network locality in MPI-based HPC applications. In: 49th International Conference on Parallel Processing-ICPP, pp. 1–10 (2020)
64. Zar, J.H.: Spearman rank correlation. In: Encyclopedia of Biostatistics, vol. 7 (2005)
65. Zhang, Y., Groves, T., Cook, B., Wright, N.J., Coskun, A.K.: Quantifying the impact of network congestion on application performance and network metrics. In: 2020 IEEE International Conference on Cluster Computing (CLUSTER), pp. 162–168. IEEE (2020)
66. Zhang, Y., Tuncer, O., Kaplan, F., Olcoz, K., Leung, V.J., Coskun, A.K.: Levelspread: a new job allocation policy for dragonfly networks. In: 2018 IEEE International Parallel and Distributed Processing Symposium (IPDPS), pp. 1123–1132. IEEE (2018)
67. Zhou, Z., et al.: Improving batch scheduling on Blue Gene/Q by relaxing 5D torus network allocation constraints. In: 2015 IEEE International Parallel and Distributed Processing Symposium, pp. 439–448. IEEE (2015)

MCCBench: A C10M Benchmark Oriented to Interactive Network Services

Hui Song[1] , Wenli Zhang[1](✉) , and Mingyu Chen[1,2,3]

[1] State Key Lab of Processors, Institute of Computing Technology,
Chinese Academy of Sciences, Beijing, China
{songhui,zhangwl,cmy}@ict.ac.cn
[2] University of Chinese Academy of Sciences, Beijing, China
[3] Zhongguancun Laboratory, Beijing, China

Abstract. With the explosive growth of IoT and other interactive network services, billions of devices are now connected, leading to highly fluctuating traffic and diverse QoS requirements for servers. This, coupled with the C10M problem, means benchmarks for interactive services should be able to handle millions of concurrency, bursty load and multiple QoS evaluation. However, existing general benchmarks for network services cannot fully meet these requirements.

To address this issue, we propose MCCBench as a benchmark for high concurrent interactive network services. MCCBench includes a methodology for load generation, service framework, and service performance evaluation, allowing for the measurement of over 10 million concurrent connections, bursty loads, and labeling of requests with different service qualities. The performance evaluation metrics include tail latency measured on the server side, and long-lived concurrent connections. To implement MCCBench, we have developed an open-source toolset called MCCBench-IoT, which includes a load generator, an IoT service system based on a user-space network stack, and an accurate monitor for measuring tail latency.

We verified MCCBench by building a testbed with MCCBench-IoT to emulate a typical IoT service, successfully testing tail latency under a concurrency of 10.2 million on a single server node. The testbed was scaled to 300 million concurrency with cluster configuration. By providing a comprehensive benchmark for high-concurrent interactive network services, MCCBench can help improve the quality of service for such services and enable better decision-making for network infrastructure design and optimization.

Keywords: Benchmark · Interactive network services · Concurrency · Tail latency · IoT

1 Introduction

The interactive network services have been developing fast in recent years. Consequently, billions of terminal devices [1] are created and penetrate into daily

A. Gainaru et al. (Eds.): Bench 2022, LNCS 13852, pp. 143–159, 2023.
https://doi.org/10.1007/978-3-031-31180-2_9

life, including smart home, connected vehicles, social networks and online shopping [1–3]. Notably, the isolation demands of COVID-19 also promotes the development of online medical consultations [10]. For servers, the large-scale terminals and user activities have sparked the ever-increasing concurrency, with fluctuations and variety of workloads, which impacted on server performance and user experience directly [4,5]. For great commercial and research significance, it's necessary to apply a suitable benchmark to evaluate the server ability on handling these properties:

- **Mass Terminal Services.** Simply in the smart home field, the worldwide smart devices have grown 11.7% in 2021 compared to 2020 with more than 8.95 billion devices shipped [13]. The services are expected to support millions upon millions of connections increasing from the devices. To save the server investment cost, the concurrency of a server is expected to be improved from the current C10K [17] to C10M [18], which means handling over 10 million concurrent TCP connections. There have been a few preliminary achievements [25,26] on C10M.
- **Instantaneous Requests Aggregated.** Because the human activities are temporal clustering like converged commuting or collective attention, the services such as connected vehicles and social networks may receive massive requests aggregation for an instant called bursts [8,9]. For example, 99% of the taxi signal inter-arrival times (about 500) of New York Grand Central Terminal is within 2 s in a day [9].
- **Differentiated Service Demands.** The various types of interactive services make the requirements for QoS different [31]. When shopping online, the search, query and purchase requests indicate high latency sensitivity and require real-time response from the server as fast as possible, while message notifications do not.

Existing benchmarks can be classified into two categories based on usage modes: **1. Representative workloads.** This category refers to the representative workloads produced by complete toolsets or datasets [11], like Tailbench [32] and Treadmill [33]. The test implementation depends on the toolsets or datasets given, or with a minor modifications. Such benchmarks are intuitive and convenient, but the usage scenarios and timeliness are limited. The performance metrics involved in the interactive service are diverse and interrelated, including but not limited to the memory and network stack. The combination of different factors may cause considerable differences. Thus the interactive services benchmark can't be represented by finite workloads. **2. Specification.** Benchmarks of specification propose algorithms or methods to define the workload format, service framework and evaluation criteria [12]. For example, TPC-C [15], TPC-H [14] and Terasort [16] belong to this category. Their workloads and toolsets are optional and customizable by the users according to the methodology. The general character can be defined abstractly and uniformly. So a benchmark of specification is more in line with the interactive services. However, the specification benchmark satisfying the three requirements simultaneously has not yet been proposed.

For interactive network services with millions of concurrency, we have presented a C10M specification benchmark named MCCBench. Users refer to the definition methods of workloads, service framework and performance evaluation to test respective servers. MCCBench can even be extended to hundreds of millions of concurrency with multiple server nodes. For MCCBench implementation and verification, we have also developed and integrated an open source toolset called MCCBench-IoT.

(i) **MCCBench.** MCCBench is composed of the methodology to define the load generation, service function and service performance evaluation. In terms of load generation, it defines workloads with massive long-lived TCP connections, which is oriented to interactive services with over 10 million concurrency. To simulate the instantaneous traffic aggregation, the repeatable burst generation is also defined. For different latency sensitivities of the requests, MCCBench sets priority labels in the request payload. The service framework is defined to afford concurrency of over 10 million and identify the request priority by default. After configurable computation, all the requests query in-memory database in the order of priority scheduling. The database query operations are customized by users. Considering the user experience, the performance evaluation criteria based on the tail latency and concurrency have also been defined: the server-side tail latency under the given concurrency and the maximum concurrency under the tail latency threshold.

(ii) **MCCBench-IoT Toolset.** MCCBench-IoT is proposed as a case to show the MCCBench implementation on IoT scenarios in detail and intuitively. It consists of a load generator MCC [24] upgraded based on MCC V1.0 [20], and an IoT service IoTEPServer [38]. MCC and IoTEPServer are all developed on user-space TCP/IP stacks and can afford the concurrency of over 10 million. IoTEPServer identifies the request priority and schedules them to randomly query multiple Redis processes on a single server, similar to the Redis cluster. We also introduced a monitor HCMonitor to calculate the response tail latency in real time on server side [41]. MCCBench-IoT has strong augmentability, which can also be used to benchmark on more applications with a few simple modifications. For example, MCC can be extended to the workload generation for web application like Lighttpd by altering payload format. HCMonitor can be used for web or IM (Instant Messaging) traffic test by changing the configuration.

With MCCBench implementation on MCCBench-IoT system, we have measured the tail latency (20.27 ms) of the IoT requests querying Redis under 10.2 million concurrent connections, and the upper limit of concurrency up to 12 million under tail latency threshold 50 ms. We also tested the number of active connections and latency in server cluster with over 300 million concurrency. The results verify the rationality and effectiveness of MCCBench.

2   Motivation

2.1   Benchmark Design

Benchmarks are used to provide reference test for service performance optimization, with the fundamental purpose of improving user experience. Now the user experience has been influenced by millions of concurrency, fluctuating aggregation and different QoS levels in interactive services. To keep up with these advances, a measurement standard benchmark for them needs support:

High Concurrency Measurement. The existing C10M achievements suggest it will benefit for cloud service providers (like Google Cloud [27]) with a scale of millions of users. It also brings a demand for service benchmarks on affording high concurrency, as the concurrency will be an important metric affecting the user experience in the large-scale services. So we design a benchmark in adaption to over 10 million concurrency flexibly to save the cost on server performance optimization. It can be scaled to test the concurrency of over 100 million for more universality.

Bursts Handling Measurement. Owing to factors such as commuting or social focus, the interactive traffic indicates substantial requests sent to the servers in some instant periods, which is called bursts [8,9]. It's essential for a service benchmark to design the method of burst generation that conforms to the interactive workload characteristics.

Priority Scheduling Measurement. The various interactive service types make the request sensitivities for response latency different. In other words, the requests have unequal QoS (Quality of Service) priorities. To restore the scenario of multiple QoS priority, the benchmarks for interactive services should simulate multi-priority workloads, as well as their identification, scheduling and performance testing.

2.2   Benchmark Implementation

Since the benchmark for interactive network services is based on measurement standard, it needs tools to verify the feasibility. To provide a reference for the benchmark implementation, we investigate the existing tools in Table 1. Benchmark tools can be divided into two categories: hardware-based and software-based, and three challenges can be revealed:

C10M Challenge. Due to performance bottleneck of kernel stack, the general tools like wrk anf Apache benchmark [30] produce concurrency up to C10K on a single server. The upper limit for concurrency generated by MCC is around 3 million. The C10M is inaccessible to them yet. Even though we can upgrade MCC V1.0, the general service for handling C10M is still missing. For example, Redis-server [22] and Nginx [23] handle concurrency up to C10K on a single server.

Economic Applicability Challenge. The load generators based on specific hardware such as Spirent TestCenter [29] can generate millions of concurrent connections, burst loads and requests with multiple QoS priorities. It's to be confirmed (TBC) whether they support C10M concurrency. They are not open source, and expensive. Meanwhile, they are developed by firms, which leads to a lack of flexibility. Thus the existing hardware-based tools have not achieved the economic applicability on interactive service benchmarking.

Server-Side Measurement Challenge. Millions of concurrency may result in hundreds of thousands millions of requests per second (RPS). Due to the processing delay and queuing in client side stack, the test gap between the client side and server side can be 87% under 1.2 million [41]. From the perspective of benchmark precision, it's lacking in tools measuring the response delay under high concurrency on server side.

Table 1. Related work to benchmark tools.

Category	Benchmark tools	C10M (currently)	Repeatable bursts (currently)	QoS evaluation (currently)	Comments
Hardware -based	Sprient	TBC	√	√	Expensive (>$100,000)
	IXIA [28]	TBC	√	√	Expensive (>$100,000)
Software -based	Netperf [21]	×	√	×	Concurrency not configurable
	Wrk [19]	×	×	×	Close-loop, poor concurrency scalability
	MCC V1.0	×	√	√	Open-loop, millions of concurrency
	Redis-server	×	√	×	close-loop, poor concurrency scalability
	Nginx	×	√	×	close-loop, poor concurrency scalability

To evaluate the user experience economically and accurately, we are promoted to develop a open source toolset implementing the benchmark methodology as a typical study case. The toolset will meet the following requirements: C10M workloads generating, serving and server-side monitoring.

3   MCCBench Design

To cover the whole service system composed of client, server and test side completely, MCCBench proposes the methodology for load generation, service framework and performance evaluation. The setting rules and working principles of parameters are defined for load generation. For the server side, MCCBench designs a default service framework adaptive to high concurrency, fluctuating traffic and QoS-aware. The service performance evaluation criteria is based on concurrency and tail latency.

3.1 Workload Definition

In large-scale interactive network, the factors directly affecting the service performance are complex and diverse. At the beginning phases of the design, the test cycle T is defined at the as the effective test time of each round. It's used for periodic statistics and results output. We firstly determine the workload parameters and the configuration rules in Fig. 1 based on the workload features.

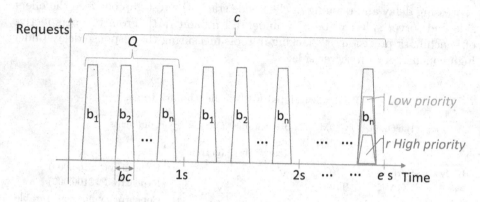

Fig. 1. MCCBench workload definition.

High Concurrency. First, we need to define the basic workload parameters: concurrency and RPS throughput, which is positively related to the service response latency. The concurrent connections c means the number of sustained connections between clients and servers in every T. To be consistent with the high concurrency of C10M, c is specified more than 10 million. The request packet length l can be configured. We refer to the request sending period of each connection as an epoch e, to flexibly control the RPS. Considering e is measured in seconds, the RPS defined as Q is

$$Q = c/e \tag{1}$$

Bursty Loads. Second, sending mode of the requests need to be determined. To measure the server capacity of handling bursts, MCCBench prefers to forming repeatable bursty traffic for server. According to [9], the workloads indicate substantial requests to services in milliseconds, which is called a burst. For each burst, b is the number of requests sent by the client instantaneously, and bc is the duration width of b. Q requests in each second are sent to the server in several bursts instead of evenly within 1 s. Therefore, the conditional constraint for burst b is

$$b \leq Q \tag{2}$$

Generally b is modified in proportion to c. A burst must be sent within the limited time bc to ensure the effectiveness of polymerization pressure. The bc is determined by the specific needs of service users. For example, if we require a burst to be sent in about 100 ms, the default bc is 100 ± 5 ms.

Multi-priority. In the real interactive scenario, the requests sensitivities for response latency are different. In accordance with this, MCCBench designs the requests composed of multiple priority. Given the RPS Q and the high priority ratio r, the requests of high priority per second Hr is

$$Hr = Q * r \tag{3}$$

We set the label in the pre-defined field of the request payload to represent the priority. There are many distributions of the request priorities in a burst. The scheduling of each priority based on the distribution will inevitably affect the response latency. We define the requests of multiple priority are evenly distributed in each burst so as to approach the real network traffic.

3.2   Service Framework

The service framework of MCCBench is designed to be interactive, which can handle workloads with high concurrency, high burst and multiple priority. For convenience of implementation and description, we choose the requests querying in-memory database as the default service in the measurement. The service framework extracts the random contents in the request payload and handles them with computation operation as the key to query the database. The specific computation procedures can be customized by users. Each request queries the database with read/write operations (configurable). The access scope of the requests is all the database processes on the server node or database cluster. To simulate multi-priority processing, the framework is defined to identify the label in request payload to schedule the high priority requests Hr every second, which take precedence to access database and respond. The scheduling and disposal of each priority are also configured by users. Response packet length can also be configured. Users can refer to the working principle of the service framework for own applications.

3.3   Performance Evaluation Criteria

With the explicit design of test parameters and service, we specify a criterion for the evaluation of service performance. Under high concurrency, a minor part of response latency is higher than the average. This part is called tail latency. For the massive distributed systems, the impact of tail latency is particularly serious. For example, in search engines like Google, the requests may be sent to thousands of servers, and the search system is forced to wait for the tail response before replying to users, which greatly affects the user experience [34, 35]. Thus, we measure performance in terms of tail latency measured on server side and concurrent connections:

1. **Tail latency:** Given the concurrent connections c, we evaluate the CDF of response latency, and tail latency TL. The tail delay percentile P is user-defined.

2. **Concurrent connections** : To test the maximum concurrency of a server, we change the concurrent connections until the tail latency reaches the threshold Th. Th is also user configurable.

4   MCCBench Implementation

For the first MCCBench implementation case, we have developed and integrated an open source toolset MCCBench-IoT, including a load generator named MCC, an IoT service–IoTEPServer and a real-time performance monitor called HCMonitor. We will show MCCBench-IoT system tested with MCCBench, which represents MCCbench benchmarking on a typical IoT scenario.

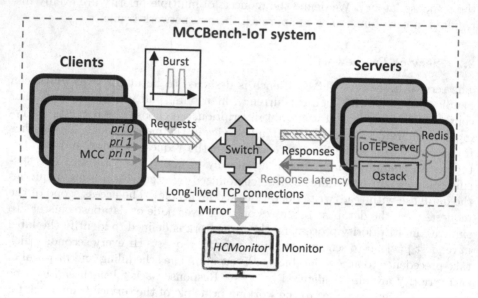

Fig. 2. MCCBench test case of IoTEPServer service.

4.1   Workloads

According to MCCBench methods, we design workloads for IoTEPServer in Table 2: 1) TL test under given c. We define the 99th percentile latency as the tail latency ($P = 99$). Because the heartbeat packets frequency of a connection in real IoT services is usually once a minute, so e is 60 s. Taking $T = 60$ s as a test cycle of HCMonitor. Each request payload length is 140 bytes. We configure the Q to be sent with a burst within 100 ± 5 ms. Thus only one burst is generated per second. To perform the QoS evaluation, MCC generates requests of two priorities. The requests are classified to queries standing for high priority demanding responses, and heartbeats for low priority. The ratio r is set to 5%. The remaining 95% are heartbeat requests for connections long-lived, which don't need to be responded. The packets of the two priorities are evenly distributed in a burst. 2) Upper limit of c test under Th. Since the average reaction speed of human body is greater than 0.1 s, we set Th = 50 ms as the threshold from the perspective of good user experience [36]. With other parameter configurations remain unchanged as the TL test, we keep b proportional to the modifying c until TL has reached to 50 ms.

Table 2. MCCBench-IoT workload configurations.

Parameter	Configuration	Meaning
c	-	Concurrency
e	60 s	The epoch of each connection
l	140 bytes	The request payload length
b	c/e	Burst
bc	100 ± 5 ms	Duration width of a burst
r	0.05	The ratio of high priority
P	99	Tail latency percentile
TL	-	Tail latency
Th	-	Tail latency threshold

4.2 Architecture

As shown in Fig. 2, the MCCBench-IoT service system works on processing multi-priority IoT requests to query the Redis, and responding to clients.

MCC. MCC is a highly scalable network load generator, which can generate bursts and multi-priority requests. To solve the C10M challenge on workload generating and scale to over 100 million concurrency, we analyzed the performance bottlenecks of the original MCC. Then we expanded its functionality and performance from two aspects: **1. multi-core scalability.** One of the issues is MCC can't obtain linear performance growth with more than 10 cores, We modify the load allocation algorithm to gain better balance among multi-cores. The memory configuration strategy has been redesigned for the improved algorithm. It now produces over 10 million concurrency with 15 cores on a single server. **2. distributed scalability.** MCCBench-IoT is designed to support over 100 million concurrency, so as to simulate real scenarios in large-scale interactive networks. Thus we developed the MCC distributed system. At the same time, to maintain the load pressure at server side, we realized burst aggregation among multiple nodes by optimizing the synchronization, so that all the bursts produced by distributed nodes can be sent synchronously and aggregated destined to servers as shown in Fig. 3.

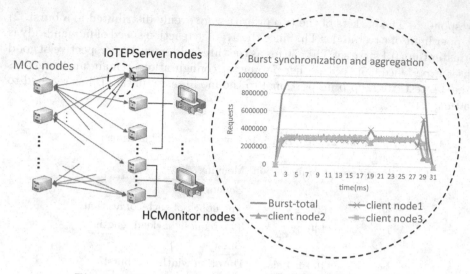

Fig. 3. MCC multi-node synchronization and aggregation.

IoTEPServer. IoTEPServer is an IoT service with Redis query. IoTEPServer correctly parses priority labels in request payload. As shown in Fig. 4, we improve the IoTEPServer performance by adopting zero-copy I/O calling based on the user-level TCP/IP stack Qstack [39]. A distribution framework D-W is developed on multi-thread for scheduling requests of multiple priority. The D-W consists of several distributors and workers, between which there are lock-free and fully interconnect queues. To simulate the K-V query common in the interactive services, the D-W connects with multiple Redis processes on a server, similar to the Redis cluster. Therefore, each request can query any Redis process through D-W for read or write operations. For example, after a read operation in Redis-server 2, a request continues writing and reading once in Redis-server 4 through D-W. All the requests query the Redis, but the server only responds to query requests. IoTEPServer can serve more than 10 concurrent connections on a single node with these optimization measures.

HCMonitor. To measure the real-time performance with little interference, we have applied an open source tool HCMonitor [40]. HCMonitor is a monitor system for high concurrent network services, which is developed on user-level and estimates response latency from requests input to responses output, called server-side latency. The measurement of HCMonitor is transparent for network services by switch mirroring traffic, and finally displays the real-time results including latency CDF distribution, concurrency, and average delay, etc.

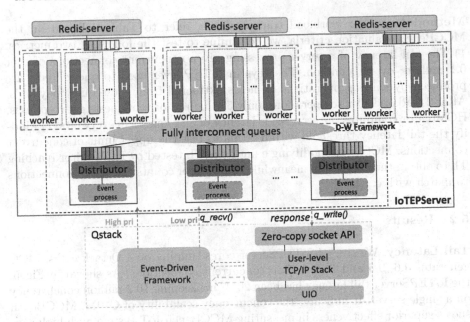

Fig. 4. IoTEPServer Architecture.

4.3 Case Study

Example: Figure 2 indicates a case to illustrate the MCCBench method: 1. The users determine the test cases based on MCCBench: TL test of IoTEPServer querying Redis under c = 10.8 million. 2. The parameters in Table 2 are given. MCC generates 10.8 million concurrent connections. The RPS is Q = 180000. b is equal to Q (b = 180000). 3. In a burst, the requests of each priority are evenly distributed. 4. IoTEPServer extracts the keys from all the request payloads for XOR operations, then apply the keys to query Redis undergo two read and one write operations. The server responds to the high priority requests. 5. HCMonitor calculates the response delay CDF within every 60s, and read the tail latency. Compare it with 50 ms, and draw a conclusion whether it meets the performance requirements.

5 Evaluation

5.1 Experiment Setup

Testbed. To verify the effectiveness of MCCBench, we have built a testbed as Fig. 2 composed of a client, a server and a monitor node with MCCBench-IoT deployed. Each server is equipped with Intel (R) Xeon(R) 6130 CPU and Intel 82599ES 10 Gbps NICs. There are also 16 Redis processes connected with IoTEPServer on the server node. The 3 servers are connected with a HW-C16800 switch.

Methodology. For workload configurations, refer to Table 2. Based on the MCCBench evaluation criteria, we determine to test the following two metrics: 1) The tail latency of a server processing given concurrent connections of over 0.1 million~over 10 million. The keys in IoTEPSever used to query Redis are produced by shifting operations on fields extracted from the request payloads. After 2 read and 1 write operations, only 5% high priority requests get responses. HCMonitor computes the server-side latency of all requests in every 60 s. 2) Modify the tail latency threshold within 50 ms to test the upper limit of concurrent connections. MCC keep modifying c until the TL tested by HCMonitor reaching Th to obtain the maximum, meanwhile HCMonitor counts the active connections to match with c.

5.2   Results

Tail Latency. We start 4 IoTEPServer cores running on 4 Qstack cores. MCC generates 0.6, 9.6 and 10.2 million concurrent connections. As shown in Fig. 5, the IoTEPServer tail latency has been 20.27 ms keeping 10.2 million concurrency on a single server. It indicates the concurrency scalability of C10M. MCCBench shows superior effectiveness in measuring MCCBench-IoT system with high concurrency of over 10 million.

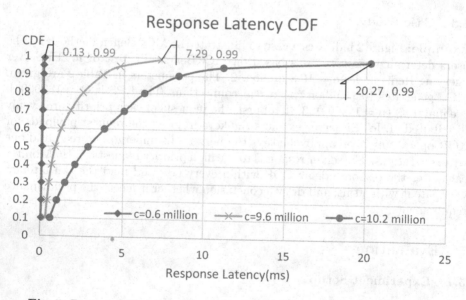

Fig. 5. Response latency CDF of the IoT service under given concurrency.

Concurrency. We modify c according to the TL to approach the upper limit of concurrency. The results are shown in Fig. 6. The maximum c is gradually increased from 7.2 million to 12 million as the Th changes from 3 ms to

50 ms, and the TL is positively correlated with the concurrency, which increases from 2.30 ms to 49.93 ms. The latency CDF of the IoTEPServer shows a tail of 49.93 ms when processing 12 million concurrent connections. Therefore, it can be concluded that the IoTEPServer can carry up to 12 million concurrency under the tail latency threshold 50 ms. MCCBench has successfully tested the upper limit of concurrent connections in an IoT service.

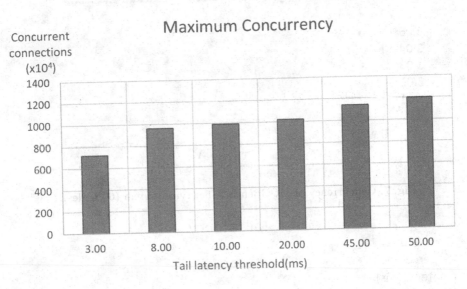

Fig. 6. Concurrency trend of IoT service with tail latency threshold.

5.3 Expansion Experiment

In terms of high concurrency adaptability, MCCBench can also expand to hundreds of millions of connections. To verify this feature, we applied MCCBench on the MCCBench-IoT service system built by 60 server nodes with Hygon C86 7285 CPU, which aims to dynamically testing the real-time performance. There are 30 client nodes keeping 300 million long-lived TCP connections to 30 server nodes every minute through switches. Each MCC on client node generates a burst per second. The bursts from multiple client nodes are aggregated to each server in about 100 ms through synchronization. The workload includes 5% of high priority requests and 95% of heartbeat packets. Each server node has deployed IoTEPServer running on Qstack and querying Redis with keys extracted directly from the request payloads.

We dynamically draw the graph of concurrent connections and tail latency with the running time. The Fig. 7 shows the trend of the long-lived connections in every minute. It can be concluded that the concurrent connections can be stabilized at more than 300 million. In Fig. 8, it indicates the trend of the tail latency

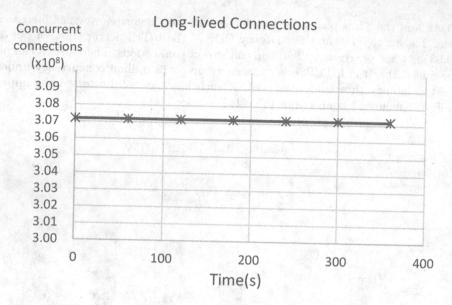

Fig. 7. Concurrency of MCCBench-IoT service system (60 nodes).

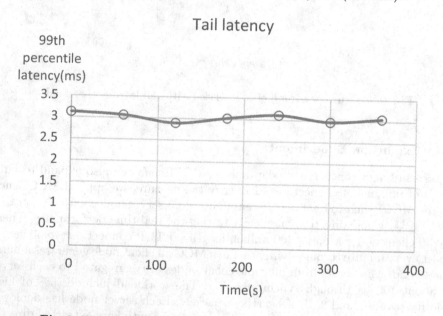

Fig. 8. Tail latency of MCCBench-IoT service system (60 nodes).

changing. It can be seen that when the number of concurrent connections is stable at over 300 million, the tail latency is around 3 ms. Therefore, MCCBench can be applied to the performance test of services with over 100 million concurrency.

6   Conclusion

MCCBench is a benchmark for the prospect of high concurrent interactive network services at over 10 million connections. It provides a test methodology involving in load generation, service function and service performance evaluation based on the server-side tail latency and sustained concurrency, for interactive scenarios like IoT or web services. A toolset MCCBench-IoT is developed for implementation, including a load generator tool MCC and a default service IoTEPServer. MCCBench measures the server performance in dealing with bursts and multiple priorities. Experiments show the concurrency of 10.2 million on single server node under the tail latency threshold in emulated IoT service testbed, and the scale to server cluster with over 300 million concurrency.

In the future, we plan to expand the MCCBench methodology of workload generation with various statistical distributions, so as to test a wider range of interactive service scenarios. The load model of MCCBench-IoT for more interactive services need to be developed, which is not limited to IoT services.

Acknowledgment. Thanks to Ms. Xiaohong Wang for her valuable support and suggestions on the use of OneITLab. The work was supported by the National Key Research and Development Plan of China under Grant No. 2022YFB4500403, the Strategic Priority Research Program of the Chinese Academy of Sciences under Grant No. XDA0320000 and XDA0320300.

References

1. Smarter Planet. https://www.ibm.com/ibm/history/ibm100/us/en/icons/smarterplanet/. Accessed 4 Jul 2022
2. Global Smart Transportation Market Size Report (2030). https://www.grandviewresearch.com/industry-analysis/smart-transportation-market. Accessed 4 Jul 2022
3. Rzadca, K., et al: Autopilot: workload autoscaling at Google. In: Proceedings of the Fifteenth European Conference on Computer Systems (EuroSys 2020). Association for Computing Machinery, pp. 1–16. 2020. https://doi.org/10.1145/3342195.3387524
4. Botta, A., De Donato, W., Persico, V., Pescapé, A.: Integration of cloud computing and internet of things: a survey. Future Gener. Comput. Syst. **56**, 684–700 (2016). https://doi.org/10.1016/j.future.2015.09.021
5. Roy, A., Zeng, H., Bagga, J., Porter, G., Snoeren, A.C.: Inside the social network's (datacenter) network. In: Proceedings of the 2015 ACM Conference on Special Interest Group on Data Communication (SIGCOMM 2015), pp. 123–137. Association for Computing Machinery (2015). https://doi.org/10.1145/2785956.2787472
6. Huang, D.Y., Apthorpe, N., Li, F., Acar, G., Feamster, N.: IoT inspector: crowdsourcing labeled network traffic from smart home devices at scale. In: Proceedings of the ACM on Interactive, Mobile, Wearable and Ubiquitous Technologies, pp 1–21. ACM (2020).https://doi.org/10.1145/3397333
7. Lu, S., Yao, Y., Shi, W.: Collaborative learning on the edges: a case study on connected vehicles. In: 2nd USENIX Workshop on Hot Topics in Edge Computing (HotEdge 19) (2019)

8. De Domenico, M., Altmann, E.G.: Unraveling the origin of social bursts in collective attention. Sci. Rep. **10**, 1–9 (2020)
9. Tadakamalla, U., Menascé, D.A.: Characterization of IoT workloads. In: Zhang, T., Wei, J., Zhang, L.-J. (eds.) EDGE 2019. LNCS, vol. 11520, pp. 1–15. Springer, Cham (2019). https://doi.org/10.1007/978-3-030-23374-7_1
10. Abdel-Basset, M., Ding, W., Abdel-Fatah, L.: The fusion of internet of intelligent things (IoIT) in remote diagnosis of obstructive Sleep Apnea: a survey and a new model. Inf. Fusion. **61**, 84–100 (2020). https://doi.org/10.1016/j.inffus.2020.03.010
11. Jianfeng, Z.: Call for establishing benchmark science and engineering. arXiv preprint arXiv:2112.09514 (2021)
12. I. BIPM, I. IFCC, I. IUPAC, O. ISO, The international vocabulary of metrology-basic and general concepts and associated terms (VIM), 3rd edn. JCGM 200: 2012, in: JCGM (Joint Committee for Guides in Metrology) (2012)
13. Worldwide Smart Home Devices Market Grew 11.7% in 2021 with Double-Digit Growth Forecast Through 2026, According to IDC. https://www.idc.com/getdoc.jsp?containerId=prUS49051622. Accessed 4 Jul 2022
14. TPC-H. https://www.tpc.org/tpch/. Accessed 15 Jul 2022
15. TPC-C. https://www.tpc.org/tpcc/. Accessed 15 Jul 2022
16. TeraSort benchmark. https://hadoop.apache.org/docs/stable/api/org/apache/hadoop/examples/terasort/. Accessed 15 Jul 2022
17. The C10K problem. http://www.kegel.com/c10k.html#related. Accessed 15 Jul 2022
18. C10M. http://c10m.robertgraham.com/p/blog-page.html. Accessed 15 Jul 2022
19. Wrk. https://github.com/wg/wrk.git. Accessed 15 Jul 2022
20. Wu, W., Feng, X., Zhang, W., Chen, M.: MCC: a predictable and scalable massive client load generator. In: Gao, W., Zhan, J., Fox, G., Lu, X., Stanzione, D. (eds.) Bench 2019. LNCS, vol. 12093, pp. 319–331. Springer, Cham (2020). https://doi.org/10.1007/978-3-030-49556-5_29
21. Netperf. http://www.cs.kent.edu/~farrell/dist/ref/Netperf.html. Accessed 15 Jul 2022
22. Redis-5.0.4. https://download.redis.io/releases/redis-5.0.14.tar.gz. Accessed 15 Jul 2022
23. Nginx. http://nginx.org/en/index.html. Accessed 15 Jul 2022
24. MCC. https://github.com/acs-network/mcc. Accessed 15 Jul 2022
25. Migratorydata server. http://migratorydata.com/. Accessed 15 Jul 2022
26. Zheng, C., Tang, Q., Lu, Q., Li, J., Zhou, Z., Liu, Q.: Janus: a user-level TCP stack for processing 40 million concurrent TCP connections. In: IEEE International Conference on Communications (ICC), pp. 1–7. IEEE (2018). https://doi.org/10.1109/ICC.2018.8422993
27. Yilmaz, Y.S., Aydin, B.I., Demirbas, M.: Google Cloud Messaging (GCM): an evaluation. In: 2014 IEEE Global Communications Conference, pp. 2807–2812 (2014). https://doi.org/10.1109/GLOCOM.2014.7037233
28. Ixia breakingpoint. https://www.ixiacom.com/products/breakingpoint. Accessed 4 Jul 2022
29. Spirent TestCenter Benchmarking. https://www.spirent.cn/assets/u/datasheet-spirent-testcenter-benchmarking-bundle. Accessed 4 Jul 2022
30. ab-Apache HTTP server benchmarking tool. https://httpd.apache.org/docs/2.0/programs/ab.html. Accessed 4 Jul 2022

31. Chen, S., Delimitrou, C., Martínez, J.F.: PARTIES: QoS-aware resource partitioning for multiple interactive services. In: Proceedings of the Twenty-Fourth International Conference on Architectural Support for Programming Languages and Operating Systems (ASPLOS 2019), pp. 107–120. Association for Computing Machinery, New York, NY, USA (2019)
32. Kasture, H., Sanchez, D.: Tailbench: a benchmark suite and evaluation methodology for latency-critical applications. In: 2016 IEEE International Symposium on Workload Characterization (IISWC), pp. 1–10. IEEE (2016). https://doi.org/10.1109/IISWC.2016.7581261
33. Zhang, Y., Meisner, D., Mars, J., Tang, L.: Treadmill: attributing the source of tail latency through precise load testing and statistical inference. In: Proceedings of the 43rd International Symposium on Computer Architecture (ISCA 2016), pp. 456–468. IEEE Press (2016). https://doi.org/10.1109/ISCA.2016.47
34. Dean, J., Barroso, L.A.: The tail at scale. Commun. ACM **56**, 74–80 (2013). https://doi.org/10.1145/2408776.2408794
35. Vulimiri, A., Godfrey, P.B., Mittal, R., Sherry, J., Ratnasamy, S., Shenker, S.: Low latency via redundancy. In: Proceedings of the ninth ACM conference on Emerging networking experiments and technologies, pp. 283–294 (2013)
36. Lindgaard, G., Fernandes, G., Dudek, C., Brown, J.: Attention web designers: you have 50 milliseconds to make a good first impression! Behav. Inf. Technol. **25**(2), 115–126 (2006)
37. Wu, W., Feng, X., Zhang, W., Chen, M.: MCC: a predictable and scalable massive client load generator. In: Gao, W., Zhan, J., Fox, G., Lu, X., Stanzione, D. (eds.) Bench 2019. LNCS, vol. 12093, pp. 319–331. Springer, Cham (2020). https://doi.org/10.1007/978-3-030-49556-5_29
38. Qstack. https://github.com/acs-network/Qstack. Accessed 4 Jul 2022
39. QStack: Re-architecting User-space Network Stack to Optimize CPU Efficiency and Service Quality. https://arxiv.org/abs/2210.08432. Accessed 19 Oct 2022
40. HCMonitor. https://github.com/acs-network/hcmonitor. Accessed 4 Jul 2022
41. Song, H., Zhang, W., Liu, K., Shen, Y., Chen, M.: HCMonitor: an accurate measurement system for high concurrent network services. Concurrency Comput. Pract. Experience, **34**(12), e6081. https://doi.org/10.1002/cpe.6081

STAMP-Rust: Language and Performance Comparison to C on Transactional Benchmarks

Felix Suchert[✉][iD] and Jeronimo Castrillon[iD]

TU Dresden, Dresden, Germany
{felix.suchert,jeronimo.castrillon}@tu-dresden.de

Abstract. Software Transactional Memory has been used as a synchronization mechanism that is easier to use and compose than locking ones. The mechanisms continued relevance in research and application design motivates considerations regarding safer implementations than existing C libraries. In this paper, we study the impact of the Rust programming language on STM performance and code quality. To facilitate the comparison, we manually translated the STAMP benchmark suite to Rust and also generated a version using a state-of-the-art C-to-Rust transpiler. We find that, while idiomatic implementations using safe Rust are generally slower than both C and transpiled code, they guarantee memory safety and improve code quality.

Keywords: Software Transactional Memory · Memory Safety · Parallelism

1 Introduction

Software Transactional Memory (STM) is a well-established method for synchronizing access to shared state in parallel programs. With the advent of emerging technologies such as Non-Volatile Memory (NVM) transactional operations on memory have found new importance [5,13,30]. However, the original *tl2* framework [14] and many subsequent frameworks have been written in C. The language itself has proven to be notoriously unsafe, requiring manual memory management and regularly exposing pointers to developers.

Rust [4] is a system programming language that has been designed with memory safety as one of its main goals. Its main selling point is the strong type system based on *Ownership types* [8,9]. This ensures that any well-typed program will not exhibit unsound behavior such as dangling pointers or data races through aliased references. Prior work has shown that such a strict type system can substantially simplify the specification and verification of system software [2]. By now, Rust has become a well-established language that is used

This project is partially funded by the EU Horizon 2020 Programme under grant agreement No 957269 (EVEREST).

in the development of systems applications like browser engines [1] and operating systems [24,25]. Rust's versatility also makes it an appealing language for GPU programming [20], writing HPC applications [10] and as source language for accelerator programming [32]. In the context of transactional memory, the recent `rust-stm` library [6] offers STM functionalities. In contrast to the rich body of work on STM using C, there is, however, a lack of studies and benchmarks that help understand the impact of the Rust programming model on STM performance.

In this paper, we analyze the Stanford Transactional Applications for Multi-Processing (STAMP) suite [11], a benchmark collection specifically tailored towards Transactional Memory frameworks. Using accepted and recommended programming practices, we re-implemented the STAMP applications, which were originally developed in C/C++. We provide details on the challenges brought by the ownership and borrowing semantics of Rust to ensure a safe re-implementation of the benchmarks. The effort invested in creating safe implementations of the applications allows us to gage the impact of the programming model on the execution performance. To compare against plain unsafe implementations, we use the c2rust transpiler [12] to automatically generate Rust implementations directly from the original C applications. We discovered that Rust's strict borrowing semantics require the code to strictly adhere to using transactions for all variable accesses. While this generally improved the code's safety, it significantly decreased performance compared to C and unsafe Rust implementations.

This paper makes the following contributions:

1. Building atop the STAMP benchmark suite (Sect. 2), we manually implement a Rust version for the benchmarks, STAMP-Rust (Sect. 3).
2. We provide a qualitative comparison between the manually translated code and the code generated by `c2rust` (Sect. 4).
3. A performance evaluation of both Rust versions against the original C implementation using the `rust-stm` framework (Sect. 5).

2 Background and Related Work

Transactional Memory (TM) [19] is a synchronization mechanism for parallel programming. The key idea of this concept is to encapsulate sections of code that should run in parallel while modifying a shared data structure in *transactions*. During execution, each transaction keeps a log of all modifications and accesses to shared data which are played back once the transaction completes. From the outside, transaction blocks then seem to execute atomically, as all changes related to a transaction are either committed at once, or not at all. The latter case can occur when another transaction running in parallel is committed beforehand and has changed a shared variable that is also read or modified by the current transaction. Such write conflicts are resolved by reexecuting the transaction until it is successfully committed. This approach to synchronization is often referred to as *Optimistic Parallelism* [22]. Several potentially conflicting operations are scheduled in parallel under the assumption that conflicts are rare enough that occasional repeated computations of single transactions will not impact overall performance. These applications form their own sub-genre of parallelization problems and usually involve large data structures based on pointers.

STM has been established more than 20 years ago. Since then, different approaches have been taken to test the performance of the mechanism. However, STAMP [11] has since prevailed and is still used today, more than 10 years after its inception [5,27,34]. It improves over existing approaches like RSTMv3 [31] and STMBench7 [17] by providing a wider variety of applications and better portability. Other works have resorted using microbenchmarks [13,15], which are not suitable as real-world examples. Additionally, the YCSB benchmark suite [30] has been used as benchmark to test key-value stores; however, a similar database-like application, i.e., vacation, is part of STAMP as well.

The rest of this section presents the STAMP benchmark suite and describes the `rust-stm` framework used to implement the benchmarks in Rust.

2.1   The STAMP Benchmark Suite

STAMP [11] is a benchmarking suite specifically tailored towards the needs of TM applications. It consists of 8 real-world applications. The suite tries to cover a wide spectrum of properties, such as varying transaction lengths, contention and time spent in transactions. Additionally, all applications are taken from different application domains, such as engineering, machine learning and scientific computation. For our comparison, we discuss the following benchmarks:

Labyrinth implements a path-finding algorithm in a three-dimensional maze, a variation of Lee's algorithm [23]. A set of paths is to be mapped in that data structure based on a set of points provided as inputs. Paths between those points are found using a breadth-first search. With STM, this is implemented by guarding manipulations on the shared grid structure using a transaction. Hence, when a conflicting path mapping occurs, the faster of both transactions may commit while the second has to attempt to find another path.

Genome implements a whole-genome shotgun sequencing algorithm [29]. The goal is the sequencing of a complete genome from a set of nucleotide sequences provided as input. The algorithm first deduplicates the set of DNA segments provided as input and then uses overlap matching with a decreasing overlap size to stitch the genome sequence back together. On an abstract level, the core workload of this benchmark is the construction of an acyclic graph from a set of nodes by finding neighboring elements. Transactions are utilized here to guard the forward and backward links of individual nodes (i.e., nucleotide sequences) in that graph.

K-Means is a popular algorithm for cluster analysis in data mining and for data classification. It partitions a set of n observations into k clusters [26]. A list of observations and the desired number of clusters to sort the data into are provided as inputs. The algorithm then iteratively assigns a cluster to each observation and recomputes the cluster center from all assigned points. This is repeated until a convergence threshold is passed. Transactions are used here to guard access to the individual centroids, which are accessed as part of the processing of each observation.

Intruder implements a signature-based network intrusion detection system. It detects malicious activities and policy violations by inspecting live network traffic. The application implemented as part of STAMP is based on design proposal number five of Haagdorens et al. [18]. Due to the architecture of today's networks, namely the maximum size of network packets, individual network flows sometimes are split into multiple packets which may be transmitted and received in any order. Hence, all incoming network packets are captured and reassembled in parallel using a shared hashmap guarded by a transaction. The reassembled flows are then processed by the signature detection pass, in which a simple pattern matching is performed on the input.

Ssca2 implements kernel 1 from the Scalable Synthetic Compact Applications 2 [3]. It constructs a directed weighted multi-graph in parallel using adjacency and auxiliary arrays. Nodes are added in parallel to the graph, whereby the adjacency arrays are guarded by transactions to ensure safe parallel accesses.

Yada is *Yet another Delaunay application* and implements a Delaunay mesh refinement. The algorithm modifies a mesh of triangles such that all interior angles of the triangles are larger than a certain threshold. If a triangle violates this criterion, it is merged with surrounding triangles and split into a set of new triangles. These operations are performed in parallel and the replacement of the formed cavity with new triangles is guarded by transactions.

2.2 Software Transactional Memory in Rust

The Rust implementation of STM used for our comparison is Rust-STM [6]. It abstracts over the transactional synchronization aspects by providing a dedicated type for transactional variables, TVar. The type encapsulates the variable to be protected and provides an interface to modify it during a transaction. Trans-

```
1  let val = TVar::new(42);
2  atomically(|trans| {
3      let mut x = val.read(trans)?;
4      x /= 2;
5      val.write(trans, x)?;
6      Ok(())
7  })
```

Listing 1: Working with Transactions in Rust-STM.

actions itself are implemented as functions that accept as argument a closure[1] that forms the transaction. Listing 1 shows this function on line 2. Within that closure, protected variabled may be accessed using a special transaction context variable. All these access functions return a type that indicates whether the operation is found to be in collision with another already-committed transaction. The ? operator will enforce a retry on the transaction upon failure.

3   STAMP on Safe Rust

To facilitate a comparison between STM applications in Rust and C, we manually implemented the whole STAMP benchmark suite[2] in Rust and have published it under the name STAMP-Rust[3]. During translation, we followed the recommended coding practices put forth by Blandy et al. [7]. This section discusses how using Rust as implementation language impacts program performance and safety.

3.1   Type-Level Safety

The C-based tl2 library provides opt-in transaction semantics that can easily be violated. Users are cautioned to not access shared data structures outside of transactions as it can easily lead to data races. In Rust-STM, however, this danger is alleviated by the type system. Sharing data between threads in Rust is guarded by its *trait system*, which behaves similarly to interfaces in other languages. A particular type T may only be safely shared between threads when it implements the Sync trait. This property holds if and only if a read-only reference &T of that type can be sent between threads safely. In other words, there must not be any possibility for undefined behavior (which includes data races) to occur if a reference to some data is shared among threads. Therefore, data shared among threads may not be mutated as no mutable references can be derived safely from an immutable one. A known workaround is to define a type that implements so-called *interior mutability*. These types can safely mutate their interior data even through a shared reference. A number of types in Rust's Standard Library implement this behavior and have been proven to be safe [21].

Rust-STM encapsulates transaction variables in a dedicated structure constructed from such types with interior mutability. Since the wrapped data is not exposed, accessing it is only possible through methods implemented on the container type. However, these methods require to be executed as part of a transaction. It is, therefore, impossible to circumvent Rust's safeguards regarding data sharing or to violate transaction semantics.

---

[1] Closures in Rust are comparable to Lambda functions in other languages. They can have arguments and capture variables from the outside context. The implications of the latter are not relevant for this paper.

[2] The code base for the original STAMP applications can be found on https://github.com/robert-schmidtke/stm.

[3] https://github.com/tud-ccc/stamp-rust.

3.2   Composable Transactions

The strong typing of transaction variables further leads to better composability of transactions. In the t12 implementation, it is not transparently visible whether a function needs to be executed in a transaction context or spawns one itself. This can lead to problems when accidentally calling functions that expect to be run in a transaction context or calling a function that creates a transaction from an already-running transaction

Rust-STM addresses this problem in part by requiring a &mut Transaction type for all its non-atomic transaction variable modifications. Therefore, functions expecting to be run from a transaction context must accept such a type as function argument, clearly indicating the required context. Nesting transaction blocks, however, cannot be detected by the type system and, hence, will only result in a runtime error.

3.3   The Overhead of Safety

Although Rust's Ownership type system enforces transactional safety throughout the program, it can also lead to computational overhead compared to t12. Every time a transaction variable is read, the reader receives a full copy of the underlying data structure. This is necessary as the variable must retain ownership of the data in case another transaction commits a change in the meantime. Depending on the size of the data structure, this copying gives transactions a substantial memory footprint besides internal data structures like logs. To bypass this copying, transactions can also receive an immutable pointer to the current value of the transactions internal data[4]. However, this is only feasible when the data will not be modified by a transaction.

The performance implication of this type safety becomes apparent in the *Labyrinth* application. Here, when mapping a path through the maze, many fields of the maze are read to determine the shortest path. A naïve implementation would read all fields of the maze on the go. But this inevitably leads to duplicated reads and a generally higher probability for the transaction to fail. Its read set gets blown up by the many read accesses to fields that are not even part of the final mapped path in the end. This is circumvented in both the C and the Rust implementation by creating a local copy of the maze before attempting a mapping. In Rust, we opted to use TVars read_atomic function to create the copy, as shown in Listing 2. This incurs a high overhead, since each individual cell in the maze is copied individually, but the TVar type does not offer more efficient methods to access its contents.

In C, however, there are no safeguards regarding accesses to transaction variables as there is no strict notion of such a type. Instead, the labyrinth implementation of the original STAMP suite resorts to copying the data structure as

---

[4] This internally uses an atomically reference-counted pointer. When a new value is written by another transaction, the TVars internal pointer is replaced, not changing the contents of the shared pointer.

```
1    type StmGrid = Vec<Vec<Vec<TVar<Field>>>>;
2    type Grid = Vec<Vec<Vec<Field>>>;
3
4    fn create_working_copy(grid: &StmGrid) -> Grid {
5      grid.iter()
6       .map(|y_grid| {
7         y_grid
8          .iter()
9           .map(|z_grid| z_grid.iter().map(|pt| pt.read_atomic()).collect())
10          .collect()
11       })
12       .collect()
13   }
```

Listing 2: Creating a local copy in Rust incurs a high overhead due to the cumbersome data accesses.

a whole using a single invocation of memcpy. This potentially brings increased performance but violates the STM concurrency model. It has been shown that such behavior increases the potential for deadlocks and memory races and is often done to circumvent limitations of the concurrency model used [33].

In the *ssca2* benchmark, we run into a similar problem: The C version utilizes thread barriers to synchronize individual threads and switch between data-parallel and transaction contexts. During transaction contexts, the adjacency and auxiliary arrays are accessed and updated as part of a transaction. Outside of that context, both arrays are frequently read by all threads to continue their computations without any memory overhead. In Rust, we can only implement a similar behavior by joining running threads periodically to update data structures before spawning new threads. This, of course, incurs additional overhead but does not violate the transactional model.

3.4   The Complexity of Using Associative Arrays

Using more complex data structures from external libraries as part of a transaction may quickly lead to a performance bottleneck in Rust due to data copying. As a rule of thumb, transactional variables should always encapsulate as few data as necessary to keep the memory footprint low. However, even using associative arrays from the standard library, such as Hashsets, then poses a challenge, as they offer no access to their intrinsics. As a result, these data types cannot be accessed unsafely due to Rust's type system, but also not efficiently out of the box.

The C implementation circumvented that problem. Since Cs standard library does not include such data types anyway, the authors of STAMP opted to write their own transaction-aware associative arrays. A similar solution could be implemented for Rust in the future, based on a suggested efficient algorithm by Paznikov et al. [28].

4   Analysis of Automatically Generated Benchmarks

Since the advent of Rust and similar memory-safe languages, the question has been raised whether or not its promises of safety could be leveraged automatically for larger code bases written in C. As a result, transpilers have been implemented that can translate C to Rust code. As part of our analysis of the STAMP benchmark suite, we used c2rust [12] to automatically generate Rust code for our selected benchmarks. In this section, we discuss the quality of the generated code and why automatic transpiling can as of now not serve as a replacement for manually translated Rust code.

The c2rust transpiler is built atop the clang compiler frontend and is designed to process individual files adhering to the C99 standard. clang emits the Abstract Syntax Tree (AST) of the input file, which is then transpiled and emitted in the form of Rust code.

```
1    pub unsafe extern "C" fn router_solve(mut argPtr: *mut libc::c_void) {
2        let mut routerArgPtr: *mut router_solve_arg_t =
3            argPtr as *mut router_solve_arg_t;
4        let mut routerPtr: *mut router_t = (*routerArgPtr).routerPtr;
5        let mut mazePtr: *mut maze_t = (*routerArgPtr).mazePtr;
6        let mut myPathVectorPtr: *mut vector_t = Pvector_alloc(
7            1 as libc::c_int as libc::c_long,
8        );
9        // ...
10   }
```

Listing 3: Beginning of the path-finding function from the *Labyrinth* application, generated by an automatic transpiler.

Unfortunately, this literal translation of programs results in code that still is more similar to C semantics than idiomatic Rust code. Listing 3 shows the code for the entry point of the path-finding function in the *Labyrinth* application. It has been declared as unsafe, as it internally mainly relies on the use of what Rust calls *"raw pointers"*, pointers not guarded by the languages safety guarantees. The existence of such pointers itself does not violate these guarantees; however, dereferencing them does, which happens in lines 4 and 5. Also, the generated code contains frequent uses of type casting, which is also unsafe. Previous work has found that the inability to generate safe code is one of the key drawbacks of these automatic approaches [16]. Additionally, automatically generated Rust code makes no use of the more sophisticated features of the Rust language such as struct member functions. This would require a deep understanding of the code structure and meaning on part of the transpiler that is hard to achieve.

Since the source code for this transpilation used to be C code, which uses manual memory management via malloc and free, this concept also surfaces in Rust. This is especially problematic since most generated code operates outside of Rusts safety boundaries. As a result, it cannot be ruled out that double-frees and other undefined behavior occur in the Rust code if the C sources already contained such bugs.

As the transpilation happens file by file, all generated Rust files expose their data types and functions using the `extern"C"` calling convention. This is also shown in Listing 3 in line 1. This not only creates significant bloat in the code, but it also means that all generated Rust functions communicate with one another through C standard calling conventions.

As `tl2` is used as an external library in the STAMP suite, our transpiled STM code still relies on this library. We are thereby be forced to adhere to the C framework's general architecture or would need to restructure the code base significantly to use Rust-STM.

All in all, the code generated by automatic tooling is in this case inferior to a manual sound translation. The generated code needs extensive refactoring to remove all occurrences of unsafe code. We, therefore, deemed a manual rewrite as preferrable in our work as it allowed us to construct the applications from the bottom up in an idiomatic way. The generated code is still useful to gage the cost of switching to the Rust programming language.

5   Evaluation

To evaluate the performance of the different implementations of the STAMP suite, we execute all benchmarks with varying configurations. We then compare the resulting runtimes and speedups and classify both Rust approaches in terms of their code quality.

5.1   Methodology

To run the benchmarks, we use input data sets originally put forward by Minh et al. in their original work [11]. The paper describes three different input sizes for each benchmark: 'small', 'medium' and 'large'. Since the creation of the benchmark suite, numerous advancements in hardware have significantly increased processor speeds. Hence, for most applications, the 'small' and 'medium' sized inputs are ill-suited for a comparison. Most of these inputs are so small that the applications terminate after significantly less than 100 milliseconds. In such a small range, the measuring noise introduced by the operating system dominates the results. We thus use the 'large' or '++' data sets from the benchmark suite for our measurements of k-means, labyrinth, ssca2 and genome. For intruder and yada, we use the medium-sized input data set, as execution times of the STM implementations were extremely long for the large input set. The k-means application additionally provides a low-contention and high-contention input set differing in the number of clusters to be computed.

Additionally, we made some changes to the k-means code. Originally, the benchmark terminated either upon convergence or after 500 iterations. However, due to variations in the floating point accuracy of the C and Rust implementations, both versions converge only after a wildly varying number of iterations. For the large input data set, convergence was always reached at the latest between 150 and 200 iterations. For a meaningful comparison between the Rust and C implementations, we hardcode the termination after 200 iterations.

As we pointed out in Sect. 4, automatically translated benchmarks also use the tl2 library through a C interface. As a consequence, optimized non-debug builds fail execution due to memory faults, which are probably caused by API instabilities. For that reason, we conduct the rust-tl2 measurements using debug builds only. Resulting speedups are still valid, as the baseline is also measured from a debug build. For the runtime comparison, however, we exclude the rust-tl2 measurement results to not distort the plot. Instead, we only show the sequential execution time of the rust-tl2 applications to compare general language overheads in runtimes.

We run all measurements on a workstation with an Intel Core i9-10900K CPU, 32 GiB DDR4-2933 RAM and Ubuntu 22.04 LTS installed. All measurements are repeated 30 times to minimize the effect of random jitter caused by system processes.

To measure the speedup of STM applications, we run all measurements for 1, 2, 4, 8 and 16 threads. This limitation stems from the original C-based STAMP implementation requiring the thread count to be a power of 2.

5.2 Performance Comparison

Figure 1 shows the mean speedups achieved by all three implementations compared to their respective sequential baselines. Additionally, Fig. 2 shows the mean execution times of all configurations. We observe that the manually implemented Rust version generally performs worse than the C implementation when transactions are used more frequently.

For Labyrinth, the manually implemented Rust version only manages to achieve half the speedup of the C implementation. This is mainly caused by the high overheads induced by repeatedly cloning the grid data structure, as outlined in Sect. 3.3. Almost 50% of the total time spent inside transactions is used for creating local copies of the maze. The C version circumvents that by unsafely copying the memory of the grid to a new location, undetected by any transaction. Rust-tl2 and c-tl2 are on par in terms of speedup. However, Fig. 2 reveals that the Rust version executes almost 50% faster than the C implementation. This hints at Rust in this case being generally more efficient, which can also be seen in the other benchmarks.

In Genome, we observe a similar pattern of Rust-STM underperforming in comparison to the C version. While the speedup increase is generally there, it is offset by a factor two from the other implementations. This can directly be attributed to Genome's internal use of complex associative arrays, namely HashMaps and HashSets. As pointed out in Sect. 3.4, the C version (and therefore the transpiled Rust version, too) implements its own transaction-ready hash-based data structures. The Rust-STM library does not come with such data

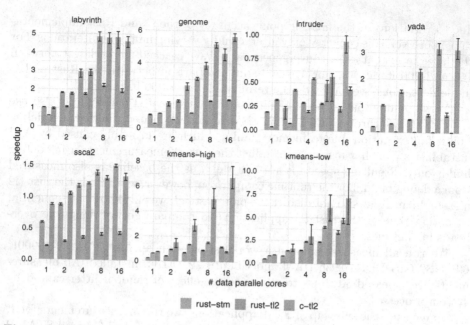

Fig. 1. Speedups of different benchmark implementations over their respective sequential implementations for a varying number of threads.

structures and therefore has to resort to constructing a HashSet alternative using Standard Library methods. We implemented a transaction-aware HashSet and HashMap that internally uses a fixed number of buckets, each containing a HashSet or HashMap protected by a transaction variable. The performance then decreases because this is significantly less efficient than constructing such a type from scratch. Future work should re-evaluate these benchmarks with a data structure leveraging more efficient implementation approaches [28].

The Intruder benchmark reveals the same performance issue in Rust-STM. However, the Rust-STM implementation manages to overtake all other implementations when using more threads. This indicates that the transaction overhead for HashSets can indeed be offset in some cases by the use of more threads, although speedups still do not exceed 1.0 for this benchmark.

Yada's Rust-STM implementation indeed performs significantly worse than the two competing versions. Here, HashMaps and HashSets are used very prominently to store the mesh's triangles and depict neighborhood relations between different elements. Thus, every modification of the graph requires the copying and writing back of one or multiple buckets of our self-implemented Hash data structure. While this is slightly more efficient than having a single HashMap that is modified every transaction, it still incurs a huge overhead compared to specialized data structures.

In ssca2, the performance difference is rooted in more fundamental differences between C an Rust, however. As outlined in Sect. 3.3, this benchmark has various

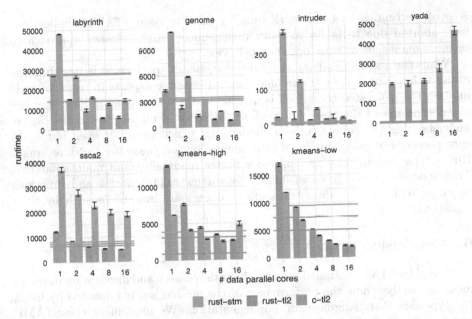

Fig. 2. Runtimes of the different benchmark implementations and their respective sequential implementations. The horizontal lines indicate the sequential execution time for comparison. Runtime data for parallel rust-tl2 executions has been omitted as no data could be obtained for non-debug builds.

synchronization points at which execution switches between transactional and data-parallel computing. Furthermore, data structures are frequently written to in parallel without synchronization, heavily imparting any safety guarantees. In Rust, neither of both is safely doable as the type system strictly prohibits both unguarded accesses to transactional variables and shared mutability. Consequently, the Rust-STM implementation has to terminate threaded execution to synchronize after data-parallel sections. This added computational overhead is clearly visible both in the speedup and even more clearly in the running time of the benchmark. Rust-tl2 and c-tl2 however, are both on par in terms of speedup.

For k-means, both Rust versions outperform the C implementation. While the Rust-STM version executes generally slower than the C version, the Rust-tl2 implementation terminates significantly faster. Therefore, the speedup can be attributed to the Rust runtime's more efficient handling of contention and more radical vectorization of numerical computations.

5.3   Qualitative Analysis

Despite the performance problems Rust-STM shows in some of the benchmarks, it improves significantly on the safety of the applications. On the other hand, the C implementation, which in and of itself already lacks any safety guarantees, has chosen to trade further safety aspects by violating the STM concurrency model.

A small percentage of benchmark runs for the C-version STAMP applications were aborted due to faulty memory management. Rusts cleaner approach to memory management rules out such behavior.

While the automatically-transpiled code generally performed better than the native C implementation, it combines several negative aspects in terms of code quality. The generated code itself is non-idiomatic as discussed in Sect. 4, while it still contains all the possibly undefined behavior of unsafe Rust code. Hence, understanding the source code is challenging, which makes it even harder to spot potential bugs. The manual implementation, on the other hand, leverages Rust's type system fully and provides better readability and maintainability: Transactions are clearly encapsulated into `atomically` blocks; and functions requiring to be run inside a transaction context are marked as such by their signature.

6   Conclusion

Motivated by STMs continued presence in both research and application development, we analyze how the performance of the mechanism is impacted by using the type-safe Rust language for implementation. We implement the STAMP benchmark suite in Rust (STAMP-Rust) and find that the existing C implementation regularly performs unsafe memory operations and violates the STM concurrency model. Hence, Rust-STM implementations of STAMP benchmarks are up to 50% slower than their C implementations in transaction-intensive benchmarks. On the other hand, automatically generated, unsafe Rust code regularly outperforms the C equivalents, hinting at Rust being generally more efficient. We think that our safe re-implementations of the prominent STAMP suite along with the presentation of our design rationale can serve as baseline for further research on STM applications using the Rust programming model. We leave it as future work to explore more efficient implementations leveraging fine-granular transactions on complex data structures, such as genome and intruder.

Acknowledgements. The authors would like to thank Sebastian Ertel for his valuable input.

References

1. Anderson, B., et al.: Engineering the servo web browser engine using Rust. In: Proceedings of the 38th International Conference on Software Engineering Companion, pp. 81–89. ACM, Austin Texas (2016). https://doi.org/10.1145/2889160. 2889229
2. Astrauskas, V., Müller, P., Poli, F., Summers, A.J.: Leveraging rust types for modular specification and verification. Proc. ACM Program. Lang. 3(OOPSLA), 1–30 (2019). https://doi.org/10.1145/3360573
3. Bader, D.A., Madduri, K.: Design and implementation of the HPCS graph analysis benchmark on symmetric multiprocessors. In: Bader, D.A., et al. (eds.) HiPC 2005. LNCS, vol. 3769, pp. 465–476. Springer, Heidelberg (2005). https://doi.org/10. 1007/11602569_48

4. Balasubramanian, A., Baranowski, M.S., Burtsev, A., Panda, A., Rakamarić, Z., Ryzhyk, L.: System programming in rust: beyond safety. In: Proceedings of the 16th Workshop on Hot Topics in Operating Systems, pp. 156–161. ACM, Whistler (2017). https://doi.org/10.1145/3102980.3103006

5. Beadle, H.A., Cai, W., Wen, H., Scott, M.L.: Nonblocking persistent software transactional memory. In: 2020 IEEE 27th International Conference on High Performance Computing, Data, and Analytics (HiPC), pp. 283–293. IEEE, Pune(2020). https://doi.org/10.1109/HiPC50609.2020.00042, https://ieeexplore. ieee.org/document/9406709/

6. Bergmann, G.: Software Transactional Memory (2022). https://github.com/ Marthog/rust-stm. original-date: 2015-09-15T14:45:14Z

7. Blandy, J., Orendorff, J.: Programming Rust: Fast, Safe Systems Development. O'Reilly Media, Sebastopol, first edition edn. (2017). oCLC: on1019128949

8. Boyapati, C., Lee, R., Rinard, M.: Ownership types for safe programming: preventing data races and deadlocks. In: Proceedings of the 17th ACM SIGPLAN conference on Object-oriented programming, systems, languages, and applications - OOPSLA 2002, p. 211. ACM Press, Seattle(2002). https://doi.org/10.1145/582419. 582440, http://portal.acm.org/citation.cfm?doid=582419.582440

9. Boyapati, C., Salcianu, A., Beebee, W., Rinard, M.: Ownership types for safe region-based memory management in real-time Java. In: Proceedings of the ACM SIGPLAN 2003 Conference on Programming Language Design and Implementation - PLDI 2003, p. 324. ACM Press, San Diego (2003). https://doi.org/10.1145/ 781131.781168, http://portal.acm.org/citation.cfm?doid=781131.781168

10. Bychkov, A., Nikolskiy, V.: Rust language for supercomputing applications. In: Voevodin, V., Sobolev, S. (eds.) RuSCDays 2021. CCIS, vol. 1510, pp. 391–403. Springer, Cham (2021). https://doi.org/10.1007/978-3-030-92864-3_30

11. Minh, C. C., Chung, J., Kozyrakis, C., Olukotun, K..: STAMP: Stanford transactional applications for multi-processing. In: 2008 IEEE International Symposium on Workload Characterization, pp. 35–46. IEEE, Seattle (2008). https://doi.org/ 10.1109/IISWC.2008.4636089, http://ieeexplore.ieee.org/document/4636089/

12. Contributors, C.: C2Rust (2022). https://github.com/immunant/c2rust. original-date: 2018-04-20T00:05:50Z

13. Correia, A., Felber, P., Ramalhete, P.: Romulus: efficient algorithms for persistent transactional memory. In: Proceedings of the 30th on Symposium on Parallelism in Algorithms and Architectures, pp. 271–282. ACM, Vienna Austria (2018). https:// doi.org/10.1145/3210377.3210392

14. Dice, D., Shalev, O., Shavit, N.: Transactional locking II. In: Hutchison, D., et al. (eds.) DISC 2006. LNCS, vol. 4167, pp. 194–208. Springer, Heidelberg (2006). https://doi.org/10.1007/11864219_14

15. Dragojević, A., Harris, T.: STM in the small: trading generality for performance in software transactional memory. In: Proceedings of the 7th ACM European Conference on Computer Systems - EuroSys 2012, p. 1. ACM Press, Bern (2012). https:// doi.org/10.1145/2168836.2168838, http://dl.acm.org/citation.cfm?doid=2168836. 2168838

16. Emre, M., Schroeder, R., Dewey, K., Hardekopf, B.: Translating C to safer Rust. Proc. ACM Program. Lang. 5(OOPSLA), 1–29 (2021). https://doi.org/10.1145/ 3485498

17. Guerraoui, R., Kapalka, M., Vitek, J.: STMBench7: a benchmark for software transactional memory (2006). http://infoscience.epfl.ch/record/89706

18. Haagdorens, B., Vermeiren, T., Goossens, M.: Improving the performance of signature-based network intrusion detection sensors by multi-threading. In: Hutchison, D., et al. (eds.) WISA 2004. LNCS, vol. 3325, pp. 188–203. Springer, Heidelberg (2005). https://doi.org/10.1007/978-3-540-31815-6_16

19. Herlihy, M., Moss, J.E.B.: Transactional memory: architectural support for lock-free data structures. In: Proceedings of the 20th Annual International Symposium on Computer Architecture - ISCA 1993, pp. 289–300. ACM Press, San Diego (1993). https://doi.org/10.1145/165123.165164, http://portal.acm.org/citation.cfm?doid=165123.165164

20. Holk, E., Pathirage, M., Chauhan, A., Lumsdaine, A., Matsakis, N.D.: GPU programming in rust: implementing high-level abstractions in a systems-level language. In: 2013 IEEE International Symposium on Parallel & Distributed Processing, Workshops and PHD Forum, pp. 315–324. IEEE, Cambridge (2013). https://doi.org/10.1109/IPDPSW.2013.173, http://ieeexplore.ieee.org/document/6650903/

21. Jung, R., Jourdan, J.H., Krebbers, R., Dreyer, D.: RustBelt: securing the foundations of the Rust programming language. Proc. ACM Program. Lang. 2(POPL), 1–34 (2018). https://doi.org/10.1145/3158154

22. Kulkarni, M., Pingali, K., Walter, B., Ramanarayanan, G., Bala, K., Chew, L.P.: Optimistic parallelism requires abstractions. In: Proceedings of the 2007 ACM SIGPLAN Conference on Programming Language Design and Implementation - PLDI 2007, p. 211. ACM Press, San Diego (2007). https://doi.org/10.1145/1250734.1250759, http://portal.acm.org/citation.cfm?doid=1250734.1250759

23. Lee, C.Y.: An algorithm for path connections and its applications. IEEE Trans. Electron. Comput. EC 10(3), 346–365 (1961). https://doi.org/10.1109/TEC.1961.5219222

24. Levy, A., et al.: Ownership is theft: experiences building an embedded OS in rust. In: Proceedings of the 8th Workshop on Programming Languages and Operating Systems, pp. 21–26. ACM, Monterey California (2015). https://doi.org/10.1145/2818302.2818306

25. Levy, A., Campbell, B., Ghena, B., Pannuto, P., Dutta, P., Levis, P.: The case for writing a kernel in rust. In: Proceedings of the 8th Asia-Pacific Workshop on Systems, pp. 1–7. ACM, Mumbai (2017). https://doi.org/10.1145/3124680.3124717

26. Macqueen, J.: Some methods for classification and analysis of multivariate observations. In: In 5-th Berkeley Symposium on Mathematical Statistics and Probability, pp. 281–297 (1967)

27. Pasqualin, D.P., Diener, M., Du Bois, A.R., Pilla, M.L.: Online sharing-aware thread mapping in software transactional memory. In: 2020 IEEE 32nd International Symposium on Computer Architecture and High Performance Computing (SBAC-PAD), pp. 35–42. IEEE, Porto (2020). https://doi.org/10.1109/SBAC-PAD49847.2020.00016, https://ieeexplore.ieee.org/document/9235046/

28. Paznikov, A., Smirnov, V., Omelnichenko, A.: Towards efficient implementation of concurrent hash tables and search trees based on software transactional memory. In: 2019 International Multi-Conference on Industrial Engineering and Modern Technologies (FarEastCon), pp. 1–5. IEEE, Vladivostok, (2019). https://doi.org/10.1109/FarEastCon.2019.8934131, https://ieeexplore.ieee.org/document/8934131/

29. Pop, M., Salzberg, S., Shumway, M.: Genome sequence assembly: algorithms and issues. Computer 35(7), 47–54 (2002). https://doi.org/10.1109/MC.2002.1016901, http://ieeexplore.ieee.org/document/1016901/

30. Ramalhete, P., Correia, A., Felber, P.: Efficient algorithms for persistent transactional memory. In: Proceedings of the 26th ACM SIGPLAN Symposium on Principles and Practice of Parallel Programming, pp. 1–15. ACM, Virtual Event Republic of Korea (2021). https://doi.org/10.1145/3437801.3441586
31. Scott, M.L., Spear, M.F., Dalessandro, L., Marathe, V.J.: Transactions and privatization in delaunay triangulation. In: Proceedings of the Twenty-sixth Annual ACM Symposium on Principles of Distributed Computing - PODC 2007. p. 336. ACM Press, Portland (2007). https://doi.org/10.1145/1281100.1281160, http://dl.acm.org/citation.cfm?doid=1281100.1281160
32. Takano, K., Oda, T., Kohata, M.: Design of a DSL for converting rust programming language into RTL. In: Barolli, L., Okada, Y., Amato, F. (eds.) EIDWT 2020. LNDECT, vol. 47, pp. 342–350. Springer, Cham (2020). https://doi.org/10.1007/978-3-030-39746-3_36
33. Tasharofi, S., Dinges, P., Johnson, R.E.: Why do scala developers mix the actor model with other concurrency models? In: Castagna, G. (ed.) ECOOP 2013. LNCS, vol. 7920, pp. 302–326. Springer, Heidelberg (2013). https://doi.org/10.1007/978-3-642-39038-8_13
34. Xu, Y., Izraelevitz, J., Swanson, S.: Clobber-NVM: log less, re-execute more. In: Proceedings of the 26th ACM International Conference on Architectural Support for Programming Languages and Operating Systems, pp. 346–359. ACM, Virtual USA (2021). https://doi.org/10.1145/3445814.3446730

Author Index

© The Editor(s) (if applicable) and The Author(s), under exclusive license
to Springer Nature Switzerland AG 2023
A. Gainaru et al. (Eds.): Bench 2022, LNCS 13852, p. 177, 2023.
https://doi.org/10.1007/978-3-031-31180-2

Printed in the United States
by Baker & Taylor Publisher Services

Printed in the United States
by Baker & Taylor Publisher Services